Cinema and History

Anthony Aldgate

CINEMA
AND HISTORY

British Newsreels and the Spanish Civil War

Scolar Press
London

First published 1979 by
Scolar Press, 39 Great Russell Street, London WC1B 3PH
Copyright © Anthony Aldgate 1979

ISBN 0 85967 485 1 (cloth)
ISBN 0 85967 486 x (paper)

Typography by Alan Bartram
Printed in England by
Western Printing Services Ltd, Bristol

Contents

List of Plates

Acknowledgements

Many people have helped me with advice during the course of researching and writing this book. But my greatest debt of gratitude must undoubtedly go to Paul Addison and Owen Dudley Edwards in the Department of History at the University of Edinburgh. By inviting me to edit and direct Edinburgh University's compilation film on the Spanish Civil War, they offered me a unique opportunity to pursue research within the realms of film and history. Furthermore, they then continued to supervise the doctoral research upon which this book is based. I am deeply grateful to them for the kindness and understanding they showed to me, and for the friendship which has grown out of our ventures together.

Professor George Shepperson of Edinburgh University, Professor Geoffrey Best of Sussex University and Professor Arthur Marwick of the Open University were kind enough to read and comment upon the final drafts of the thesis. Their comments were succinct and always valuable.

Lord Asa Briggs, the Provost of Worcester College, Oxford, and Professor Paul Smith of Southampton University took the time and the trouble to suggest ways in which the research might be modified to turn it into a book. Their efforts are greatly appreciated. And I am especially grateful to Penelope Houston at the British Film Institute who put a good deal of personal time and care into editing the various drafts of the book. Her suggestions were invaluable.

The work could not possibly have been completed, of course, without the assistance of the various newsreel archives and I would particularly like to thank the following individuals for allowing me to view the films and papers contained in their libraries: Pam Turner of Visnews Ltd; Ted Candy and Pat Holder of British Movietonews Ltd; and Harry Wynder of the EMI-Pathé Film Library. Extracts from newsreel commentaries are included with acknowledgements to the above companies. Some extracts from *The Content of Motion Pictures* by Edgar Dale are included with acknowledgement to the Payne Fund, New York. Irene Sullivan of Movietone and Roy Drew, formerly of Gaumont, kindly helped to provide some of the photographs. Pat Wyand, formerly of Movietone, and Ray Perrin, formerly of Visnews, were equally forthcoming in offering me advice and information.

Finally I would like to thank my wife, Jane, who was a constant source of support and reassurance throughout.

A.A.

Introduction

x Introduction

The historian of the twentieth century has a new-found wealth of source material at his disposal in the form of cinematograph film, which has not been available to observers of previous ages and epochs. With the advent of motion pictures and the cinema, it became possible seemingly to traverse time and space, and to see at first hand the events and personalities which were shaping history.

In recent years, more particularly since 1968 in Britain, historians have at long last given serious thought and detailed attention to this material which has been accumulated and housed in the world's various film archives and libraries.

This study attempts to engage in that same process. The purpose is threefold. First of all it seeks to fill in the background to the debate, current among historians in Britain, about the usefulness of film as a primary source for historical study and to assess the value of archive film as a historical source. Secondly, it attempts to investigate the emergence of the British newsreel during the 1930s as a medium for mass communication and as a means for the dissemination of news. Both these tasks serve as a necessary prelude to the major purpose: a detailed examination of the film coverage of one particular event, the Spanish Civil War, by the British newsreel companies operating during the years 1936–9.

The Spanish Civil War broke out on 17 July 1936 with the rising of the garrison at Melilla in Morocco, and by 18 July the rising had spread to the Spanish mainland. From that point until the war came to an official end on 1 April 1939, the Spanish people were locked in a struggle to determine who was to govern the country. But during those years, and indeed for a long time after, the Spanish Civil War also influenced the thoughts and actions of governments and peoples in many countries beyond the frontiers of Spain.

In attempting to assess the impact which the Spanish War had upon foreign opinion, historians have quite naturally looked towards the archives of the various European newspapers in print during the period. For example, David Wingeate Pike chose to examine the French press as part of an analysis of French public opinion on Spain.[1] Similarly, Kenneth Watkins surveyed British press reactions in his study into the effect of the Spanish Civil War on British political opinion.[2] To some extent, Franklin Reid Gannon also touched upon the British press response to Spain as part of his larger investigation into the British attitude towards Germany in the years from 1936 to 1939.[3]

Yet what is most noticeable about all three accounts is that their respective authors see the press reaction during this period as constituting the only major source for a study on the dissemination of news. To be fair, it should be added that two of the authors readily acknowledge the limitations imposed upon their work, which they ascribe to a lack of extant sources. Pike, for instance, makes a point in his preface of stating that, in the absence of opinion polls and radio commentaries, the only source of public opinion and news dissemination for France must be the French press. Gannon implies the same with regard to Britain when he points out on the first page of his book that Britain at the time was just experiencing the development of radio as a news medium, had not yet got television on a significant scale, and therefore for the majority of people the only means of information about the outside world was the newspaper press.

What both failed to take into account, however, is the existence of another far-reaching and potentially influential medium of news transmission, the cinema newsreel, which was on view in most European countries throughout the period from 1930 onwards. It is easy enough to produce statistics, as Gannon does, which reveal that in 1934 every 100 families in Britain bought 95 morning and $57\frac{1}{2}$ evening newspapers every day, and 130 Sunday newspapers every week, or that in 1937 the British press was producing a total of 1,577 newspapers and 3,119 magazines and periodicals. It is just as easy to cite figures which show that in Britain there were by 1934 some 4,300 cinemas providing four million seats and showing newsreels to an average weekly audience of eighteen and a half million paid admissions, an audience which by 1940 had risen to a weekly average of twenty-one million. And that there were five newsreel companies, each producing two news-reel issues per week in every year, thereby showing many thousands of feet of news film to the British cinemagoing public.

But arguments on such points of comparison are fruitless, other than perhaps to reinforce the point that the cinema newsreel provides one further area for historical study, which should not be so easily ignored.

After all, in any study of the newspaper press or the cinema newsreel the problems are basically the same. In both instances it is a comparatively light task to prove that these media reached a large audience. But it is another thing to prove that the media, in whatever form, did necessarily communicate with the mass of people receiving them. It cannot be stressed often enough that there is a great deal of conjecture about whether the messages transmitted by the media over such events as the Spanish Civil War really came across to the audience which was presented with them. Indeed conjecture should be the keynote of any study into the mass media or mass communication, especially in a historical context. That is perhaps one reason why Asa Briggs has been prompted to suggest:

To talk of 'mass communications' is to mislead: the agencies of so-called 'mass communication' are really agencies of mass or multiple trans-mission.[4]

Furthermore, care should be taken to remember that, while it is possible to isolate and identify the messages emanating from the media, conjecture and speculation are once again the inspiration for any ideas one might have with regard to the motives of the people who formulated those messages. For as David Pike has put it:

Conjecture, therefore, is the primary interest, and above all, conjecture on what can never be proven, on what in fact historians largely ignore: the motivations of the actors on the stage, the inner thoughts they never expressed or dared to express in written form, and the considera-tions which moved them to action or held them to inaction as they sprang from hope or fear.[5]

This study, therefore, attempts to investigate how the British newsreels covered the Spanish Civil War, what messages were transmitted by them on Spain, and what the motives of the men in charge of the newsreels were when forming these messages. To this end the study has examined the newsreel coverage of five companies throughout the duration of the war.

The film material housed in the archive for Gaumont British News and British Paramount News was viewed first, and in both instances all the extant stories relating to Spain for this period were seen. In the case of Gaumont, the scripts of the spoken commentaries for all the stories have also been examined. In the case of Paramount, very few written commentaries were extant but those that exist have also been examined, along with the shot lists for all the stories. A cursory investigation was made of the same companies' stories relating to Spain for the period before the Civil War. Most of this material was viewed during the research and production of a historical compilation film on the Spanish Civil War, which was made by the Department of History at the University of Edinburgh. This film constituted No. 3 in the series of British Universities Historical Studies in Film. The film had a commentary which was written and narrated by Paul Addison and Owen Dudley Edwards, and it was edited and directed by myself.

Since that time a further examination has been made of the stories on the Spanish Civil War which were produced by the British Movietone News and the Pathé Gazette. Many though by no means all the stories relating to Spain from these two companies were viewed, though once again in both instances the written scripts for all spoken commentaries were used to supplement the viewing sessions.

In the case of Universal News no material on the Spanish War has been seen. However every Universal story on Spain is extant in the form of commentary scripts and these have been examined.

Chapter 1 | Film as a Primary Source

Ever since the invention of cinematography the question has been raised again and again whether and to what extent it would be possible to use films as a way of documenting contemporary history.

Fritz Terveen, 1955[1]

It is the intention here to take up Fritz Terveen's point and to trace briefly in what ways film has been regarded as a means of documenting history. Only then will it be possible to ascertain at what point in time historians became interested, for their own part, in using film as a potential source of historical study, to see what kind of films it was that took their attention, and what questions they asked of film.

Of course the advent of films and the cinema is a comparatively recent technological development. Yet at different times and from various quarters numerous views have been put forward on film and its possible value as an additional record of documentation. And as might be expected, in the earliest days of the film industry it was the founding fathers of cinematography who spoke upon the subject, not the historians.

By 1889 the first cinematographers, like William Friese-Greene, were providing moving pictures, examples of what later came to be called 'actuality' film, 'short scenes of everyday people and events, unmanipulated activity of more or less general interest'.[2] The events themselves were hardly of newsworthy interest, being little more in the case of Friese-Greene's material than scenes of Londoners wandering through Hyde Park on a Sunday morning. Yet within the space of six years the French brothers Louis and Auguste Lumière were exhibiting a programme of similar scenes to an audience in the basement of a café on the Boulevard des

Capucines in Paris. The fruits of their 'Cinématographe' took the form of actuality material with titles like *Arrival of a train at a station*, *A Blacksmith* and *Bathing Beach*.

In that same year of 1895, the first claims that actuality film might be of more use than simply for entertainment purposes were being made by W. K. L. Dickson, who had worked with Thomas Edison on the standardization and perforation of film. It was Dickson who suggested that the advantages of film to students and historians could be immeasurable if the motion picture cameras were turned upon those great national scenes 'instinct with all the glowing personalities which characterised them'. Archives would be enriched by such vitalized pictures, and gone would be 'the dry and misleading accounts, tinged with the exaggerations of the chroniclers' minds'. Dickson's hope for the future was boundless. There were no limits to what the motion picture camera might achieve. Its potential was enormous 'in the promotion of business interests, in the advancement of science, in the revelation of unguessed worlds, in its educational and recreative powers, and in its ability to immortalise our fleeting but beloved associations.'[3]

Just as optimistic was the Pole, Boleslaw Matuszewski, who in 1898 boldly declared the cinema to be *'une nouvelle source de l'histoire'*. While it is evident that his general statements were meant to enhance his own cinema endeavours in Paris, Matuszewski did at least show great foresight in suggesting the establishment of an archive of actuality films for the use of historians. Furthermore, he went one step further than Dickson in pinpointing certain limitations to film as a document of history when stating that 'History is far from consisting only of solemn occasions which have been planned and foreseen and which are organised in advance all ready to be photographed.'[4] As he went on to elaborate, history also consists of the beginnings of actions, initial movements and unexpected events which escape the camera, just as they are hidden from other methods of recording.

However Matuszewski considered that this limitation should be overcome simply as a result of the fact that the cinematographic photographer is indiscreet by the very nature of his profession. He is watchful for every opportunity, and his professional instinct will help him to determine what events to cover that might grow into 'the history of tomorrow'. Furthermore, he is helped by the potential mobility of his camera, for 'even in a war one can easily imagine its apparatus being carried on the same shoulders that bear rifles.'

In isolating the potential for physical mobility of the motion picture camera, yet at the same time hinting at the inability to forecast what events may or may not be of paramount importance to cover, Matuszewski put his finger on what would prove to be one of the greatest problems to confront the newsreel cameramen of the future. When concentrating on the practical side of cinematography, he displayed some useful insights. But when he tried to step also into the shoes of the historian he tended to become much too lyrical about the potential value of film and the vistas it would open up, as is evident from his statement that:

The cinema may not give a complete history, but what it gives is incontestably and absolutely true. Ordinary photographs can be retouched to the point of transformation. But just try to retouch, in a uniform way for each figure, those thousands of almost microscopic negatives.

It is noticeable that this last emphasis on 'cinematographic truth' is what distinguishes the writings both of Matuszewski and, before him, W. K. L. Dickson. With understandable naïveté and undaunted optimism, they welcomed the advent of motion pictures, and of course their own enterprises which went with them. They saw the moving picture as heralding the arrival of a pictorially reproductive art which they believed was synonymous with the events it deigned to recreate. Here was a process, as they saw it, which could honestly and faithfully hold a mirror up to nature and come away with a pure reflection, untainted by the interposition of the artist's hand. It is easy in retrospect to conclude, as does the German historian Fritz Terveen, that 'They were impressed by the fact that it was possible to preserve present day life faithfully in moving pictures. It was thought that would be of particular interest to the historians.'

It was inevitable that the fathers of cinematography should have enthused, as they did, to one and all about the potential merits of their respective inventions. They were, after all, in business and the cinema industry has always had an exploitative side to its nature. Yet even in their own day events were to catch up with the first cinematographers' claims for visual truth and sincerity. Such events were to prove that the manipulation of film, whether at the command of commercial or ideological pressures, would more than likely win the day.

In the very year that Matuszewski was speaking in Paris, for instance, François Doublier was touring Russia exhibiting numerous pieces of actuality film which had been shot by the Lumière brothers. From the varied material he had with him, Doublier put together a scene of a French army parade, street scenes in Paris, film of a Finnish tug going out to meet a barge and shots of the Nile Delta. With the help of a live commentary, Doublier used this sequence of shots supposedly to show the story of the Dreyfus case, a popular topic at the time. The film was then devised to depict Dreyfus before his arrest, the Palais de Justice where he was court-martialled, the ship which carried him to captivity and Devil's Island where he was imprisoned, all purporting to take place in 1894.[5] As Doublier sardonically recounted, 'People actually believed that this was a filming of the famous case.'[6]

Faking was at hand and money was to be made. Furthermore, during the period from 1896 to 1910 the French film pioneer George Méliès concocted a whole series of theatrical recreations of the more important and newsworthy events of the day; the events which he reproduced in his film studios included the assassination of President McKinley, the sinking of the Maine, the coronation of Edward VII and, once again, the trial of Alfred Dreyfus. Trick photography was in fact Méliès's stock-in-trade and his initiative was to destroy Matuszewski's adage that it would be impossible to retouch 'those thousands of almost microscopic negatives'. For Méliès's studios employed girls to tint film by hand, frame by frame. Of course he was looking to introduce colour into films, not so much to alter their provenance or distort their faithfulness. But in the process his studios, more so than any others at the time, revealed the immense potential for manipulation of the cinematographic image.

Throughout this early period in the history of the cinema, the historical profession paid little attention to the cries of the first cinematographers for vindication of their films as a potential source of historical documentation. In the light of the immediate capture of the film industry by those members within its ranks who had more of an interest in its business potential, it is perhaps easy to understand the lack of a response. Indeed it was not until the 1920s that historians felt compelled to make any kind of concerted comment, and in the meantime the First World War had shown how film could be developed and put to further use, this time as an instrument of political propaganda.

Between 1926 and 1934, at the various meetings of the International Congress of the Historical Sciences, a small but significant band of historians began to take an interest for their own part in film as a historical document. At one of their congresses they even went so far as to establish an International Iconographical Commission, with the expressed intention of dealing with the problems of collecting and sorting out film material for historical purposes. The papers of such historians as Lhéritier, Fruin and Glotz, among others, were published intermittently in their Committee's bulletin.[7]

First and foremost, these men were interested in the practical task of setting up the right conditions for the preservation of film, through the establishment of film archives. Then they set about the problem of deciding what films should be preserved. Towards this end Fruin undertook an enquiry covering many countries, including Germany, France, Belgium, Canada and Great Britain, in order to find out what archives were already in existence, how they were kept, whether they comprised 'historical' films, and under what conditions films were deposited in them. His use of the term 'historical' films was in no way begging the question 'what constitutes a historical film?', since the Iconographical Commission had also gone some way towards a definition of that very term. Quite early in their proceedings, the Commission had decided that what the cinema industry called historical films would not serve as a possible source of material for the historian, since they were open to so much dramatic licence on the part of their creators. Thus feature films, generally along the lines of epics such as *Ben Hur* starring Ramon Navarro, were considered to provide very little scope for historical analysis.

As far as the Iconographical Commission was concerned, the term historical film could only justifiably be used to describe those films 'which record a person or period from the time after the invention of cinematography and without dramaturgical or "artistic" purposes: those films which present a visual record of a definite event, person or locality, and which presuppose a clearly recognisable historical interest inherent in the subject matter.'[8]

Clearly, what concerned these historians were not feature films, documentaries or any other kinds of filmed reconstructions, but more the actuality films of their day, or as they were called by that time, the topicals, later to become known as the newsreels. The Commission thought that films were of most interest to the historian as 'illusions of objective reality, of events and people, a visual version of newspapers'.[9] Once again, however, it is obvious that the stress lay heavily upon the idea of cinematographic truth. The prevalent idea was that by removing feature films from consideration, and by concentrating upon actuality material, one thereby somehow excluded the interference which might ensue from personal interpolation by the film-makers.

In Britain it took many years before the professional historian began to investigate or associate himself with the realm of film, perhaps because of the lack of a strong film culture in this country, perhaps also because the film industry tried for so long to push forward its feature products for the historian's consideration. Such interest as there was manifested itself in discussions on the accuracy or otherwise of films like *The Private Life of Henry VIII* or *Catherine the Great*, amounting to no more than condemnation of these distorted versions of history, and offering nothing further in the way of constructive suggestions towards understanding the value of film as a historical source.[10] The emergence during the 1930s of a strong documentary film movement in Britain, offering an alternative and respectable form of cinema for the disenchanted intelligentsia, only served to divert what little interest there was.

Much the same story can be told of the response in America, where the first serious thoughts, since W. K. L. Dickson, on the value of film as a historical source emanated from an archivist, the motion picture consultant to the Library of Congress. Though, interestingly enough, John Bradley's comments in 1948 suggest that very little had happened between the time of Dickson's early statements, full of unbridled enthusiasm, and his own. There is still the same insistence on finding in motion pictures a new and flexible medium for recording the history of people, things and events 'so that they attain a realism never attained before'. Bradley draws comparisons with the ancients documenting their history on tablets, with other ages utilizing monuments, paintings and folk tales, and with the printing press serving the basic urge to be remembered whether as nations or individuals. Now, he continues, we live in an age whereby we record in motion and sound on film. And such documentation has a 'fidelity' not found in any other medium. The printed word is based on an acquired art and is an artificial thing, but motion pictures transcend these limitations so that 'History so recorded will not only have a new fidelity but a present tense value not found in other mediums.'[11]

In view of the massive amounts of film expended by American, British, German and many other national governmental agencies during the Second World War on propaganda, Bradley's insistence that film is not an artificial thing and is invested with a new-found fidelity seems surprisingly blinkered. Furthermore his implication that the production of film is not based on an acquired art reveals a sad misunderstanding of the methods of film-making. Indeed his apparent lack of knowledge on the nature of film and the methods of film production suggest that he had hardly advanced one jot beyond Dickson. And the pioneering efforts made some twenty years earlier by historians in Europe would appear to count for nothing.

It took a film-maker with the experience of Sir Arthur Elton to understand both these facets of film and to appreciate most of all that 'films can be used, as other historical source material can be used, for various and different historical purposes.' Like Bradley, Elton drew historical parallels between film as a record of the twentieth century and the records left by bygone ages. But his points of comparison were more carefully scrutinized. For he considered that film should be regarded as source material for historical studies 'in the sense that palimpsest and parchment, hieroglyph and rune, clay tablet and manorial roll are source materials, fragments, sometimes fragments of fragments, often defaced by time, and applied to purposes of historical reconstruction rarely contemplated by the original authors.'

In a paper entitled 'The film as source material for history'[12] Elton's examination of the maxim that film provides an image of objective reality is nothing if not thorough and searching. After making a personal lament that there is 'no film *Times*, no *New Statesman* or *Spectator* and, virtually, not even a *Daily Express*', he takes up the point that film is an illusion of external reality, of objective reality, and comments:

For at least the first thirty years the content of the newsreels was determined mainly by the passing fads and fancies of the time. . . . Of scenes of one-legged men pushing turnips with their noses from Paris to Rome there is much; of boat races, crowned heads, bathing belles, railway smashes, the glossier phases of war, fashion parades, fires, murders and dance marathons, more; but of industry, technology, sociology, art, poetry, agriculture, only accidental glimpses. There are miles of men biting dogs, but much less of the stuff of history, dogs biting men. . . . Taking a parallel from written sources, it is as if the historian of the early twentieth century had little more to guide him than the *Daily Mirror*, *Old Moore's Almanac*, *Tit-Bits* and a run of Nelson's Sevenpenny Novels.

His first-hand experience of producing films led him quite naturally to mistrust the truthfulness of film as a visual record. 'Let one piece of film be joined to another,' as he put it, 'and something new comes into existence, some quality shared by neither piece alone.' He could not fail to appreciate that film is not an objective, faithful reproduction untouched by human hand, but that selection and manipulation are inevitable in the process of film production. He concluded that it was in the nature of film to be manipulated and that it was in the nature of film production to do the manipulating. Furthermore, Elton had also introduced a new argument into the proceedings, as far as the historian was concerned. For he had suggested that selection and manipulation played as strong a part in the area of the newsreel as they did in the feature film. Yet for all that he was by no means willing to write off entirely the value of such film at the purely depictive level.

It was Christopher Roads who collated the findings on the value of film at the depictive level of photographic reality, during the course of a paper he delivered in 1965.[13] Roads began by isolating what he saw as five significant classes of film, each of which he considered held varying degrees of interest for the historian. The first such class he singled out was the original film record in a completely unedited condition, after it had been removed from the film camera and exposed, though with all its attendant technical failures and excess footage. The second class consisted of the same film in a semi-edited condition, with its excess footage and technically inadequate sequences excised. Thirdly, there is what he called edited record film, in which category he included the newsreels. The drawback, as he saw it, to this material was that it had generally undergone 'censorship' of one sort or another, and therefore reflected more in the way of contemporary attitudes or prejudices. Ironically, whilst admitting that film can in this sense gain in value as historical evidence, Roads considers that tampering with film in this way means that it has sacrificed much of its status as a basic record. The fourth category was the documentary whose purpose was to tell a story and which culled film of varied provenance from many sources to put across this story to the viewer. Once again Roads's feeling was that there was very little chance of using such film as direct historical evidence, since the original context in which the various pieces of film had been shot was lost. Finally there is the vast field of the feature film, which Christopher Roads dismisses as offering little more than a 'distorted perspective'. He does willingly concede for feature films, as he did for the newsreels, that they must be considered as important evidence of 'the attitudes to certain problems of the generation that created them'. But the fact that they are complete re-enactments obviously means that they are in no sense evidence of the events they attempt to portray. These are the films which Roads calls the 'secondary' sources, whereas what he believes the historian ordinarily prefers is the 'primary' material.

Roads's arguments show very clearly that his personal preference was for the first two classes of film. He does to some extent weigh the sort of arguments put forward by Elton about the nature of film and film production largely militating against film's capacity for a 'true reflection'. This is evident from his remarks concerning newsreels and feature films, where in both instances he concedes that the purposes for which such films are used can reveal a great deal about the attitudes of the people making them and the period within which they were produced. But in the final analysis Christopher Roads firmly believes that film is of most value to the historian as a basic record. And he goes on to cite several important ways in which, when such film has been thoroughly researched and authenticated, it can 'not only record invaluably but uniquely innumerable aspects of the social, economic, administrative, military and political history of this century.' These ways have been summarized as follows:[14]

(a) Film can depict the attitudes of the people shown towards the events being depicted.

(b) Film can describe the physical conditions and geography of people and places.

(c) Film can record the measurement and effectiveness of machinery or act as a record of experiments in the development of technology.

(d) Film can effectively show the personality of political leaders.

In their respective papers, Arthur Elton and Christopher Roads had adequately rehearsed the arguments and probed the issues which were to occupy both commentators and historians alike in subsequent years when it came to debating the value of film as a historical source. It will be seen that to a great extent these debates, particularly among historians, revolve around a choice of emphasis between Elton's views on the nature of film and the selection and manipulation inherent in the process of its production, and Roads's view that 'It is true that the film which survives may be biased, even to the extent of deliberate misrepresentation, but where it does show aspects, such as human conduct and behaviour, technical equipment and topographical features, it adds substantially to the historian's understanding.'

It is noticeable, for instance, that the film critic Penelope Houston, in an article written for *Sight and Sound* on 'The nature of the evidence', elaborates upon many of the features which Elton had outlined by pinpointing some of the shortcomings of the film image.[15] As she put it, 'Cameramen have provided us with a shorthand visual imagery for this century.' British political crises are symbolized by a crowd outside Number 10 Downing Street; the Depression by shots of cloth-capped men on street corners; the General Strike by idle machinery or empty railway lines; and the Battle of Britain is conjured up with the help of clips from Humphrey Jennings's *Fires Were Started*, with fire-hoses snaking down a London street after an air-raid. But the questions remain unanswered. 'Look behind the shots and the film image can't help you. What political crisis? How many men out of work? Which air-raid, and which street?'

Miss Houston's observations are of course correct. So much of what interests the historian is not on film. The cameras were not allowed behind the closed doors where the political decisions were made. Her conclusion that this makes film 'untrustworthy, superficial, vulnerable to every kind of distortion' is well justified. But her assertion that film is 'at the same time irreplaceable, necessary, a source material that no twentieth century historian ought to disregard, though many still seem prepared to', remains unproven. She does, however, suggest one path which might be followed up when she adds that 'one thing, it seems to me, that historians are going to have to reckon with is the unfixed nature of the image, and its partisanship.' And when, after 1968, historians in Britain did finally apply themselves to an examination of film as a historical source, this was the area for study which first captured their attention.

In his inaugural lecture at the University of Birmingham, Professor John Grenville chose to examine the subject of 'Film as History'[16] in order to determine just what kind of evidence film put forward for consideration by the historian, and to establish whether it constituted a primary or a secondary source. In fact he came to the conclusion that film provides a primary source of evidence in two basic ways. To illustrate his point he used the example of a Gaumont British newsreel story on Neville Chamberlain's visit to Hitler and his return from Berchtesgaden during the Munich crisis in September 1938. He noted that these film sequences 'provide evidence of the manner in which Chamberlain read an important statement at Heston on the results of his visit' and that it is possible 'to form conclusions for instance from his general demeanour and from his reception by the German crowds in Berchtesgaden and in Downing Street.' At this level film can be seen to impart certain basic 'information'.

But Grenville also proposes that this newsreel imparts further and more useful primary evidence if the question is asked of the material: 'What were the British public told at the time and how was the Munich crisis presented to them?' For then one is looking at the archive film in order to determine what 'messages' were being put across to the public by this very important medium of communication. In conclusion, he considers that the historian's task would then be to weigh this new film evidence in relation to the knowledge gleaned from the traditional array of sources at his disposal, in order that the new evidence could be made the basis of a point of view which might not otherwise have been possible.

The distinction between the information and the messages which a piece of film might contain, between what might be denoted and connoted from a piece of film, is a simple but successful one. It draws together the differing ideas on film as evidence that had been put forward previously by Elton and Roads. Film offers a primary source of evidence on the one hand because of the amount of basic information it displays at the purely depictive level, and on the other hand because it manifests general and particular messages on matters of historical import. For John Grenville it is obviously the latter which is the more important, for he states, 'It is in the study of attempts to mould public opinion on political, social and international questions that research in film (and later television) will find its first important academic application.'

Professor Arthur Marwick draws a different conclusion during the course of an article entitled 'Archive Film as Source Material'.[17] He also makes a distinction between information and message, and addresses himself primarily to the newsreels. Only for Arthur Marwick the message that such a film wishes to put forward is described as 'the witting testimony', and the term used to describe the amount of information a film might contain is 'the unwitting testimony'. It is the latter perhaps that interests him most:

All historians must be essentially interested in what I call 'the unwitting testimony' of the sources. However much filtering has been done by the cameraman, however much reality has been distorted by cutting, editing, and many other devices, it is still possible for the historian to deduce from the film evidence facts about past situations which indeed he might well find it hard to derive from any other source.

Then, like Christopher Roads, he goes on to list the points he would include under his heading of unwitting testimony. These include:

1. The environment.
2. Life-styles and patterns of behaviour.
3. Portraiture. Film frequently shows us more of the real character of past individuals than any other source can.
4. The 'crash course' function of archive film. If we want to know

immediately what some technological, or specialist, operation was really like, film can more readily give us a 'crash course' in this experience than any other possible type of source.

5. The concrete reality of particular situations. If the historian is to deal in the actual and the concrete, as he must, instead of becoming enmeshed in verbal mystique and fancy, then film is a vitally helpful source.

What is perhaps most interesting is that around both John Grenville and Arthur Marwick two bodies of historical film production have also grown up, each attempting to put its ideas into practice. For several years historians have acted as consultants on such archive compilation series as the BBC's *The Great War*, Granada's *All Our Yesterdays* and Thames Television's *The World at War*. But recently historians have also decided to take the tools of film production into their own hands. In Britain the result has been a succession of archive film compilations, drawing upon the resources of the newsreel libraries, and emanating from two organizations in particular. The first such body, the Inter-University History Film Consortium, has so far produced two series of films.[18] These films were produced by historians in different universities and were intended for use primarily on courses in modern history. The second body was the Open University, where historians have used archive film on two courses thus far, intended in the first instance once again for students of history.[19]

This growing interest in the use of film as a historical source has also resulted in a series of seminars and conferences arranged by the British Universities Film Council, the Imperial War Museum and the Open University.[20] At the research level, so far, the main concern has been with the actuality film material housed in the various newsreel archives and with the newsreel companies which produced it, but historians are also beginning to work on the much more tricky subject of the feature film.[21]

No longer is it quite as true to say, as one historian felt compelled to only a few years ago, that historians have been slow to recognize and identify the methods of film distortion and that this has delayed the development of suitable methodological approaches to the film medium. Or that scant work has now been done in devising proper methodologies for historians' use of film and in conceptualizing the relationship of film and history.[22]

For historians are increasingly aware when viewing newsreel material that what they are seeing is a fabricated statement and that distortion plays a great part in the conjuring up of the newsreels' messages. At the present moment, it would be more to the point to suggest that the maxim being adopted is one which states that:

The essential and simple point to grasp then is that a piece of film is not some unadulterated reflection of historical truth captured by the camera.[23]

Furthermore, the historian has attempted to conceptualize the relationship of film and history by trying to understand first of all the nature of film and the nature of film production, in order to find out what areas in the production of the newsreel, for instance, were open to manipulation. For only when one has a thorough grasp of this side of the process is it possible to begin to speculate upon what constituted the 'news', in filmic terms, upon what messages and images were put before cinemagoing audiences on current affairs, and ultimately upon questions of film and history.

Film is first of all an art form, an art form firmly married to the world of mass entertainment, but an art form nonetheless;[24] and this means that all the biographical materials which are ordinarily useful in the study of the other arts are as useful in the study of film. Thus, papers, letters, diaries, memoranda, all provide insights into the personalities of the film-makers and help to reveal the educational, social, political and psychological elements from which that film was fashioned.

Film is also a corporate art. As such this means, and particularly with regard to the newsreel, that no one person can be held responsible for its production. Everybody from the assignment editor, the cameraman, the editor, the scriptwriter and the commentator, to the sound effects man and the musical director could and indeed did influence the outcome of a specific newsreel.

Film is also a business. As Nicholas Pronay has put it:

The newsreel companies were run by their parent companies as a break-even advertising unit to keep their names before the cinema-goers and to keep off others who would undoubtedly have filled their timespan on the screen.[25]

Film is a technological art; no other art form interposes so much technical know-how between the artist and his audience. So if film is to be understood, so also must the equipment and the technical processes involved in its production. The limitations of its technology can sometimes impose a severe burden on the credibility of film as a record of what actually happened.

These characteristics then, and more, define the nature of film as a medium of communication, and cognizance should be taken of them in any analysis of film as a historical source. But these characteristics in themselves invite further questions. For as Hans Magnus Enzensberger notes:

Every use of the media presupposes manipulation. The most elementary processes in media production, from the choice of the medium itself, to shooting, cutting, synchronisation, dubbing, right up to distribution, are all operations carried out on the raw material. . . . The question is therefore not whether the media are manipulated, but who manipulates them.[26]

If, as the defining characteristics of film suggest, it was in the nature of the newsreels to be manipulated, then this study will also need to investigate who it was that manipulated them, what their purposes were and whether they acted on their own initiative.

To this end this study attempts to investigate the following factors:
1. The historical evolution of the newsreel.
2. The ownership of the newsreel companies, their relationships with their parent companies and the financial state of the newsreel industry.
3. The organizational structure of the newsreel companies, their personnel and production techniques.
4. The nature of the technology and the technicians at their disposal.
5. The structure for the exhibition of the newsreels and the characteristics of the cinema audience.
6. The content of the newsreels.
7. The relations between newsreel companies, the public and the government of the day with regard to matters of censorship.

After such an investigation, the survey will then go on to look at a case study of the Spanish Civil War in order to determine what value film might have as a historical source on that particular topic. In this instance the purpose will be to determine what messages and what information might be gleaned from newsreel coverage on Spain, and how far the newsreels were attempting in fact to manipulate public opinion.

Chapter 2 | Inside the Newsreels

THE EVOLUTION OF THE NEWSREEL

By the advent of the Spanish Civil War, the newsreels were well established. However, in view of the massive amounts of film and resources which were by that time being spent on feature film production, it was all too easily forgotten that:

Newsreels are not an extraneous branch of cinematographic work, grafted on to the essential business of film production. On the contrary, the cinema itself developed out of the presentation of topical events.[1]

The Lumière brothers had begun the process of showing actuality film of everyday events and happenings to 'cinema' audiences in 1895, and within a very short time collections of such film reportage on more specific subjects were being assembled and shown under the title of 'topicals'. Among the earliest examples of this material in Britain was film of the 1896 Derby, which was shot by Robert W. Paul; and the Pathé film library also has coverage of the Jubilee of Queen Victoria in 1897. Kenneth Gordon, a newsreel cameraman in his day, maintained that the first regular topical coverage was made by an American firm, the Biograph Company, which established itself in London with laboratories in Great Windmill Street, on the site of the Windmill Theatre, and began by covering such events as the Derby and the Boat Race.[2] In 1895 the Lumière films had never exceeded sixty-five feet in length,[3] but within two years the Biograph stories were as long as 160 feet.[4]

In these early days of film, the news was mostly covered by private showmen for use in peep-shows or music halls. Their films were not rented, but sold to exhibitors, who screened the prints until they were worn out. Such film-makers were quick to appreciate the commercial value of filming famous personages and historic events. By 1898 A. J. West had started combining topicals with interest films of the Royal Navy, and these were shown under the title *Our Navy* for several years in the West End of London. Charles Urban, Will Barker and W. Jeapes started the Warwick Trading Company, and later the Charles Urban Trading Company, both of which covered in one-reel issues such events as the Grand National, for exhibition at London music halls. Topicals were shown at Gatti's in Westminster Bridge Road, and at the Old Standard which became the Victoria Palace. Robert Paul introduced his 'Animatograph' into the Alhambra and the 'Bio' was shown at the Palace.[5] Topical companies arrived and disappeared with some frequency during these years. W. S. Barker founded the Autoscope Company, while W. C. McDowell and A. Bloomfield left the Biograph Company to set up their own British and Colonial Films. At the same time a Biograph cameraman, W. K. L. Dickson, was showing the potential for war coverage with film of the Boer War. Other events of note that were filmed included President McKinley's inauguration in 1897, Gladstone's funeral in 1898 and Queen Victoria's funeral in 1901.[6]

But it was the French, always the pioneers of film and film culture, who set up the newsreel organizations which were to cover the world and set the example for the rest to follow. In 1908 Charles Pathé started his Pathé Journal in Paris, with offices soon to follow in London, Berlin, St Petersburg, Milan and Barcelona. By 1910 his British newsreel, the Animated Gazette, was in full operation, although at first the British material was filmed in Britain and processed in Paris. Soon afterwards Léon Gaumont started the British Gaumont Graphic. The third French competitor, the Eclair Journal, also started a British company but it quickly disappeared. The home-grown competitors included the Warwick Chronicle, founded by Charles Urban, the Topical Budget, founded by W. Jeapes and W. Wrench, and the Williamson News.[7] The birth of these companies coincided with two important changes in the film industry. The first was the changeover from travelling shows to permanent cinemas where, because the audience remained largely constant, the topical programme had to be renewed frequently. The second was the changeover from outright sales of material to film-renting.[8]

The nature of the content is adequately conveyed by the subjects contained in Pathé's first issue, which comprised a sculling contest, a strike of Camden factory girls and Queen Alexandra leaving to visit Italy.[9] Because the film was developed and printed in France, the pictures of British events could in the early stages take several weeks to cross the Channel and come back again for exhibition. But the service was soon speeded up, particularly after rivals appeared in the topical field, and very quickly a system of releasing a new reel every week became established. This was shortly followed by a service whereby two newsreels were provided every week. Of course since there was no sound on the film, all the messages describing the people, places and content had to be served up by the use of captions, both before and during a particular story. Such limitations meant, however, that the best visual footage, which was acknowledged to speak for itself and engage the audience's attention, was considered to be film of catastrophes or war.

The coming of the First World War provided a lot of such material, although the cameramen were limited by government instructions about what they could film. During the war the newsreel firms banded together and formed the Cinematograph Trade Topical Committee in an attempt to secure as much film as possible. But this organization was absorbed into the War Office Cinematograph Committee, under the chairmanship of Sir William Jury, as a result of which film shot by individual newsreels was generally distributed under government control to all the companies. In fact the British Government even went so far as to buy up the Topical Budget in November 1916, and to run it as an Official War News, though after the war Jeapes bought it back. The Government discovered the possibility of using film in general and newsreels in particular for the purposes of home front propaganda and for the dissemination of knowledge, always biased, upon matters of governmental interest. Somewhat late in the day, they set up a Ministry of Information, in March 1918, under Lord Beaverbrook, which had a cinematographic branch with the capacity to make films for various government departments. Theoretically the Ministry had no concern with opinion within Britain, since one department was aimed at American and Allied opinion, one at the neutrals and another against the enemy.[10] However, the Ministry did conduct propaganda on the home front, to such an extent that one MP felt compelled to raise a question in

Parliament concerning 'the possibility that public propaganda may be misused for commercial and class purposes' and expressing his fears that 'capitalistic interests had suborned national propaganda'.[11] The point of his remarks was contained in a speech which read:

I have a record of a very extraordinary film which is being performed now. . . . The title of the picture was *Once a Hun, always a Hun*. It first of all depicts two German soldiers in a ruined town in France. They meet a woman with a baby in her arms, and strike her to the ground. The two German soldiers then gradually merge into two commercial travellers, and are seen in an English village after the war. One of the travellers enters a small village general store, and proceeds to show to the shopkeeper a pan. The shopkeeper at the beginning is somewhat impressed by what is offered to him for sale, when his wife comes in and, turning the pan upside down, sees marked on it 'Made in Germany'. She then indulges in a good deal of scorn at the expense of the commercial traveller and calls in a policeman, who orders the German out of the shop. A final notice, flashed on the screen, was to the effect that there cannot possibly be any more trading with these people after the war and under this statement were the words, 'Ministry of Information'. The question of the policy of trade after the war has got to be decided by this country, but I hope the Ministry of Information does not intend to decide it before we have an opportunity even of discussing the Government policy.[12]

For all such fears that the Ministry of Information was committing the country in advance to a policy which Parliament had not yet decided upon, it would appear that in the short term the propaganda effort and the use of film in particular during the First World War met with great success.[13]

But by 1919 the content of newsreel releases was almost back to the normal fare of celebrities, royal personages and notable events. They simply reverted, slowy but surely, to what had won the public's interest prior to 1914. The Pathé Gazette content checklist for 3 July 1919[14] was full of material concerned with the end of the war and the signing of peace:

Peace Day: Huge crowds throng Trafalgar Square at 3.00 pm. Mr Lloyd George announces 'Peace is signed'. Thousands flock to acclaim the King at Buckingham Palace. The King and Queen and Royal Family appear. The King meets and drives back with Mr Lloyd George who brought us 'Peace with Honour'.

The Historic Scene at Versailles: The German delegates arrive and are conducted to the Hall of Mirrors. The Big Four are seen to the left of the picture. The Signing. The Prime Minister and Mrs Lloyd George home again at Downing Street.

Yet the very next Gazette hinted at the sort of story which would once again come to occupy most of the newsreel space, with pieces on Henley and a transatlantic airship. It contained:

Another air triumph: The R34, the first transatlantic air liner. (Approved for publication by the Air Ministry.) Sixteen American officers decorated by Sir Douglas Haig on the Horse Guards Parade.

The Proclaiming of Peace: The old-world ceremony at Temple Bar. A fanfare announces the arrival of Bluemantle to the Lord Mayor who gives permission for the cavalcade to enter. Reading the proclamation at the Royal Exchange. Chilly Henley: Bad weather mars opening day's racing. Scuttled: All that is visible of the once proud German 'High Seas' Fleet at Scapa Flow.[15]

It was with the arrival of peacetime conditions and the onset of the 1920s that rivalry between the newsreel companies for the attention of the cinemagoing public became intense. During this period the Gaumont Graphic was dubbed 'The Gruesome Graphic' by malicious competitors, the Empire Screen News became 'The Impure Screen News', and the Topical Budget was renamed 'The Comical Budget'. In order to win and hold their audience figures, the Pathé and Gaumont reels started special women's editions. Fate sometimes took a hand in dispensing with rivals, as when Topical Budget's offices were burned down in a fire which also damaged the façade of their neighbour's building at Pathé. But Pathé was by now an international concern and could afford to rebuild. Although Topical Budget had been a domestic success, it simply did not have enough financial backing to be able to sustain such a loss and start again. It collapsed as a newsreel company soon after the fire.

Most of the newsreels were constantly expanding. Out of the small 300-foot newsreel of 1910 grew the 'super' British reel of 1926, some 750 feet long. The three- or four-item Gazette had become six or seven items by 1920. Such an unprecedented demand for newsreel reportage necessitated an increase in staff and capital expenditure for coverage on the spot, which some of the small British concerns were not able to accommodate during a period of economic crisis. But what finally killed the smaller companies was the advent of sound and the subsequent increase, once again, to an average newsreel length of 850 feet, comprising some eight, ten or even twelve stories.[16]

As with the rest of the film industry, the newsreel companies, with the exception of Fox Movietone of America, hoped that the 'talkies' would be no more than a passing fad. But Movietone, grasping the opportunity to go ahead of their rivals, decided to expand their American operations and arrived in Britain in 1929 with British Movietone News. Movietone equipped their newsreel entirely with sound, which meant travelling to locations with several hundredweight of equipment such as microphones and cable, in a sound van, all of which could cost as much as £10,000 for each unit. None but the bigger companies could afford this new outlay in expenditure. Furthermore, the advent of sound also saw an increase in pay to cameramen, in an attempt to secure the services of the more experienced men who might be able to manage the new technical accomplishments. In his book *Useless if Delayed*, Paul Wyand tells how in 1928, as a British cameraman for American Fox in London, his pay was £5 a week. In 1929 he joined the British branch of Pathé at a salary of £9 a week, but later in the same year he rejoined Fox, this time as a cameraman for British Movietone, at a starting wage of £10 per week, rising at six-monthly intervals to £14.[17]

At the very beginning of their venture, British Movietone insisted upon shooting everything with sound. They set themselves up in offices in Berners Street, brought over half a dozen American cameramen for good measure and bought a fleet of left-hand drive Rio Speedwagons to ferry their equipment around. But they did not have to travel far to find people willing enough to commit themselves to sound on film, for as Paul Wyand put it:

One of the first people to appreciate the pack-'em-in value of 'talking' newsreels was the then Prime Minister, Ramsay MacDonald, who invited us to make a film in the garden at Downing Street. In it he introduced his Cabinet Ministers, each of whom mouthed a few platitudes into the microphone. The film resulted in queues outside every cinema at which it was shown, not due to some sudden awakening of the political consciousness, but because this was a newsreel with the additional marvel of sound.[18]

The other stories contained in the very first sound newsreels included items on rowing, Army horse-trials, and a piece on the Duke of York, later King George VI. At the time Movietone had five silent British counterparts—Pathé, Gaumont, Topical Budget, Empire News and British Screen News. Within a short while those that had not assimilated sound into their newsreels were to die or to be bought out. Gaumont Graphic was the second company to introduce sound, though they continued their silent edition for a while and allowed exhibitors a choice between the two. Pathé followed suit soon after. Paramount set up production facilities in Britain in 1931 and were the fourth company to accommodate for sound recording. The Empire Screen News failed to do so, and they were bought up by Universal, who were also looking for British opportunities to extend their American operations.[19]

By the beginning of the 1930s, then, the lines were drawn and the stage was set for domination of the British newsreel industry by five companies, all affiliated to major international film corporations, a situation which was to last until the demise of the cinema newsreel itself. Gaumont, Pathé, Movietone, Paramount and Universal were the big five and seemed intent to remain so, by fair means or foul, for many years to come. For, if the 1920s had been distinguished by a strong sense of rivalry within the newsreel industry, then the early 30s could only be described as the era of 'the newsreel war', prompted by the arrival on the scene of the large American film corporations. One reason for the war was put forward by Paul Wyand when he commented:

In the twenties, it must be remembered that there was no television, picture magazines such as *Illustrated* and *Picture Post* were still many years away and newspaper production of photographs was, in the main, both technically poor and editorially unimaginative. Consequently there was a tremendous demand for newsreels and this in itself stimulated rivalry.[20]

But that reason by itself does not adequately explain the deep feelings of mutual animosity which reached their height during the first half of the decade which followed. The main cause of the trouble was the sudden granting of exclusive rights for coverage of various events (the Grand National, important football matches) which all the newsreels had habitually attended. Once the desire to 'scoop' these events got into full swing, the rivalry to secure exclusives manifested itself in every area of newsreel activity. It achieved such notoriety that the feature film industry incestuously determined to capitalize on it with a 1938 film entitled *Too Hot To Handle*, starring Clark Gable as an intrepid newsreel cameraman who risks losing his loved one, Myrna Loy, rather than sacrifice a good story.

Many commentators have noted the existence of this rivalry between the newsreels, but few have pinpointed the cause, after 1930, as lying with the granting of exclusive rights, and the opening up of the opportunity to bid for them, something that was actually brought about by the action of organizations outside the film industry. The responsibility really rests with those bodies who felt they could capitalize upon the desire of the newsreels to be present at important occasions in order to extort large sums of money from them. For by 1936 a big event was costing Gaumont British up to £2,000 on rights alone, apart from their weekly budget which amounted to £3,000 for two editions.[21] The competition between the newsreel companies simply intensified, not only in the race to secure exclusive rights, but also in their attempts to pirate material at events for which one company alone was supposed to hold a monopoly.

The evidence relating to this pirating remains purely anecdotal in character and generally emerges from the reminiscences of former newsreel cameramen who took part in the numerous encounters. It is therefore only fitting that it should be summed up by one of their number, Kenneth Gordon:

Then Gaumont entered the war, buying up all the rights they could, some of which they shared with Movietone. Pathé lost the rights of the Grand National by being outbid, and we had to become a pirate at this fixture. Pathé used scaffold towers: fights took place around these, although they were outside the course. The towers were built at the last minute; on our stand were Jock Gemmell, with his range of long-focus lenses, and myself with the slow-motion camera. Then the fight was on. Our opponents got hold of the rope which we used to lift our gear, and started to pull the tower over. Just as this 60ft. tower was about to topple over, someone cut the rope and we just managed to get our cameras lined up. The race had started. Then we were attacked for a second time. Fireworks were started in front of the cameras, which frightened the horses, causing the favourite, Golden Miller, to fall in front of our slow-motion camera. That season's Test Matches brought out balloons, heavy net, and many other tricks to stop filming. The balloons were punctured by air-gun fire, and the pictures stolen.[22]

However by 1936, because of the competitive and ever-increasing spiral of bidding, the price being demanded for exclusive film rights had risen out of all proportion to the budgets of the newsreels. And as a result of a conference called by the Cinematograph Exhibitors' Association in that same year, all the newsreels agreed to co-operate on big national events for a period of one year. Not surprisingly, the situation was immediately eased and the newsreels showed a degree of harmony which nobody, least of all themselves, could have foreseen. This was borne out when between them the newsreels offered a sum in the region of £2,000 for the rights to film the 1936 Cup Final. Wembley Stadium held out for more money and refused to grant such rights. So the newsreels got together and decided to withdraw their first offer, substituting in its place a smaller one. Needless to say, Wembley now rejected the offer outright and started making plans to film the match for themselves. They intended to release the completed film in the form of featurettes which would be distributed at £12 10s. per booking. The newsreels responded by hiring planes and autogyros which they were finally given permission to use, since they were on good terms with the Air Ministry. Because the Wembley authorities rarely, if ever, had cause to consult the Air Ministry, their attempts to dissuade the latter body from granting permission to hover and fly over Wembley Stadium quite naturally fell upon deaf ears. The outcome was as *World Film News* recounted:

Came the day. Under the command of the intrepid Campbell Black, the flying armada took to the air and the sky was black with long-focus lenses. Everybody got a picture, the cinemas had it by early evening and democracy was saved.[23]

The harmony manifested by the newsreels over this particular incident took them completely by surprise. For a while the Football League, who were quite innocent of what ensued over a Football Association Cup Final, were worried by a retaliatory threat from at least one newsreel company that during the following League season it might feel compelled to boycott the film coverage of all soccer matches. However such a threat never materialized, and soccer continued to be shown in the cinemas and on the newsreels, though newsreel cameramen and producers never quite forgot their capacity for working together, should the occasion ever arise.

This then was the position in which the newsreels found themselves by the mid-1930s, at the beginning of what might be termed, to borrow a phrase, the 'golden age' of the newsreel. By 1936 the British newsreels manifested all the characteristics of the modern newsreel. Little was to change between that point and the very death of the cinema newsreel itself. And when in January 1938 the Board of Trade was to ask for a suitable definition of the term 'newsreel', the Newsreel Association of Great Britain and Ireland could readily reply:

A Newsreel is one of a series of films published not less than once weekly, compiled, produced or issued by a recognised Newsreel Company, and
(a) mainly composed of items of 'up-to-the-minute' news or matters germane thereto, or
(b) covering a current event of such importance as to warrant a special edition relating to that particular item only.[24]

Of course there were slight variations between one company's product and the next. It will be seen, for instance, that some newsreels cleverly related one item or topic in an issue to another, in order to make a certain point or emphasize a particular contrast. Furthermore, the presentation of these items was not always so straightforward, and the newsreels manifested a capacity for interpretation just as much as any of the other media. This was appreciated by some film critics early in the day. In 1933, for example, Donald Fraser commented:

British Movietone strives after a BBC impartiality, although it is a BBC jockey trying to ride a Wardour Street horse. Paramount News approximates very closely to the American tabloid. Gaumont Graphic suggests a bourgeois atmosphere, redolent of public houses. While Universal Talking News inclines more and more to the funny page of the Chorlton-cum-Hardy Gazette.[25]

One thing, however, was beyond dispute. By 1936 the newsreels in Britain had evolved to a point where five major companies were in command of the news-bearing potential within the cinema industry.

THE MONEY BEHIND THE NEWSREEL SCREEN

At the beginning of 1936, the five major newsreel companies were self-contained production units of large British and American film corporations whose main interests were in the production of feature films. Gaumont British News was a subsidiary of the Gaumont British Picture Corporation, which also controlled Gainsborough Pictures; Pathé Gazette was part of the Associated British Picture Corporation, which also had interests in British International Pictures; British Movietone was controlled in part by the American film company 20th Century-Fox; Paramount News was owned by a subsidiary of the American Paramount company; and the Universal News was produced by British Pictorial Productions and affiliated to the Universal Film Company of America.

Yet for all their undoubted independence of each other and their respective parent companies at the production level, financial inter-relations were known to exist between several of these companies, and that fact in itself may go some way towards explaining how 'the big five' secured a monopoly of the newsreel industry from 1936 onwards.

The Gaumont British Picture Corporation was formed in March 1927. The original Gaumont concern in London had been formed as early as 1898 by Lt-Col A. C. Bromhead but had at that time only served as an agency for Léon Gaumont of Paris. By 1922 the Gaumont Company had come entirely under British control, with the major interest being acquired by Bromhead and his British associates. In 1927 the Gaumont British Picture Corporation was formed to acquire the Gaumont Company and Bromhead was appointed chairman of this new company, though he resigned from the position in 1929.[1]

By January 1936, the Gaumont British Picture Corporation
Ltd was controlled by the Metropolis and Bradford Trust Co Ltd.
It owned 2,915,000 ordinary ten-shilling shares out of a total issue
of 5,000,000. However of those 2,915,000 shares 2,100,000 were
held on behalf of the 20th Century-Fox Film Corporation, and
815,000 were held on behalf of three brothers, Maurice, Mark and
Isidore Ostrer.[2] The board of directors of GBPC consisted of the
following members:

Isidore Ostrer (President)
Mark Ostrer (Chairman and Managing Director)
Maurice Ostrer (Assistant Managing Director)
S. R. Kent
Dixon Broadman
O. H. C. Balfour
J. Maxwell
Col H. A. Micklam
C. H. Dade
I. P. Little[3]

If the Gaumont interest was reflected in the presence of the
Ostrers, then the 20th Century-Fox concern was reflected in the
presence of S. R. Kent, O. H. C. Balfour and D. Broadman. For
Kent was at the same time the president of 20th Century-Fox,
while Balfour and Broadman were chairman and managing
director respectively of Balfour, Broadman and Co, who were the
Fox bankers in this country.[4] It should also be noted that one of
the directors, John Maxwell, was in turn the chairman and
managing director of the Associated British Picture Corporation,
which ran the Pathé Gazette.

The same triple interest manifested itself in the ownership of the
controlling company, Metropolis and Bradford Trust, where the
shares were divided among the following members:[5]

'A' shares (*Voting*)
5,100 by Isidore Ostrer
4,700 by 20th Century-Fox
100 by W. J. Hutchinson (Manager, Fox)
50 by S. R. Kent (President, Fox)
50 by R. B. McDonald (Solicitor, Fox)

'B' shares (non-Voting)
750,000 by United American Investment Corporation (for Fox)
250,000 by John Maxwell on behalf of Associated British Picture
Corporation

The 250,000 'B' shares had been owned by the Ostrers until October 1936, when they sold them to John Maxwell on behalf of ABPC. In return they received 300,000 ordinary shares in ABPC. Maxwell's intention was not only to participate in the financial benefits that might accrue from the Metropolis and Bradford but also to obtain control of Gaumont British. To this end in November he also acquired a five-year option on the 5,100 voting shares, but Fox objected to such a takeover and the control of Gaumont British remained unchanged.[6] The proposed takeover would have severely affected the nature of the newsreel industry in Britain and these considerations must have weighed heavily in Fox's deliberations over the matter. For the Movietone newsreel was shown at a percentage of Gaumont British cinemas. If Maxwell had secured the shares, there was a strong likelihood that the Pathé Gazette would have replaced the Movietone reel in those Gaumont cinemas, as well as being shown in their own ABC theatres. In such an eventuality Movietone would have been blocked from entry into either of the two largest cinema circuits then operating in Britain. For a while the cinema's trade press was full of talk about this 'Guy Fawkes Deal'[7] and about Gaumont and ABC being 'past rivals, future brothers'.[8] But the final outcome was that nothing changed on the newsreel front. The major threat throughout this period to the stability of three of the big five newsreel companies was scotched by the control which one of them held over the share ownership of one of its rivals.

Apart from their holdings in Gaumont, 20th Century-Fox still of course retained a controlling interest in their own newsreel product, the British Movietone News. But here the Harmsworth family also held a strong influence. For Movietone News was jointly controlled by Fox and the Hon. Esmond Harmsworth, who was chairman of Associated Newspapers Ltd, *Daily Mail* and General Trust Ltd, as well as being a director of Imperial Airways Ltd. Fox held 25,498 shares at 7s. 6d., and Harmsworth held 21,500 shares of the 50,000 shares available. The board of directors included the names of two men already familiar to Gaumont, S. R. Kent and R. B. McDonald, who represented Fox, the Hon. E. Harmsworth and G. W. Price, on behalf of Associated Newspapers, and a fifth member, F. L. Harley.[9] The Movietone reel was the newsreel most closely associated with the world of journalism through Harmsworth and G. Ward Price, then leading foreign correspondent of the *Daily Mail*.

The Pathé Gazette comprised part of the mammoth Associated British Picture Corporation. With the exception of John Maxwell, the chairman and managing director, none of the other five directors was represented on the boards of rival film companies. The largest single block of ordinary shares, amounting to a total of 1,569,000, was held by Cinema Investments Ltd, a private company controlled and owned by Maxwell and four of his associates.[10] However, after 12 October 1936, the largest individual shareholders of the company were the Ostrers, who had obtained their 300,000 ordinary shares as part of the exchange deal with Maxwell for their non-voting Gaumont shares.

Universal Talking News was produced for the American parent company of the same name by British Pictorial Productions Ltd, which had no financial interaction with any of the other newsreel companies in the way that Gaumont, Movietone and Pathé had. British Pictorial Productions had been registered as a company in 1926 with a £5,000 share capital of £1 each. In the beginning it had produced the Empire News Bulletin, but that reel was subsumed into the Universal Talking News with the advent of sound film. The directors were three in number: W. C. Jeapes (managing director), C. W. Jeapes and A. P. Smith, who were also the only shareholders.[11] However Universal News had strong links with perhaps the most rapidly expanding cinema corporation during the years from 1936 to 1939, J. Arthur Rank's General Cinema Finance Corporation (GCFC).

Immediately after its formation in March 1936, GCFC took over one of the largest film distributors in Britain, General Film Distributors, which had been founded in June 1935 by C. M. Woolf after his resignation from Gaumont British. Furthermore, over the next few years it added the Odeon chain of cinemas and the County Cinemas circuit to its small GCFC circuit to become the third largest exhibitor after Gaumont and ABC. Early in 1936 the major American company, Universal, was wrested from the control of its founder, Carl Laemmle, by a group of American and British financiers, including Rank. As a result of this transaction Universal News passed into the domain of the GCFC, was distributed by General Film Distributors and shown in many of the Odeon cinemas.[12] And at Gaumont, meanwhile, the euphoria and over-investment encouraged by the world-wide success of Korda's *The Private Life of Henry VIII* had resulted in the company suffering setbacks and deciding that it was no longer economic to run their production studios at Shepherd's Bush, or their distribution facilities. So General Film Distributors also acquired the rights to distribute the Gaumont newsreel. From April 1937 Universal News therefore became inadvertently wedded with the Gaumont British Newsreel, albeit only at the level of distribution.[13]

The only newsreel that remained completely free of any ties with its fellow competitors was the British Paramount News, which was the property of American Paramount pictures. It sought an exhibition outlet through the many independent cinemas up and down the country, thereby precluding the necessity for forging any links with its rivals either at the level of distribution or large circuit exhibition.

These five newsreels held a monopoly so strong that it became virtually impossible for control to be taken away from any one of them or for a new arrival to impose upon their dominance. It has already been seen how John Maxwell's attempts radically to alter the status quo came to nothing. The circumstances surrounding the short-lived and ill-fated National News reveal how difficult it was for a newcomer to survive.

The National News was the idea of Norman Loudon, the chairman of Sound City Ltd. It had gained a reputation as 'one of Britain's smaller but thoroughly efficient production and distribution companies'.[14] In July 1937, Loudon engaged as his editor-in-chief Cecil R. Snape, who had spent thirteen years as the editor of the Empire News, later the Universal Talking News. Their intentions were sufficiently interesting and different. It was their desire to break away from the almost obligatory length of 850 feet per newsreel, and to print three different lengths in order to offer variety for exhibitors. There would be a five star reel, running for 1,200 feet, a four star of 800 feet, and a three star of 500 feet. The hiring costs would vary accordingly. The make-up of the reel would consist of a smaller number of bigger stories, thereby dispensing with the Roving Camera Reports section put out by Gaumont, for example, or the News in Flashes as used by Paramount. It was hoped that these longer stories would allow for more news in depth, along the lines of the monthly *March of Time* newsreel compilation. Finally, it was proposed that the commentator would be allowed to collaborate in the writing of scripts for stories before they were shot and that he would work in close co-operation with the editors and cutters. Their intention here was to emulate a style of commentating cum editing similar to that so successfully evolved at Gaumont, where Ted Emmett was in charge of both functions. Their commentator was to be Tommy Woodrooffe, a BBC announcer who had made something of a name for himself when he was sent to Spithead for the Coronation Naval Review of May 1937. Night fell, fireworks were started, and Woodrooffe was heard to say in his commentary: 'The fleet's all lit up', only to add as a corrective rejoinder, 'When I say lit up, I mean, with lights.'[15]

The first National News release was issued on 11 October 1937, and withdrawn on the afternoon of 13 October. In November it tried an 'experimental' Armistice edition, but the cinema managers were not interested in trying it out in their cinemas. It closed down that same month. Two reasons accounted for its failure. First of all it received a critical panning and 'Terribly disappointing' was the unanimous verdict.[16] But most of all it failed because it could not secure regular distribution to cinemas which already had strong ties with other newsreels. There can be little doubt that the existing newsreel companies exerted pressure on their distribution outlets not to take up the new product. It was rumoured that National News had pinned its hopes most of all upon encroaching into the Odeon circuit,[17] but the Odeons already had the choice between Universal News and Gaumont British News, as offered to them by General Film Distributors. This factor, together with the poor quality of its first issue, meant that National News never really had much chance of succeeding in the close-knit world of the newsreel.

But what chance did the big five newsreel companies have of success? Did the uncertain situation in film finance during the years between 1936 and 1939 affect the outcome of newsreel production at all and did they suffer any cutback?

Both these questions are impossible to answer with any degree of certainty, for, as *The Factual Film* put it in 1947, 'The balance sheets of the newsreel companies are the private concern of their parent companies and no separate disclosures of newsreel budgets are made.'[18] However, for all the lack of information where budgets are concerned, there is some evidence available to enable one to speculate generally about the state of newsreel finance.

Perhaps the most important point to be made at the outset is that whether the newsreels made money or not, it is highly unlikely that they would have suffered any cutback, even during a period of financial stringency, either in the resources at their disposal, or in economic backing. Two reasons have been put forward to help in reaching this conclusion. The first argument states:

What is of significance is that the newsreel companies were run by their parent companies as a break-even advertising unit to keep their names before the cinemagoers and to keep off others who would undoubtedly have filled their time span on the screen.[19]

The second argument is similar in scope and suggests:

The most important feature of newsreel finances is that whether they make a profit or not, they always have the backing of the parent company and would probably continue production for the sake of prestige even in the face of a financial loss.[20]

Advertising and prestige then are two reasons why it is generally accepted that, regardless of the financial state of the newsreel industry, the standards of newsreel production were not likely to suffer. Nor indeed was there any likelihood of them closing down, at least not in the face of competitors from within the film industry alone. Since the newsreels were in some way allied to feature film companies, it was more than likely that an audience would see one particular company's name several times during the course of an evening's entertainment. And the film companies lived in as much hope of an audience associating quality with their product, whatever form it took, as did the cinema managers of generating an ABC audience, an Odeon audience, or a Gaumont audience.

In an interview for *World Film News*, Castleton Knight, who was in charge of production at the Gaumont newsreel, maintained that by May 1936 their weekly budget for two editions ran to about £3,000, although he stressed the figure was exclusive of specials, where the rights to a big event could cost up to £2,000 extra.[21] But in 1937, figures released by the Board of Trade showed that overall the newsreels produced 577 reels with a total length of 606.5 thousands of feet, and at a cost of £296,000.[22] Those Board of Trade figures reduce to an average sum of £513 per edition or £1,026 for a week's run of two editions, less than half the figure suggested by Castleton Knight.

Certainly, the five newsreel companies did not spend an equal amount of money, and undoubtedly Gaumont would have spent more on their reels than Universal, for example, which was renowned for its economic stringency. However, by 1937 Castleton Knight's figure of £3,000 would have been somewhat reduced. For by that time the newsreel companies were increasingly sharing many costs. If both these factors are taken into consideration, it is probable that the cost per week to Gaumont during 1937 for two editions was somewhere in the region of £2,000–£3,000. Of course there are no figures available to reveal how much Gaumont took in return for their product during this period.[23] Yet it is noticeable that despite the fact that the Gaumont Corporation suffered a bad financial year overall in 1936, there was no talk at all of closing down their newsreel during the Annual General Meeting which was held on 2 November 1936. It was believed, however, that 'with the cessation of the production of films other than the Gaumont British Newsreel', and 'with the additional revenue from the newsreel', then 'the heavy losses incurred in the current year could be non-recurring.'[24]

All deliberations upon the state of newsreel finances must in the final analysis remain tentative. But it does seem that what killed the newsreels finally was not so much the lack of money to sustain them, but more the competition from television which could report the news that much more quickly.

THE ORGANIZATIONAL STRUCTURE OF THE NEWSREELS
In order to determine what value newsreel film might have for the historian, it is essential to know precisely what effect the structure

of the newsreel-bearing organizations had upon the content of their products. For only then will it be possible to ascertain what areas of manipulation there were inherent in the very process of newsreel production. Such an examination would need to look closely at the personnel who staffed the newsreel companies, how these men produced the newsreels and what latitude there was for influencing content at the various stages of production.

It has been suggested that 'The newsreels of the 1930s belonged much more to the world of journalism than to the film-world.'[1] To some extent this observation is correct. It has already been seen that in the ownership of at least one newsreel company, British Movietone, there was a strong connection with the *Daily Mail*. But how far was it also the case that the newsreel companies were staffed by 'ex-Fleet street men'?[2] And where did the men come from who constituted the personnel of the newsreel companies at all levels?

There was strong criticism at the time that 'newsreel policies and organisations are under the control of men who, in fact, are not newsreel men. In only two cases have qualified newsreel men got executive positions and one of these is burdened by non-technical control.'[3] But if it can be seen that the men in control of the newsreel companies were not newsreel or even film men, then neither were they necessarily newspaper men. At the executive level it is evident that the bigger the company, especially if it formed part of an international combine, the less likelihood there was of finding a man in charge who had experience of either the film or newspaper world. Of course it was only to be expected that such companies would fill their executive positions with men whom one might have confidently found in similar positions anywhere within the world of large-scale business.

At Movietone, for example, the Harmsworth influence was obvious. Gerald Fountaine Sanger occupied the position of executive producer. He was educated at Shrewsbury, served in the Royal Marines from 1917 to 1919 and then went to Keble College, Oxford. From 1922 to 1929 he was secretary to the Hon. Esmond Harmsworth before taking up his position with British Movietone. He was a member of the Windham Club.[4] Sir Malcolm Campbell, MBE, was the editor-in-chief and occasionally took on the role of commentator.[5] Sir Gordon Craig was the general manager. He had been born in 1891 and knighted in 1929. He was a Liveryman of the Gold and Silver Wyre Drawers Company, vice-president of the 'Old Contemptibles' Association, and president of the Hackney Branch of the British Legion. His clubs were the Royal Thames Yacht Club and Sunningdale.[6]

The men who ran the production side, especially at Gaumont British and Universal News, had stronger connections with the film industry, though none with the world of journalism. Cecil R. Snape, for instance, who was editor-in-charge at Universal, had been in the film industry for most of his life. Born in 1888, he joined the trade in 1911, becoming the general manager and secretary of the Kinematograph Trading Company Ltd, and its associated concerns. During the war he served as a photographer in the RFC and the RAF, and afterwards spent some time in America in feature film production. He returned to Britain as editor-in-chief of the Empire News Bulletin and later of the Universal Talking News, both of which he ran from the very first issues.[7] Similarly H. W. Bishop joined the trade in 1910, specializing on the technical and production sides of the industry, first in processing in the laboratories, and then for ten years as a cameraman for newsreel, scientific and studio productions. He was at first technical adviser to the old Gaumont company, and later became production manager for Gaumont British News.[8] Even the news contact manager, H. T. Bromige, was not, as might have been expected, a former Fleet Street man, but had spent his working life in the film industry, first in the accounts and film library departments at Gaumont and later as a cameraman.[9]

At Movietone the actual production ranks had plenty of experience of film, though once again little of journalism. Thomas F. Scales, their assistant editor, had been on the topical side of the business since 1905, starting in the dark room of the Warwick Trading Company before joining Barker's Gaumont and then spending seventeen years with Pathé Gazette.[10]

But if the newsreel executives came from the world of business, and the majority of general and production managers from the early days of the film industry, then it is certainly the case that most of the cameramen had at some point in their lives worked as press photographers.

Kenneth Gordon, for example, who was invaluable as a

cameraman to Pathé, had intended to take up a career in engineering but started working part-time as a projectionist. From there he served an apprenticeship in photography with Bolak's Press Agency. He was one of the first photographers on the *Daily Mirror* to use photo-telegraphy. He later joined the *Bristol Evening News* as a photographic reporter, then worked with the Gaumont Company for King Edward vii's funeral and King George v's Coronation. He filmed the Delhi Durbar and returned to experiment with early colour processes such as Kinemacolour, Biocolour and Chronochrome. As a photographer in the Balkan War with the Turks, he filmed and took press photographs for the London News Agency and the *Illustrated London News*. With the advent of the First World War, Gordon joined the army but acted as the official cinematographer on the Royal Tours to the Industrial North in 1917. After the Armistice he joined the official newsreel of the Ministry of Information and was a war cameraman with the British North Russian force before finally joining Pathé, for whom he was the staff photographer in Ireland during the troubles.[11]

Either the cameramen went to the newsreels with experience of 'photo-journalism', like Gordon, or they went after gaining experience of camerawork for the British Government in the First World War. Jock Gemmell of Pathé Gazette was an example of the latter, having joined the RAF and become a photographic officer, then leaving to work for Topical Budget in May 1919, only to join Pathé in June 1920.[12] Harold H. Jeapes had left England in December 1920 to accompany the Duke of Connaught on his Indian Tour as Official Kinematographer. Jeapes had held a similar position for two and a half years with the Egyptian Expeditionary Force in Palestine, where he filmed the entry into Jerusalem and Damascus, before returning to Universal News.[13]

It would appear then that the personnel who made up the staff of the various newsreel companies had only tenuous connections with journalism, apart from the cameramen who might easily have worked in both fields of reportage at some point in their careers. Yet for all that it is evident 'the ethical and professional aspects of newsreel-reporting are the same as those of the Press, and the organisations are also similar.'[14] This can be seen from a study of the newsreel operation and process of production.

Certainly the organization of a newsreel had to be as quick and efficient as that of Fleet Street. Gaumont British News, for example, circulated in 1,750 cinemas throughout Britain by June 1936. In order to accommodate such a demand it gathered its news from all over the world. Gaumont had a cameraman ready to cover local events in every town of importance in Britain. Two tape-machines provided a twenty-four-hour-a-day service in their London office and in addition they claimed a network of 4,000 local correspondents ready to telephone in whenever a story broke. Gaumont British had its own office at Heston Aerodrome with a plane and pilots on permanent stand-by. It had soon perfected a system of air distribution to its cinemas for scoops and specials which enabled a total distance of 1,400 miles to be covered in three hours. Gaumont had twenty-seven cameramen and five mobile recording trucks permanently employed by the company.[15] Universal News was the only company not actually in possession of any recording trucks. Universal was financially the poor cousin of the newsreel industry and had never bought any sound equipment for outside coverage, thereby becoming totally dependent upon manufactured studio sounds and so losing the opportunity to turn from being Universal Talking News into Universal Sound News.[16]

The newsreel companies covered foreign news in a variety of ways. Gaumont, for example, had cameramen available in all the large continental towns, these freelance 'stringers' being paid for the amount of footage they shot which was used by the company. In America Gaumont had a tie-up with Fox Movietone and the Hearst Newsreel. Since it did not in fact have a complete foreign service of its own, Gaumont obtained many world-wide pictures via British Movietone and the world-wide service of Movietone of America, in return for which the latter's reel was shown at a percentage of Gaumont cinemas in Britain. Pathé Gazette had its own foreign service and was linked with Pathé News of America, with Pathé Journal of France, with UFA, the official German newsreel, with the government newsreel in Russia and with others in South Africa, Australia and New Zealand.[17] Paramount also had its own world-wide organization. Of course most of the newsreels also had working arrangements with one or other of the big British news agencies such as Reuters, the Press Association, the Exchange Telegraph Co, and Central News, or the American agencies, Associated Press, United Press or International Press.

The hub of any newsreel company was undoubtedly its central office and it was this part which most closely resembled the office of a daily newspaper, with its editorial rooms, caption writers, developing rooms, printing department, all very much the same as in any Fleet Street office.[18] Generally speaking, it was divided into two main departments known as assignment and make-up. It was the assignment or news editor who had to be in closest touch with events in the outside world, arranging what subjects should be filmed and allocating the work to the cameraman and sound recordist. It was the job of the latter men to journey to the spot where the picture was to be shot, with a sound truck, a motor van which carried the sound recording apparatus including microphone, cameras, cables and all. The assignment editor's job was at its easiest with such stock subjects as the Derby and Wimbledon, which occurred year in and year out at pre-set times. But of course it was the unexpected happening, the sudden catastrophes and disasters, that caused the most trouble, calling for more than a small measure of personal resource and initiative from assignment editors and, most of all, cameramen.

In practice, the process of newsreel coverage allowed for a great deal of latitude in the areas of selection and decision-making, both on the part of the news editor with regard to what should be covered in the first place, and on the part of the cameraman, with regard to how it should be reported. On the whole the cameramen did a straightforward job of covering their assignments as best they could, but occasionally the camera's inevitable selectivity was obviously enhanced by the location chosen for the shots and by the angles chosen to shoot from. A British Paramount News story for 18 October 1937[19] no longer has any of the original commentary on it, yet for all that it is obvious how, through the choice of camera angles, this film of General Franco holding a youth parade in Burgos goes out of its way to romanticize and even glorify him. The camera is positioned so that, in any shots of Franco himself, the audience is continually looking up at the dictator. The exoticism, almost Easternness, of the setting is highlighted strongly. The Moorish troops are found in extravagantly heroic postures and the close-ups of the Franco youth tend to isolate a host of beautiful Spanish girls and well-groomed men.

Once the first-hand footage was back at the head office, it was viewed in negative form by an editor, and what was considered to be the best visual material was immediately selected for possible release, and cut down to a state where it might comprise one of the eight, ten or twelve stories that together formed an issue. Where the original sound on the negative was good or where a speech had been recorded it would probably be preserved, but where the original sound did not complement the story it was wiped out and new sound from the library, more sound effects or mood music, would be added to replace it or augment the original. Music could completely change the tone of a newsreel, as with a Gaumont story for 2 February 1939,[20] where the music accompanying the entry of General Yague's troops into Barcelona is of such a stirring and martial character as to shift these shots from the realm of reportage almost towards the feature film. The drums are rolling as the flags are held aloft, and whilst it is impossible to know for sure what effect such a piece would have had on the audience seeing it at the time, the sequence is so well put together that one's attention and sympathies are engaged even now.

Of course such attempts to dramatize a newsreel story could easily lead to over-embellishment, as with a Paramount story for 17 August 1936[21] which has a series of shots of Republican soldiers firing their rifles at the statue of Christ and His Angels in Madrid, where it is obvious that the soldiers are not in fact firing their rifles at all, yet the sound effects of rifle fire have been laid over their actions. This, together with a commentary to the effect that 'you are now about to witness an event that shocked the world', casts such a heavily anti-Christian shadow over the Republican soldiers that one is tempted to wonder how far the whole action may have been staged at the request of the camera team. Worries such as those expressed in recent years by Murray Sayle, for example, in the *Sunday Times* about fabricated television news coverage of the India–Pakistan War, and the subsequent correspondence this provoked concerning shelling especially done for the benefit of CBS News men, are by no means new.[22] The newsreel teams were just as capable of asking for similar effects.

While the sound effects and music were being laid it was the job of the scriptwriter and commentator (sometimes one and the same person) to work hand in hand with the editor to evolve a commentary. Whereupon the edited film would be projected before the commentator whose voice would be piped into a mixing machine, where it joined the other sounds, which were toned down while he was speaking. Meanwhile titles would come from the print shop and such artistic effects as dissolves, wipeouts and double exposures were added. Next to the editor, the commentator and his scriptwriter had the greatest opportunity to influence the shape of an issue and to determine where its emphasis would lie. Where once 'the picture told the story', eventually, after the advent of sound, it became a matter of the commentator 'telling' and the picture 'illustrating' the most photogenic incidents.

Three British newsreels, Gaumont, Universal and Pathé, used the single commentator technique.[23] E. V. H. (Ted) Emmett at Gaumont had a style which was light, witty and tongue-in-cheek. Emmett had trained for the Stock Exchange and joined Gaumont as a cutter in their silent days. He enjoyed one enormous advantage over his rivals in that he controlled the cutting of all Gaumont stories, so that picture and commentary always matched. His voice was on many occasions instrumental in dictating the tone and mood of a story, as with Gaumont's release for 6 May 1937,[24] where a superbly edited story on the bombing of Guernica and a highly emotional commentary from Emmett ending on the line 'These were homes once, like yours' managed to point a decidedly anti-war message. R. E. Jeffrey at Universal was not in quite so powerful a position, though he was able to write his own scripts. His style was far more homely, with its strength in a slow, heavily emphasized, fireside manner. Jeffrey had been a pioneer of the British Broadcasting Company where he was better known as Uncle Jeff of Children's Hour. During the course of the Spanish Civil War, Pathé Gazette made use of the heavy, rolling dramatic voice of Roy de Groot, who at twenty joined the BBC, and became in turn studio announcer, outside broadcast commentator and programme producer. With his bass voice de Groot was strongest on drama and tragedy, reportedly putting so much feeling into his description of the funeral of King George V that Pathé News of America released the British version, with his voice on it, in their cinemas throughout the United States.

Like their American counterparts, Movietone and Paramount used the multi-commentator technique, though the criticism levelled at them in Britain was that all the voices sounded alike.[25] Paramount held rigidly to a policy of complete anonymity for its commentators. Movietone employed a host of commentators including Sir Malcolm Campbell, who made only rare appearances, Eric Dunstan, an ex-BBC announcer and journalist, Leslie Mitchell, an ex-actor whose main job was as a BBC announcer, Ivan Scott, who was also Movietone news editor for a while, and Beryl de Querton, the first woman newsreel commentator. It was British Movietone who pioneered the multi-voiced technique, and they were very good at letting the scriptwriter have a fair amount of latitude to draft his ideas first, before the negative was cut. However, their scriptwriters were not their commentators and once again the criticism was levelled that the commentators' voices were plummily indistinguishable from one another. Indeed there is an anecdote about a Movietone commentator who, while covering the Boat Race for 1937, finally decided to add, much to the delight of one audience, 'I expect you realize that I am an Oxford man myself.'[26] Once again the problems encountered by the newsreels can be seen to predate the problems now faced by television news, in this case over the pronunciation of the English language as spoken by the newsreaders.[27]

None of the British newsreels ever attained the heights of multiplicity reached by their American counterparts where, for example at Movietone, Lew Lehr would always take the comedy stories, Louise Vance the fashions, and the whole issue would invariably be introduced and summarized by Lowell Thomas (with script by his writer Prosper Burnelli); or at Pathé, where Bob Bartlett would cover travel and Clem McCarthy sport. In the States the companies very quickly realized that the personality of a commentator could easily generate a 'fan' following.

Generally, though, it was the editor's work on any one newsreel which revealed most about the newsreel coverage of the pressing topics of the day. It is from the array of cinematographic techniques at the disposal of the editor and the purpose for which he used them that it becomes possible to determine how a particular company covered a foreign event such as the Civil War in Spain.

Of course an editor would have at his fingertips not only the footage coming in regularly from his cameramen but also an immense library of stock-shot footage which could be used at any time to augment a story. A Universal release for 8 October 1934,[28] supposedly covering the Spanish miners' riots in Asturias, is in fact made up entirely of stock-shot footage of riots in Spain from 1932. A Paramount report on 7 October 1935,[29] covering the Italian invasion of Ethiopia, actually goes so far as to introduce some trick war material and feature film footage from America, in order to strengthen the point the editor wished to make. A similar piece of editorial manipulation occurs in Gaumont's Spanish story for 9 November 1936.[30] It purports to show the Fall of Madrid, some two and a half years ahead of time. In his attempt to scoop what was generally felt at the time to be a likely occurrence, the Gaumont editor wrongly, but consciously, ascribes certain shots of General Franco at Burgos, taken some time beforehand, to his supposed arrival as the victor of Madrid.

The potential then for misleading the cinemagoing public was enormous. It was in the very nature of film to be manipulated, and it was also in the nature of the newsreel organizations and their production process, for a number of different people to play a part in the manipulation of reportage for whatever purposes.

THE TECHNOLOGY AND THE TECHNICIANS

The motion picture industry has always been one of rapid technological change, if only in an attempt to capture the attention of the cinemagoing audience of the day by means of such passing fads as 3-D. Yet for all that, the highly cumbersome nature of the technological means of production has meant that the limitations imposed upon the newsreel cameraman, for instance, have been immense.

The requirements of camera design for the newsreel cameraman in particular were simple and straightforward. The first requisite was of course the lens and lens focusing, for it was a fact that 'the poorest lens made, well mounted, will produce a sharper image than the best lens badly mounted.'[1] For the newsreel cameraman, speed and accuracy were undoubtedly the essential prerequisites, which meant that the cameraman had to rely a lot upon his lens scale. The lens itself could not be as accurately focused, if done so visually, as it could if it were well-mounted and also calibrated.

One good example of the difference was found during 1937, when Pathé announced a few days before the Coronation that they would use a new fifty-six-inch lens.[2] It had been specially made for them by Taylor Hobson in order to take shots of the King and Queen on the Buckingham Palace balcony from the steps of the Victoria Memorial, a distance of some 400 yards. The results when shown on the screen were disappointing: the picture was distinctly unsteady because with such enormous magnification the slightest movement ruined the image; and it was obviously out of focus, a disaster which had been exacerbated by the fact that on this occasion Pathé had used an inexperienced cameraman. Yet when the giant lens was used soon afterwards at the Derby, where it was trained on the Royal Box from the opposite side of the course, the results proved to be more than worthwhile. This time the bulk of the camera and lens was supported upon a tripod specially designed for the purpose and the focus was looked after by an accomplished cameraman. Both wobble and focus difficulties were eliminated.

Other requirements for the newsreel cameraman included a means of focusing and framing up the picture; a means of changing the lenses with the least possible delay (essential for war coverage); magazines which would feed and take up the film, allowing for as much filming as possible, and a synchronous electric motor for sound purposes.

The pioneering manufacturers of all this equipment both in Britain and abroad included some of the first actuality and topical cinematographers. Robert W. Paul, who shot the earliest footage of the Derby, was one of the first engineers in Britain to produce cameras for more than simply experimental purposes. He was followed by J. A. Prestwich, Alfred Darling, J. A. Williamson, Moy, Wrench, Arthur Newman, Beck and, later, Vinten. In France the leading makers were Lumière, Debrie, Eclair and Pathé; in America they were Mitchell, Bell and Howell, Akeley and Wall.[3] It appears that Germany had little interest until the Second World War in originating camera designs, although some makers did copy models of other manufacturers such as Debrie.

The earliest coverage of events like the Boer War was made by W. K. L. Dickson for the Biograph with a Bio-Camera weighing nearly a ton, which perforated the stock at the same time as the film was exposed, and had to be transported everywhere on a bullock cart. Even earlier Biograph film produced a positive image which had no perforations on it at all, and a single frame measured two and three-quarter inches by two inches.[4] It was Dickson who along with Thomas Edison went on to develop the standard 35 mm film as we know it today.

The cameras used during these years were hand-cranked, the film running at sixteen frames per second as compared with today's sound speed of twenty-four frames per second, thereby producing the familiar jerky impression whenever they are shown on modern projectors.[5] Pathé used their French model, with outside magazine boxes, Gaumont used the Prestwich, an English model, also with outside boxes.[6] The advantage to a newsreel cameraman of an outside box for feeding in and taking up the film, as opposed to the side-by-side internal magazine, was that considerable time was saved because the film could thereby be removed without breaking. Furthermore, the advantage in not breaking the film extended to the fact that there was a saving in short ends, not an inconsiderable factor when every shot counted. These cameras were still heavy but not as bad as the old Bio-Cameras, since it was at least possible to carry them by means of a strap handle. Moys, Williamsons and Eclairs were also used by the British newsreels before and after the First World War, and later Topical Budget used Debries. The Warwick Chronicle was the first newsreel to use an automatic camera to avoid hand cranking—the Proszinski Aeroscope, which was run by compressed air. The earlier models were also fitted with a gyroscope to keep them steady when held by hand.[7]

Ironically, newsreel cameras were just reaching the stage of becoming really lightweight and exceptionally portable, despite the necessity for tripods and film magazines, when the advent of sound and the extra bulk involved in carrying around sound equipment virtually set the camera crews back to square one. The additional limitations of having to take along sound equipment in a van were immense, since a complete outfit for sound, at the time when the amplifier was attached to a truck, could weigh as much as 1,400 lb. Also the new film speed of twenty-four frames per second, demanded to extend the range of recorded frequencies, meant a slowing up of processing and added fifty per cent to the amount of material to be handled.[8] The earliest combined cameras were made by fitting an attachment to a silent motor-driven camera. The physical mobility of the newsreel cameraman was however severely curtailed because of such demands.

Sound brought with it a number of additional problems. The newsreel microphones had to be used in all sorts of conditions, and the three main sources of interference were background noises such as general murmuring and traffic, wind on 'the mike' and camera noise.[9] Background noises were unavoidable. They depended on the location of the story but could be reduced to a minimum by careful mike placing, which was of course only possible after considerable experience with various types of stories. Wind on outside coverage was the newsreel engineer's worst enemy, and the only way to overcome it was by using a wind shield around the diaphragm of the actual microphone which filtered out such interference, but at the same time also reduced the response of the mike to higher sound frequencies. Noise from the camera itself, generally a whirring sound from the motor, was apparent when close-up speeches were being shot. Provided the camera was in first-class condition, with no noisy gears, the limit for the distance between subject and camera was generally found to be about fifteen feet when close-up speeches were being filmed. This fact alone gives some idea of the constraints binding upon newsreel cameramen and sound engineers whilst working in the field. It was not simply a matter of setting up the camera and sound equipment just anywhere and then starting to roll. So many technical factors had to be taken into consideration and so much had to be seen to beforehand, particularly in the case of recorded interviews.

Yet these constraints did not impair the success of the recorded interview, and two examples of how effective these could be are to be found in the film archive of British Paramount News. Paramount's issue for 23 November 1936[10] has a story entitled 'Premier takes stock, finds Britain best' with a speech by Stanley Baldwin in which he contrasts Britain's improved trade position and general democratic tradition with conditions overseas at the time. Here the cameraman has an easy job, for Baldwin is seated at a desk in his study throughout and the conditions for recording are near perfect. Considering the ease of the interview perhaps the cameraman might be faulted for using one face-on view of the Prime Minister all the time. Such a pose was however customary during this period, and Baldwin evidently needed simplicity to combat his obvious lack of confidence before a camera.

The second example shows how well a camera team could manage in adverse conditions and was made for inclusion in Paramount's issue of 24 February 1938.[11] Here Major Clement Attlee expressed the view of the Opposition on Anthony Eden's resignation. The interview is shot in the open air in a park; although traffic noises and wind interference are in evidence, they are kept to a minimum and the cameraman even manages to get in a variety of shots which include a semi close-up and close-up of Attlee.

By the mid-30s, when the American Mitchell and Newman Sinclair cameras arrived on the British market, equipment had been reduced in size until camera and sound together weighed as little as 150 lb, with most of the weight in the tripod on which the camera rested. But even that imposed many limitations upon the agility of the cameraman on the spot, in addition to which it was only possible with certain cameras to film continuously for a maximum of three minutes before it became necessary to reload. In fact Kenneth Gordon cites one instance when he was using a Debrie 'Sept' camera which would only run fifteen feet of film at a time (some ten seconds' worth). As Gordon put it: 'I managed to get shots of the King inspecting the teams, a fair coverage of the game, and by good fortune the only goal, which was a penalty. Every roll was taken back to the office by a messenger as soon as it was ready.'[12] There are many anecdotes about these messengers, motorcyclists whose job it was to bring back the exposed film to the laboratories for processing, with a bounty of £1 for every minute they could cut off half an hour by such tricks as speeding round Trafalgar Square on the pavement.[13]

But Ken Gordon's problems of film supply were by no means as difficult as those of the newsreel cameraman on location. The freedom of choice as to where to position the camera was simply not available to the cameraman who endeavoured to get as near the front lines as possible during time of war. In these instances it was felt to be enough just to get some shots, any shots, as a note which accompanied some of Pierre Luck's Spanish Civil War footage, sent to Fox Movietone, bears witness: 'If you find on developing that the negative quality is not up to standard, please forgive me, and take into consideration that a good deal of it was shot under danger of life.'[14] When such hazards were overcome, it caused great jubilation within the company and offered a chance to sell the product to the audience as an unexpected opportunity to witness an event of technological import, as with Gaumont's release for 29 March 1937.[15] Alongside a story on British prisoners of war in Spain, there is a story heralding 'the first live interview from the trenches in Spain'. The issue spends forty-eight feet of film on the prisoners of war and sixty-six feet on the interview with a commentator on location, a sign perhaps of where Gaumont felt their priorities should lie, despite the fact that all the commentator in Spain does is identify the location and state that there is a battle going on for the adjoining territory. Similarly Gaumont's issue for 23 June 1938[16] had a story entitled 'Zoom Camera', the commentary for which ran as follows:

Gaumont British News never misses an opportunity of going one better than the other fellow, and now once again we are first in the field. We have bought a new thousand-guinea lens which performs the functions of a travelling camera without moving from its original position. Gaumont British News is the only newsreel in the world possessing this miracle of equipment. We do this sort of thing partly because we like to be the best, and partly because we can't sleep at night unless we know the exhibitors are happy. We have used this camera for the first time in this current issue, in the story of Helen Wills Moody at Wimbledon.

Despite the technical accomplishment, it is evident from the flippancy of the script that technological advance had normally to be very closely allied with stories of 'human interest'.

But what of the men behind the cameras? Were they politically committed and, if so, did this fact in any way affect their coverage of the events they were assigned to report?

The years covering the duration of the Spanish Civil War are concurrent with the growth of the Association of Cine Technicians (ACT), which in more recent times has expanded to become the Association of Cinematograph and Television Technicians (ACTT). The ACT was established in 1933 and a simple table shows its growth in the ensuing years:

31 December 1933	98 members
31 December 1934	88 members

31 December 1935   605 members
14 April 1936   845 members
31 July 1936   1,006 members[17]

By the time of the Third Annual General Meeting of the ACT in May 1936 it was reported that there were 900 members, representing 670 studio men, 180 laboratory workers and 50 newsreel technicians.[18] By the time of the Fourth AGM (30 May 1937), it was reported that there was almost 100 per cent membership of the men on the studio side and that, as of 31 December 1936, there were altogether 1,122 members.[19] However, if one considers that there were 10,000 persons normally engaged in film production in Great Britain,[20] it becomes evident that it took some time before membership of the ACT was accepted as the normal course of action by one and all.

The newsreel side of the cinema industry was certainly well represented within the ranks of the ACT, and as early as November 1935 it was decided to form separate sections inside that body to represent its most stalwart support, namely the laboratory and newsreel technicians. The composition of the first committee to represent the newsreel section shows that all the major newsreel companies were included. It consisted of:

Chairman: Mr J. G. Gemmell
Vice-Chairman: Mr A. Tunwell
Committee: Messrs F. Bassill and L. Maskell (Pathé); T. Cotter and P. Wyand (Movietone); J. Humphries and R. L. Read (Gaumont); J. F. Gemmell (Paramount); F. E. Miller and F. Wilson (Universal); J. Hodgson (March of Time); H. Starmer and J. Hutchins (Freelance).[21]

Certainly the ACT helped the newsreel side of the industry to marshal its forces more efficiently, and with the ACT's help the newsreel section organized the Press Photographers' affiliation and in May 1937 joined the International Federation of Newsreel Cinematographers.[22]

It would appear that on political matters the ACT was divided in its formative years. Certain members of its executive, like George Elvin, the general secretary, and Ralph Bond, would appear to have wanted to push its membership towards the left of the political spectrum. At its Third AGM in 1936 the ACT did agree to a non-political affiliation with the Trades Union Congress. (Elvin's father was actually to be President of the TUC in 1938.) Yet at the same meeting another successful motion pledged the ACT to pursue its 'present policy of allegiance to no one political party'.[23] Similarly another motion at the Sixth AGM on 16 April 1939 to affiliate the ACT with the Labour Party was narrowly defeated.[24]

During the years of the Spanish Civil War, the ACT was therefore unable to act as a unified body, with a coherent political commitment towards any kind of overt action. However this did not stop the more politically inspired members from making their feelings known as individuals. They offered their technical expertise, for instance, on an unofficial basis to ensure that certain things were made known which might not otherwise have been so. The *Journal of the ACT* reported that when the first contingent of the British battalion of the International Brigade returned to London late in 1938, there were no newsreels present to record the event. However several ACT and ETU members banded together, borrowed some film equipment, and filmed the events at Victoria Station for subsequent private showings at such places as working men's clubs in order to drum up support for the International Brigade Dependents and Wounded Aid Committee.[25] It would appear that this action prompted the newsreels into realizing what a good story they were missing. The ACT cited the newsreels' failure to cover the arrival of the first contingent as 'a recent example of the newsreel companies' prejudice overriding news value',[26] which may well be the case for they did display a great deal of bias in their coverage of the British battalion, as will be seen later. But be that as it may, the newsreel companies proceeded to cover the subsequent arrivals of British members of the International Brigade.

Alternatively, such ACT support as there was for the Republic in Spain manifested itself in the form of a straightforward declaration of sympathy. Their journal for March–April 1939 carried a letter, printed in full, from Felipe Pretel, General Secretary of the Federacion Espectaculos Publicos (the Spanish Entertainment Workers' Union). The letter expressed the determination of his members to fight on. It is prefaced by a short editorial expressing the ACT's solidarity with their fellow workers and stating that 'We can but admire it [the letter] and as trade unionists send our sincere good wishes to our fellow workers in Spain.'[27] But by the time such sentiments were published Catalonia had fallen, trade unions in that province were a thing of the past, and Republican Spain was on the verge of collapse.

Throughout the years of the Spanish Civil War, the ACT conducted a campaign against censorship of film, not only with regard to the Civil War in particular, but also on the wider issues of both feature film and newsreel censorship and bias. Their campaign was aimed at the British Board of Film Censors, as well as at the owners of the feature film and newsreel companies. It culminated in a long article by George Elvin entitled 'This Freedom, An Enquiry into Film Censorship'[28] where he catalogued what he considered to be the numerous attempts to curtail freedom of speech in the cinema. He noted that at the 1936 Conference of the Cinematograph Exhibitors' Association, the Film Censor, Lord Tyrrell, had stated that nothing would be more calculated to arouse the passions of the British cinemagoing public than the introduction on the screen of subjects dealing with religious or political controversy. Elvin recounted that at the time the ACT had taken grave exception to such an attitude and had thereby passed a resolution which stated that while holding:

no brief for any particular political belief whatsoever, it must sternly resist any tendency to deprive those working in the field of cinematography of the right which they should enjoy as British citizens, the right of expression in their chosen field of any view not inconsistent with the law. The attempt to limit the function of cinematography exclusively to 'entertainment' is outside the province and duties of censorship; if successful, it will establish the cinema, per se, as inferior in social value to literature and the other arts, and thereby degrade the status of technicians who devote their lives to it.

The elimination from cinematograph subject material of every controversial question deprives the cinema of the possibility of playing any useful part in the life of the nation, and will have the effect of holding it at that nickelodeon level from which the skill of generations of technicians has raised it to the heights of an art unlimited in potentiality. The underlying assumption that British audiences are incapable of witnessing material with which they disagree without riot is, further, an insult to the British people which, as citizens, the Council of the ACT must strongly repudiate.

On the matter of the newsreels Elvin noted that 'The Censor has no control over them. But it is obvious that indirectly, if not directly, very great pressure is at times exercised.' Elvin believed:

Part of the trouble is, of course, with the newsreel companies themselves. The majority of their executives are government supporters and their newsreels naturally tend to reflect that fact. (The Honours Lists are beginning to reflect it, too.) It is all the more surprising that when they occasionally give expression to a contrary view for one reason or another the reel is sometimes censored or withdrawn.

His conclusion was:

The newsreel companies should remember they are *news* reels and not propaganda sheets. They should provide news to appeal to their patrons as a whole and not let their reels be determined by the private interests of their owners or the feelings of officialdom.

The rest of Elvin's article continued to chart instances where he felt that censorship and bias were being exercised, looking in particular at the case of the proposed production of a film called *The Relief of Lucknow*. The British Board of Film Censors had let it be known that it was unlikely the film would be granted a certificate since it had been informed by the authorities responsible for the Government of India that such a film could only serve to revive memories of the days of conflict.

The next edition of the journal contained a follow-up article under the title 'Censored',[29] which assembled numerous letters of support. They included letters from A. J. Cummings of the *News Chronicle* under the title 'Newsreels will lose popular appeal', Geoffrey Mander, MP, under the title 'Pro-Fascist Bias', Clement J. Bundock, the General Secretary of the National Union of Journalists, on 'Suppression of Inconvenient Criticism', and Ronald Kidd, the Secretary of the National Council for Civil Liberties, who wrote a letter which was editorialized under the caption 'Totalitarian Frame of Mind'. But for all the ACT's attempts at making known the full ramifications of censorship in the cinema industry, they still felt the need to raise the subject once again at their Annual General Meeting for 1939 when they broached the matter of the political censorship of newsreels. A member from the Progressive Film Institute put forward a motion drawing attention to the tendency towards one-sided political partisanship in certain

1 Scaffolding towers were erected to get the best coverage (see page 24)
2 Gaumont exhibit their camera crews

3 Gaumont on parade
4 One of the first Gaumont sound vans

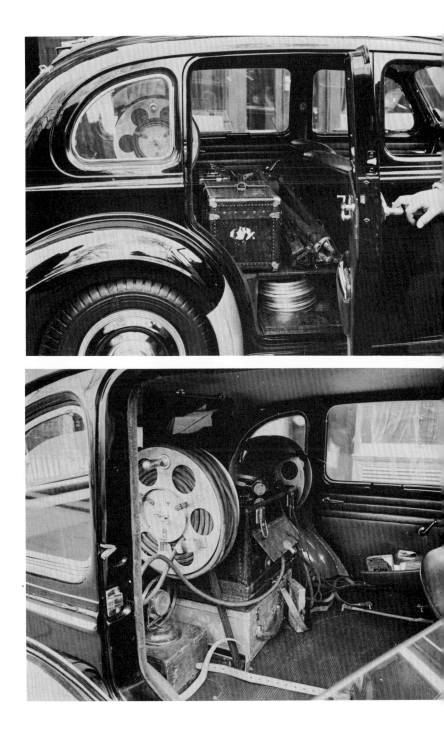

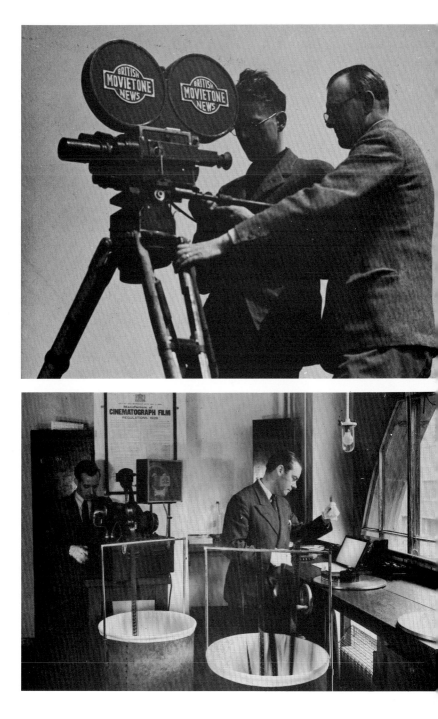

11 Movietone commentator Leslie Mitchell gets his cue
12 Roy Drew of Gaumont at the editing bench

13 Movietone's executive producer, Gerald Sanger (second from left on back row), watches results
14 Sir Gordon Craig, general manager of Movietone

15 Ted Emmett, commentator at Gaumont
16 Castleton Knight, in charge of production at Gaumont

newsreels. The resolution, which was carried unanimously, 'urged the ACT to support any efforts that may be made towards combating political censorship of the newsreels.'[30]

It would appear that there was no attempt to issue any instructions to cameramen going out on assignments to cover the story from any particular political standpoint, nor indeed does there appear to have been any attempt by the cameramen to impose their own political views upon their depiction of events. It will be seen that such bias as there was really only manifested itself when it came to editing down their material into stories for release and, most of all, when it came to adding the commentary.

For their part the newsreel cameramen saw themselves as being too 'professional' to allow their own personal judgements to influence their work. Indeed the image of themselves which they seemed to enjoy most was far removed from the realm of politics and was rather jovially encapsulated in a ditty that went under the title of 'Newsreel swindle sheet':

In Bradford she was Mabel,
She was Marjorie in Perth.
In Plymouth she was Phoebe,
The sweetest thing on earth.
In London she was Doris,
The brightest of the bunch,
But down in his expenses,
She was Petrol, Oil and Lunch.[31]

Chapter 3 | Outside the Newsreels

EXHIBITION AND THE AUDIENCE

Until 1950, the Board of Trade published very little in the way of regular statistics about the cinema industry. However, one or two surveys were published during the 30s and 40s which to some extent set about determining the size and nature of the cinema-going public. For instance, Simon Rowson conducted a statistical survey which he collated from two sources of cinema information available for 1934: the yield from the Entertainment Duty and the number of admission tickets sold in the cinemas.[1] His findings provide some valuable data.

From the figures available to him, Rowson ascertained that the total number of admissions to all cinemas in Great Britain for 1934 amounted to some 963 millions, a figure of 18.5 million per week. Rowson calculated that this total number of paid admissions represented an average of nearly twenty-two visits to the cinema each year for every man, woman and child in Britain.[2] (To make this deduction he used the 1931 Census figure for the size of the population, which amounted to 45,090,000 people.[3]) In fact Rowson went on to suggest that for persons aged fifteen and upwards, the average worked out at nearly thirty visits per year, and that 'If it were possible to eliminate all that portion of the population to whom a cinema is practically inaccessible, either because of distance or for any other reason, it is clear that the average in relation to potential patrons must be a very much higher figure.'[4]

However, as Rowson readily admits, it would be incorrect to suggest that everyone in Britain went to the cinema on an average at least twenty-two times every year. For an important distinction can be drawn between the number of admissions to the cinema in any one year, and the number of persons actually frequenting the cinema. Furthermore, it would be wrong to conclude from

Rowson's statistics, as one historian has done, that because there were 18.5 million admissions in any one week out of a population of some 45,090,000 people, then there was necessarily forty-three per cent of the population going to the cinema weekly.[5] Such a calculation does not take account of the fact that some people went to the cinema more than once a week, some people went fortnightly, and some people went at less frequent intervals. Rowson did not tabulate the habits of cinemagoers to such an extent. There were in addition seasonal fluctuations, varying from as high as 21.8 million in January to as low as 13.8 million in June, when people's recreations naturally tended to take them out of doors.[6] Rowson's statistics simply did not provide enough information to enable one to calculate the actual proportion of the population attending the cinema.

In fact the only definite conclusions which can be drawn from Rowson's survey are that in 1934 there were 4,305 cinemas operating in Great Britain, offering a total of some 3,872,000 seats,[7] and that during that particular year there were 963 million admissions to those cinemas. But Rowson's findings do give some indication of the kind of audience which frequented the cinema. For he estimated the distribution of cinema admissions with regard to price of seat and location of cinema. He was surprised to find that '43% of the entire cinema admissions are in respect of seats for which the charge last year (1934) did not exceed 7d, inclusive of Entertainment Duty, and this year (1935) did not exceed 6d; and that another 37% paid not more than 1s.'[8] His conclusion was that 'Nearly four out of every five persons visiting the cinema pay not more than 1s. (including duty) for admission.'[9] In other words, the vast majority of the people who did go to the cinema paid to go into the cheapest seats available, either because they wanted to do so or because they could not afford otherwise.

Furthermore, Rowson calculated that when the distribution of cinemas and cinema seats was compared with the various regional populations, then it was found that there were more seats per person outside of the political, economic and cultural capital than might at first have been expected. For there was one seat to every nine persons in Lancashire and Scotland, one seat to every ten persons in the North of England and South Wales, one seat to every eleven in Yorkshire and district, one seat to every twelve in the Midlands, one to every thirteen in North Wales, one to every fourteen in London (postal area) and the Home Counties, one to every fifteen in the West of England, and finally one to every nineteen in the Eastern Counties.[10] The obvious implication to be drawn from both these sets of figures is that the cinema was most popular among the urban working class, and this was borne out in the same year that Rowson began his investigation when the Social Survey of Merseyside was published. For 'The Social Survey of Merseyside was one of the many surveys which recorded the extent and the nature of the working class affiliation to the cinema. . . . The manual working class went more frequently than those immediately above them (Registrar General's Groups 4–5) and the professional and upper classes frequented the cinema the least.'[11]

Probably the most useful such survey was one entitled *The Cinema Audience*.[12] Although it was made during the Second World War, at a time of social upheaval and disruption, its findings only served to confirm the results of the earlier surveys. Indeed to judge from this Wartime Social Survey, which was made for the Ministry of Information, it would appear that very little had changed in the decade from 1934 to 1943, and that if anything a period of war only accentuated the prevailing trends in cinema-going habits.

The Wartime Social Survey acknowledged its aims in the service of propaganda by stating that 'The cinema is an important publicity medium in war time and it is, therefore, desirable to know what sort of people go to the cinema and how often they go.'[13] But because it was conducted during wartime there were several limitations imposed upon this survey. To begin with it was based upon a sample of only 5,639 people, who were interviewed during the months of June and July 1943. The method of approach was different from the one adopted by Rowson. The 5,639 men and women were interviewed by means of a questionnaire and they were selected in representative proportions from different regions and occupation groups. But because the interviews were held during what were generally considered to be quiet months by the cinema trade, there is every reason to believe that the findings might be down in numbers in comparison to other months of the year. This factor should however be balanced by the fact that people would appear to have frequented the cinema more often in time of war than they might have done in peacetime. Only civilians were included in the survey in order to compensate for this factor.

The survey found that the cinema was an important form of recreation for one-third of the adult civilian population, who went once a week or more often. A further twelve per cent went to the cinema once a month or once a fortnight and twenty-six per cent went less frequently. But thirty per cent of the population did not go to the cinema at all during the summer months.[14] In other words, seventy per cent of adult civilians sometimes went to the cinema during the months of June and July in 1943, and thirty-two per cent went once a week or more often.

The survey then proceeded to analyse the cinemagoers by economic groups, by education and by occupation. Here once again the results show that the lower income groups and those with only an elementary education went most often to the cinema. The lower group was classified as earning a wage rate of £5 or less per week, and as having experienced only an elementary education with no secondary, technical or university education.[15] The analysis by occupation revealed that relatively high proportions of factory workers, clerical and distributive workers went to the cinema more than once a week whereas managerial and professional workers went less often.[16] Furthermore, as was only to be expected, town dwellers went to the cinema more than people living in the country, due in no small part to the access and availability of cinemas. More people went to the cinema in the North, North West, the Midlands and Scotland than did so in the South East, South West and East Anglia.[17]

Finally, the survey compared the average cinema attendances per month with those people among the sample who saw a morning newspaper, bought a weekly or monthly magazine about matters of public interest, or bought a small book. Here it found that the cinema reached appreciably more people than did the other media of public communication, particularly in the lower income group.[18]

The overall conclusions which were drawn by the Wartime Social Survey bore out the implications that were inherent in Rowson's survey and more besides. There were very large numbers of people going to the cinema each week and these people were for the most part from the working class. There can be little doubt that the newsreel companies were also aware of these facts without any recourse to social surveys. And there can be even less doubt that they went out of their way to ensure that as often as there was a cinema programme on offer for this large audience, then there would also be a newsreel as part of that programme.

When a newsreel was ready for release about 200 copies would be made for distribution, each of which was expected to be seen in four or five cinemas. Each newsreel would cost £10 to rent for its first three-day run, and the cost would then decline as the news became stale, so that by the time the film reached a small cinema, two weeks or more later, it would cost only £3. After that the reels were recalled and destroyed, except for one copy which was filed in the company's library.[19] But during that time the newsreels had probably reached all the cinemas in the country, for by 1936 it was accepted that a newsreel formed part of virtually every cinema's programme.

Gaumont British News and the Pathé Gazette were backed by Britain's two largest cinema chains and they were also affiliated to the two main renters. The Gazette was distributed by Wardour-Pathé and shown in the cinemas owned by the Associated British Picture Corporation. In 1933 this organization ran only 147 cinemas,[20] but by the autumn of 1936 the circuit strength of ABPC had risen to 296 cinemas.[21] At the beginning of 1937 that figure further increased to 314 cinemas and by October 1937 it had control of over 450 cinemas.[22] The Pathé Gazette would have been shown in most of these cinemas.

The Gaumont British News was distributed in 1936 by Gaumont British Distributors, but in March 1937 Gaumont handed over all its distribution facilities to General Film Distributors, who proceeded to distribute the Gaumont News along with the Universal News.[23] The Gaumont newsreel was shown in most but not all the Gaumont cinemas. In 1933 this amounted to a chain of 287 cinemas,[24] but by the autumn of 1936 this figure had expanded to 305.[25] It should be remembered however that because Gaumont took a great deal of film from the foreign service of Movietone, in return the latter's newsreel was shown at a proportion of Gaumont cinemas, although it is not known precisely how many cinemas were involved in the deal.

By 1939 these two leading circuits of cinemas had been joined by a third, the Odeon chain. Even then it is noticeable that all three organizations still only accounted for 1,011 cinemas, amounting to about twenty-one per cent of the total in operation.[26] The remaining seventy-nine per cent of cinemas in Britain consisted of smaller chains or of independently owned cinemas. Gaumont, Pathé, Universal, Paramount and Movietone were in constant competition until 1942 to ensure that as many independent cinemas as possible took their product. Because these cinemas changed their minds regularly about which newsreel they wished to hire, and because new deals were constantly being made, it is impossible to ascertain the exact circulation figures for each of the newsreels over a long period. It was reported by *World Film News*, for instance, that in June 1936 the Gaumont newsreel was reaching 1,750 cinemas and that by January 1938, Universal News had the highest circulation figure with Gaumont second and Pathé third.[27] But such opinions are difficult to substantiate now. Indeed there are opinions to the contrary. Howard Thomas, a former newsreel executive, implies that Paramount had the largest circulation by virtue of garnering such independent cinemas as those in Sidney Bernstein's circuit.[28] Evidently all five newsreels had enough of a circulation to merit some kind of success, for as one cinema manager put it: 'There's always been room for five.'[29] Certainly it is the case that in 1952 all 4,755 cinemas then in operation in Britain took one or other of the five newsreels which were still on offer.[30]

The obvious popularity of the newsreels was perhaps best shown by the fact that from the early 1930s onwards special cinemas began to appear which were devoted exclusively to exhibiting newsreels, cartoons and other topical films, in a programme generally amounting to somewhere between fifty minutes and an hour in length. The admission price to these cinemas was 6*d* between midday and 4 pm, and 1*s* between 4 pm and 11 pm. On Sundays they were open from 6 pm to 11 pm. By December 1933 there were nine such theatres, and that year also saw the opening of two railway station news theatres at Victoria and Waterloo, both designed by Alistair MacDonald, the then Prime Minister's son.[31] The news cinema at Victoria Station was hailed as a triumph in construction design. It had been built during the night in order to interfere as little as possible with the normal activities of the station and special provision had been made for sound insulation since the theatre was suspended in mid-air within the station, with traffic passing under the floor of the auditorium. The double entrance formed an archway between platform sixteen and Buckingham Palace Road. There was a small illuminated panel near the screen giving ten minutes' notice of the arrival and departure of the principal trains.[32]

Such cinemas proved to be immediately successful, and by 1936 London had eighteen news theatres seating somewhere between 300 and 500 people, and there were other news cinemas in Manchester, Brighton, Leeds, Chester, Southampton, Sheffield and Bournemouth.[33] The cinema at Bournemouth revelled in the glorious name of The Bijou. In the same year the Pathé Gazette was actually shown on the railway route from London to Leeds, in a special projection carriage, and it was later introduced by the LNER on the London to Leeds to Newcastle to Edinburgh route.[34] In fact it would appear that the news theatres managed to secure a clientele who would otherwise not have been disposed to visit the cinema at all, and cinemas such as the Tatler, the Cameo and the Monseigneur, all in Charing Cross Road, attracted a regular stream of customers. The Gaumont-Movietone attracted as many as six million people in eight years.[35] Norman Hulbert, Member of Parliament for Stockport and a member of the London County Council, was the managing director and chairman of the Capital and Provincial News Theatre Chain, the largest newsreel theatre circuit. And in 1936 he was sufficiently optimistic about their future to express the hope that 'The day will come when every town with a population of 50,000 or more will have a newsreel theatre.'[36] But the advent of war and the subsequent emergence of television on a large scale meant that the total number of news cinemas probably never exceeded the 1952 figure of thirty-five theatres.[37]

The evident demand for newsreel theatres was one means, albeit less than satisfactory, of judging the popularity of the newsreels themselves. Unfortunately, very little was done in the way of surveys to establish what effects the newsreels had upon the audiences viewing them. There was certainly nothing done in Britain during the 1930s to equal the research conducted in America through the Motion Picture Research Council and sponsored by the Payne Fund. For all that their twelve volumes of results only dealt with the effects of film upon children, they were nevertheless invaluable in establishing the methods by which such surveys might set about achieving their objectives.

The only surveys conducted in Britain before 1939 that remotely approached the Payne Fund Studies were the annual popularity polls among both adults and children which were instituted by Sidney Bernstein purely as a business venture. Bernstein wanted to find out what was most popular among the cinema audiences in order that he might then book these films for his cinema chain. *World Film News* commented at the time:

Sidney Bernstein's famous questionnaire goes out again this month. It will ask the members of his audiences in eighteen theatres what stars, directors, types of film and programme they prefer. A quarter of a million questionnaires will be issued, and half of them will be returned. They will tell us the taste of Suburbia.

The results we expect will not differ greatly from last year, except in the names of the stars of the moment. Some stars will be up, some down. But thriller-adventure, musical-comedy and comedy will be preferred by the men, and musical comedy and society drama preferred by the women. Comedy will continue to be low on the female list.[38]

However, from 1939 and throughout the course of the Second World War, Mass Observation was to show that there might well be a great difference between the verbal responses of an audience as publicly manifested in popularity polls, and the private response as evidenced during the actual exhibition of a film in the cinema. They noted, for example:

Watching audience responses in cinemas gives the same sort of information about what is really going on in people's minds as we get from intimate war diaries, or dream studies. For instance, while public opinion polls and press letter-bags showed a heavy increase in Chamberlain's popularity after the beginning of the war, and while this popularity was superficially maintained until within a few days of his resignation, newsreel observation showed a steady and accelerating decline in favourable audience response whenever he appeared on the screen, though it is the 'done thing' to be loyal to your Prime Minister in public, especially in wartime. Similarly, direct opinion testing would always show a big hand for the King. But in the early months of the war, newsreel (and other) studies showed that his popularity was at a low ebb.[39]

Even at the level of direct opinion testing it would appear that from the onset of war the newsreels suffered a sharp decline in credibility, perhaps because they were now for the most part reporting events which the audiences were enduring for themselves under stress. The newsreel audiences were therefore able to evaluate their own response in comparison with the portrayal of events as depicted in the cinema. Evidently it was felt that the newsreel coverage simply did not match up to the events themselves, for Mass Observation found:

At the end of 1939 just under two-thirds of all persons asked said they liked newsreels, and expressed sentiments distinctly favourable to them; by August, 1940, only just a quarter of those questioned held this point of view. In 1939, 12% spontaneously criticised newsreels for having no news; in 1940, 35% spontaneously made this criticism.

The investigators, the questions, the areas and class proportions were the same each time; and the questioning was spread over several weeks in order to avoid the dominant influence of any one newsreel. A whole wealth of criticism was revealed, some of it very unfair to the newsreel companies. At the same time, we have found repeated cases where the newsreels have alienated people by their political bias, by their treatment of emotional topics, by the commentaries (which are often unsympathetic to ordinary people), and have shown by numerous indications that they are sometimes out of touch with the feeling of the moment and even, sometimes, with the permanent feelings of housewives or labourers.[40]

Of course there was, even in its day, a good deal of criticism about the methods by which Mass Observation conducted its research. Ewart Hodgson, the film critic of the *News of the World*, raised some important questions when he asked:

To be assured that Mass Observation is of any value at all, there are three questions which need to be answered.
1. What is the method of selection and of training a Mass Observer?
2. How, and through what body scientifically concerned with psychology, do they qualify for their jobs of accurately observing and recording public opinion and behaviour?
3. What are Mr Harrisson's own qualifications for the publishing of generalisations arrived at from the perusal of his Observers' statistics?

In his essays individual comments are often used as the basis for a generalisation.[41]

But then nobody was more aware of the problems involved in audience research and the inevitable shortcomings of their findings than Mass Observation. Tom Harrisson appreciated that a lot of the success of his venture depended upon the methods employed for measuring audience response. As he readily admitted, the conditions under which his observers worked were far removed from the laboratory:

Observer variation, the rapid sequence of film events, the difficulty of getting scripts as a check on observation, and the darkness in which the observer must write and record, are all difficulties.[42]

Furthermore, Harrisson always went out of his way to point out that 'These results have no absolute validity, but a comparative value.'[43] And it is therefore at the comparative level that Mass Observation's wartime findings must be understood. It is at the comparative level that Mass Observation showed the newsreels to be lacking in popularity and credibility early in the war. But it is noticeable that the newsreels later regained a fair amount of

	All replies	Boys	Girls	
Yes	71	76	61	%
No	28	23	38	
No reply	1	1	1	

AGE ANALYSIS BOTH SEXES

	Under 8	8	9	10	11	12	13	14 plus	
Yes	63	70	70	72	71	74	78	74	%
No	36	29	29	27	28	25	22	25	
No reply	1	1	1	1	1	1	1	1	

BOYS

	Under 8	8	9	10	11	12	13	14 plus	
Yes	65	76	76	77	77	81	85	86	%
No	33	24	23	22	22	18	15	12	
No reply	2	0	1	1	1	1	0	2	

GIRLS

	Under 8	8	9	10	11	12	13	14 plus	
Yes	56	60	56	64	61	64	68	58	%
No	43	39	43	35	39	35	32	42	
No reply	1	1	1	1	0	1	0	0	

their lost prestige. And a Bernstein questionnaire conducted among children in 1947 revealed that there was a new generation coming into existence which, once again, appeared to enjoy the newsreels. One question was asked of the young audience, 'Do you like newsreels?', and the results can be tabulated as on the previous page.[44]

Bernstein's questionnaire showed that the newsreels were liked by seventy-six per cent of boys but only sixty-one per cent of girls and that in both cases their interest increased with age.

Apart from a brief period during the Second World War, the newsreels had apparently succeeded in capturing the attention of the cinemagoing public in sufficient quantity to make them a popular form of mass communication. Television, however, was shortly to kill them.

NEWSREEL CONTENT

If one were to judge the content of the newsreels in the 1930s from the opinions expressed by critics, then one might well expect to find very little in them of value to the historian. Sir Arthur Elton's comment that 'for at least the first thirty years the content of the newsreels was determined mainly by the passing fads and fancies of the time' has already been noted. But Elton's comments were made in 1955 and with the benefit of hindsight.

What was the opinion on newsreel content in its day? In fact it appears to have been unanimous in its condemnation. The American film writer Terry Ramsaye commented in 1934: 'The newsreel is not a purveyor of news and is never likely to become one . . . Whether they know it or not, the newsreels, as they call them, are just in the show business.'[1] A similar comment was forthcoming from the film producer Emanuel Cohen, when he said of newsreel content: 'What kinds of pictures are most popular with audiences? Soldiers, airplanes, battleships and babies.'[2]

Both these speakers were Americans and were obviously referring first and foremost to their home grown product. It seems, however, that the situation was not considered to be any better in this country, for in 1937 John Grierson, the father of the British documentary movement, observed:

From the beginning we have had newsreels, but dim records they seem now of only the evanescent and the essentially unreal, reflecting hardly anything worth preserving of the times they recorded. . . . The newsreel has gone dithering on, mistaking the phenomenon for the thing in itself, and ignoring everything that gave it the trouble of conscience and penetration and thought.[3]

Nor can the charge be levelled at Grierson that simply because he had such a strong interest in the documentary film movement, he therefore felt less than kindly disposed to a rival in the field of actuality and reportage. For the dismissal of newsreel content was virtually universal among film critics and commentators, and articles with titles such as 'Are newsreels news?'[4] were all too frequently found in the film journals. But did the newsreels necessarily deserve such wholehearted condemnation? Perhaps one answer can be found in an article entitled 'Newsreels or real news?', written by another British film producer, Andrew Buchanan, who was strongly critical of newsreel content in 1935. Buchanan elaborates upon his points of attack when he says:

With the rapid development of the documentary picture, those inter-ested in non-fictional production are increasing their criticism of the newsreel, primarily because it presents the greatest output of 'actuality' on the screen. Nevertheless newsreel material is inadequate and cannot be regarded as a contribution to documentary production. This is lamentable, for films dealing with reality are so rare that one would have welcomed the opportunity of being able to categorise newsreel material under the dignified and important heading, Documentary. In fact if, in the beginning, the newsreel had been made intelligently, it would have expedited the evolution of the documentary, which would in turn have influenced the methods of fictional production.[5]

The major point which emerges from such an extract is the comparison that is drawn between a supposedly respectable documentary film movement and an allegedly disreputable news-reel film movement. This comparison occurs over and again throughout the critical articles on the newsreel for the period, and indeed one can understand why. The documentary film movement as initiated in Britain by Grierson and his band of talented directors, first at the Empire Marketing Board, and later at the General Post Office Film Unit, was winning a great and deserved reputation for British cinema in general. World film output had shown that the British film industry could not begin to compete in the realm of feature film production, either for standards or for sales. But with the advent of the documentary film, Britain had shown that she could rival the likes of America and France, and indeed lead the way. Inevitably the newsreel was held up in comparison to the documentary, simply because on the surface they both appeared to be dealing with the same kind of material, actuality film. So it was that Andrew Buchanan felt compelled to go on to state:

I see no reason why the best creative brains in filmdom should not be concentrated upon the production of the real newsreel, so that it shall be a first class documentary production with a topical flavour.[6]

Yet unwittingly Buchanan had put his finger upon the major cause of the dilemma. For it is interesting to note that there was never any duplication of personnel between the documentary and newsreel sides of the film industry. The reason is that they were fulfilling completely separate functions under entirely different conditions of work. News had to be covered while it was still 'hot', and the speed which was essential in getting the newsreel to the exhibitors precluded the sort of artistic endeavour that might ordinarily have gone into the making of a documentary. The documentary film-makers were first and foremost artists and poets, despite Grierson's statements to the contrary. By comparison, the newsreel makers were film 'journalists'.

Furthermore, too much was made by the critics of the supposed capacity for 'realism' inherent in the documentaries. Certainly it is true that with such films as *Drifters*, Grierson paved the way for the use of amateurs playing themselves without the 'benefits' of a feature film actor's expertise and dramatic training. Also it is true that the documentary makers often used 'everyday people in everyday settings'. But for all that, what made the success of a film like *Night Mail* was the additional efforts of acknowledged artists such as W. H. Auden and Benjamin Britten, wedded together with the sort of subtle editing which demands a lot of time, and the sort of studio help which simply did not come the way of the newsreels.

The claim to 'realism' is also undermined by recent revelations from Paul Rotha concerning the production of *Drifters*. For he reveals that to make this film a drifter, the *Maid of Thule*, was hired at Stornoway 'chiefly on the strength of the crew's supposed photogenic quality'. In fact the words are not Rotha's at all, but were drawn by him from a source attributable to Sir Stephen Tallents, Grierson's mentor, all of which goes on to show just how fabricated the 'realism' of this film was. The interior scenes, for instance, were shot on a cabin set designed by the sculptor, John Skeaping, which was erected near the harbour. A fisheries protection cruiser provided the power for the interior lighting. The underwater shots were supplied with film of dogfish chivying small roach around a tank at the Plymouth Marine Biological Station. Then when shooting on location started, the *Maid of Thule* simply could not find any herrings and all the operations had to be transferred to a completely different drifter which was fishing off Lowestoft.[7]

In reviewing Rotha's book, the film producer and critic Stuart Hood has suggested that a phrase originally coined by Arthur Calder-Marshall would better serve to describe the efforts of Grierson's film-makers. For in calling them 'false-to-life, true-to-life documentaries' one is getting closer to the point. Furthermore, as Hood goes on to point out, the documentaries simply replaced one set of feature film stereotypes with a new set of documentary film stereotypes. They 'aestheticized' reality, labour and the ordinary man and woman. The ease with which this new set of stereotypes was then taken up and assimilated into the feature film industry adequately reveals the comparative hollowness at the heart of the documentary claims for 'realism'. This was shown most of all when the Second World War engaged the documentary men as part of 'a propaganda machine, which accepted the most reactionary mythologies about British life and dealt with stereotypes of the cheerful Cockney, of the West Countryman and the Scotsman.'[8]

It was a characteristic also noticed by Charles Barr, who in his masterly study of Ealing Studios pinpointed the ease with which certain directors progressed quite logically from documentary shorts, to 'dramatized' documentary, to the more orthodox story films. He is speaking in particular of men such as Alberto Cavalcanti and Harry Watt, and the reasons for the course which they took are summarized by Barr when he says:

There was no special political or aesthetic rigour in the documentary tradition which created a barrier to its easy assimilation by a commercial studio. The social/political outlook was less than radical. Nor had a firm anti-theatrical acting tradition been formed. Perhaps the main influence was in the area of: location shooting, editing techniques, sober narratives.[9]

Perhaps it was Grierson's own aversion to 'art', and all the pretensions which the word connotes, that made him put forward his ideas on documentary as being 'the creative treatment of actuality'. Clearly, in the light of what is now known about the documentary film movement, and its methods of production, Grierson's definition needs to be re-assessed. It is equally as clear that to demand, as many contemporary critics did, that the newsreel should follow in the footsteps of the documentary, is completely to misunderstand the role which the newsreels played and the conditions under which they worked.

However, such an argument can by no means dismiss outright the many criticisms of newsreel content during the decade from 1930. It is easy to suggest that the critics were making a mistake in comparing newsreel content with documentary content, and misunderstanding the nature of documentary at that. But this does not dispose of the basic criticism that the newsreels were still for their own part trivial. The Arts Enquiry on *The Factual Film* probably encapsulated such criticism best of all when it noted:

The usual content of the majority of pre-war British newsreels was trivial, being largely devoted to reports of minor events such as the laying of foundation stones, society weddings, traffic jams on the main roads at holiday seasons, ship-launchings and all the main sporting events. Material from overseas was usually similar in character.[10]

The only way to answer the persistent criticism that the newsreels dealt with trivial subjects is by an analysis of newsreel releases. There are already in existence two surveys of the period under review, although they both refer to the content of the American newsreels. However, an examination of their results is valuable in order to determine what methodology must be applied in surveys of this sort and how best they can be used. For only then can one determine what likelihood there was of events such as those of the Spanish Civil War being covered and how well one might expect them to be reported.

The first survey was made by Edgar Dale and published in 1935 as part of a comprehensive review for the Payne Fund Studies on *The Content of Motion Pictures*. The purpose of Dale's research with regard to newsreels is best expressed in his opening remarks to the chapter, where he states:

The newsreel is a device by means of which the population can be made intelligent about the events which are current in this complex and changing world in which we live. How does the newsreel measure up to the ideal which has been set up for it? The analysis here presented attempts to answer these questions.[11]

Dale's method of enquiry appreciated that each story or 'item', as he called it, within any newsreel release, was an entity in itself. Each of these items or stories had a certain amount of film ascribed to it, which did not necessarily bear any relation to the topic that preceded or followed it. And in order to determine precisely what topics and current events these items covered, Dale decided to use the synopsis sheets of newsreel companies instead of analysing the newsreel themselves at the cinema. Furthermore, he confined his analysis to only two companies, although he never actually states their names but simply designates them as X and Y.

The X newsreel was studied from April 1931 to June 1932, a period of fifty-nine weeks providing a set of 118 synopsis sheets, since there were two issues in every week. The Y newsreel was studied from August 1931 to June 1932, for forty-four weeks with a total of eighty-seven synopsis sheets. Thus, altogether, it can be seen that the study looked at the period from August 1931 to June 1932, from the synopsis sheets made by both these particular newsreels, whereas the months from April to July in 1931 were examined from the coverage made by one newsreel alone, the X reel.

Certain other factors should be borne in mind with regard to Dale's method of approach which decidedly lessen its potential value. First of all he states that while the X reel gave the footage of each particular item, the Y reel did not do so. Therefore it is impossible to ascribe any importance, in Dale's analysis, to the length of individual stories, or to the relative importance which a story might gain by comparing its length with that of other stories. In fact, Dale does not even ascribe any value to the position a story might occupy within a newsreel release. He fails to appreciate that the opening and closing positions were generally believed by the newsreel trade to be the more important slots. It will be seen that length and position of newsreel stories are factors which are both considered important in the detailed study which follows of the British newsreel coverage of the Spanish Civil War.

It is worth citing two examples which Dale gives of stories from the synopsis sheets, for they reveal further limitations:

X NEWSREEL
'2-Gun' Slayer Caught In Desperate Battle With Army of Police.
New York, N.Y. Sought as the murderer of a policeman and a dance hall hostess, Francis Crowley puts up fight reminiscent of wild west before ammunition gives out and tear gas bombs bring his surrender.
Rudolph Duringer, accused of one killing, and Helen Walsh, 16-year-old girl, taken with him.

Y NEWSREEL
Japanese Bombs Create Havoc In Shanghai. Y News gives you a vivid picture of the devastation in the leading city of China in additional films rushed from the Orient by fast steamer and air-plane. These are the first sound pictures from the war zone made in the midst of the Chinese counter attack which retarded the Japanese advance.[12]

It can be seen immediately that a study of this sort, depending as it does upon the synopsis sheets alone, and with no viewing of the material, either in private or public, would be of little value should the investigator wish to extend his survey into the area of presentation on a particular topic or into bias of depiction. However, within the bounds which Dale set himself for his research, they are valuable, for the synopsis sheets do give a good idea of what constituted a story in content alone.

Dale proceeds to classify the stories under twenty-six subject-headings (see Table 2). His intention was to adopt what he called a 'common-sense' classification and to make certain divisions which might make it possible to answer some important questions which he felt should be asked of newsreel content. These questions were:

Is more attention given to war than peace? Are current economic conditions being treated in newsreels? Is there a tendency for crime news to be included? Are bathing girls shown more frequently than government officials? Are religious activities ever treated? What does the newsreel show us of the drama of modern industry?[13]

The one thing that Dale's twenty-six categories did not allow him to determine, however, was just how much foreign coverage there was in either of the two American newsreels he was investigating. So he conducted a preliminary survey in order to ascertain the frequency of appearance of foreign items in the two newsreels. The results were tabulated as follows:

Table 1: *Frequency of appearance of foreign items in newsreels*[14]
(The number and per cent of reels and of items which dealt with foreign countries and with the United States)

	REELS				DIFFERENT ITEMS			
	X		Y		X		Y	
Type of locale	No	%	No	%	No	%	No	%
Foreign	99	84	81	93	188	20	168	22
United States	118	100	87	100	764	80	604	78
Total	118	100	87	100	952	100	772	100

The results are revealing, for they show that stories on foreign topics appeared in ninety-nine out of the 118 newsreel releases for the X reel, and in eighty-one out of the eighty-seven releases of the Y reel. The second half of the table indicates that out of a total of 952 stories contained in all the 118 releases for the X reel, some 188 or twenty per cent were on foreign topics; and that of the sum total of 772 stories in the eighty-seven releases for the Y reel, there were 168 or twenty-two per cent on foreign topics. As Dale concluded: 'We see, therefore, that the newsreel is by no means provincial. It does deal to a significant extent with foreign countries and peoples.'[15]

But it was Dale's second survey which attempted to quantify the subject matter contained in the newsreels. And here the results prove even more interesting. The first point to be made about Dale's findings in Table 2 is that there is a strong degree of correlation between the two newsreels he studied with regard to the

Table 2: Subject matter contained in the newsreels[16]
(The number and per cent of reels and of items which dealt with each type of subject matter, arranged according to frequency of the X newsreel)

CATEGORY	RANK according to frequency X	Y	REELS X No.	%	REELS Y No.	%	DIFFERENT ITEMS X No.	%	DIFFERENT ITEMS Y No.	%
Sports	1	1	87	74	82	94	138	14	230	30
Animals, birds, fish and insects	2	12	71	60	15	17	85	9	15	2
War–army–navy	3	2	64	54	53	61	83	9	89	12
Aviation (civil)	4	4	52	44	32	37	66	7	42	5
Engineering and scientific marvels and inventions	5	20	47	40	8	9	65	7	8	1
Accidents, fires, storms, wrecks and disasters	6	16	52	44	12	14	62	6	13	2
Conventions, reunions, contests, parades, festivals, pageants	7	5	43	36	29	33	49	5	37	5
Economic conditions	8	9	40	34	22	25	43	5	26	3
Government and civic officials	9	3	40	34	52	60	47	5	77	10
Curiosities and freaks	10	25	34	29	2	2	43	5	2	.3
Police and criminal activities	11	7	37	31	25	29	42	4	32	4
Governmental–political–civic	12	8	34	29	23	26	37	4	29	4
Religion	13	19	31	26	11	13	33	3	11	1
Educational and instructive	14	14	27	23	15	17	30	3	17	2
Commerce, transportation and industry	15	18	23	19	11	13	26	3	11	1
Celebrities	16	11	22	19	16	18	22	2	17	2
Prohibition and liquor	17	6	17	14	26	30	19	2	28	4
Children and their activities	18	17	15	13	12	14	15	2	12	2
Entertainment	19	24	13	11	5	6	15	2	5	.6
Fashion shows	20	15	10	8	15	17	10	1	15	2
World peace	21	22	7	6	7	8	7	.7	7	1
Beauty contests	22	23	5	4	6	7	5	.5	6	.7
Explorations and adventure	23	26	5	4	1	1	5	.5	1	.1
Music	24	10	2	2	19	22	2	.2	19	2
Scenic splendours	25	21	2	2	8	9	2	.2	8	1
Dancing	26	13	1	1	15	17	1	.1	15	2
Total			118	100	87	100	952	100	772	100

ranking according to the frequency of topics. In fact the rank correlation is plus .54, showing that to a great extent these two newsreels agreed upon what they believed the spectator should see. Sports news is the most frequent in both newsreels and perhaps this is why critics felt the newsreel was basically trivial in content. But then it is easy to understand the feeling on the part of the newsreel companies that the public enjoyed seeing sport on the screen, and of course it should not be forgotten that sport did lend itself very well to a cinematographic representation.

What is more important with regard to the newsreels' potential for covering the Spanish Civil War is that items of war ranked third in the X reel and second in the Y reel. 'Since 54% of the X and 61% of the Y newsreel contain shots of such activities we note that the chances are greater than even that one will see some phase of war activity depicted on the screen if he sees either of these newsreels.'[17]

Other items that ranked high with both companies are civil aviation, conventions etc, government and civic officials, and economic conditions. However it is interesting that items on world peace fare badly. In fact the ratio of world peace items to war items, in the combined totals of both companies, was approximately 1 to 12. Once again the answer is simple, if somewhat macabre. For war coverage must by definition be that much more full of action, and hence more photogenic, than matters of world peace.

For the purposes of this study, then, two major points of interest arise from Dale's findings. First, the newsreels under consideration, for the period he studied, were by no means provincial in character. They did devote a fair amount of screen time to foreign matters. And second, the newsreels covered topics of war in profusion. In passing, it is perhaps worthwhile adding that the newsreels in question seem to have devoted a good deal of time to covering matters such as economic conditions, government and civic officials, and engineering inventions, which would appear to give the lie to those critics who accused them of dealing only with trivia. However it should be remembered that Dale's analysis was purely quantitative in nature and not by any means qualitative.

There is another analysis of newsreel content which should be brought under review for the purpose of determining whether Dale's findings can only be applied to one particular period and two specific newsreels. For in 1950, in his book *Hollywood Looks at its Audience*, Leo Handel examined newsreel content for the ten years from 1939 to 1948. Once again, the analysis refers only to American newsreels. But Handel's survey was more comprehensive than Dale's since it was compiled from the 1939–48 releases of Movietone

News, News of the Day, Paramount News, Pathé News, and Universal News. Of course Handel's survey also traverses the years of the Second World War, with the American commitment to fighting in both Europe and the Pacific. One would therefore expect the war coverage to be that much more pronounced, as indeed it is, with a falling off in such topics as sport. So for the purposes of this study, the examination of Handel's findings has been confined to the results for one year alone, that of 1939. The results then are as follows:

Table 3: Topical content for 1939
(Expressed as a percentage)[18]

NATIONAL NEWS:

Aviation	3.1
Disaster, fires etc.	3.4
Farm	0.2
Fashion, styles	1.8
Governmental news	5.1
Health	0.4
Industrial progress	0.7
Labour news	0.8
National defence	4.1
Political news	0.8
Religious news	1.0
Science	1.1
Sports	26.1
Weather	0.8
Miscellaneous	21.8

FOREIGN NEWS	18.3	(excluding World War 2 coverage)

WAR IN EUROPE	10.5
	100.0

Total number of clips 4,940

Perhaps the most obvious thing is the similarity of Handel's findings to those of Dale, despite an intervening gap of six and a half years. There are differences which can be accounted for by prevailing trends. For example, Prohibition and Liquor appear in Dale's survey but not in Handel's and similarly National Defence appears in Handel's survey, obviously as a result of the political uncertainties and fears throughout the middle and late 30s. Furthermore what constituted the general term 'War' in Dale's findings has become encapsulated by the end of 1939 into the specific term 'War in Europe'. Handel also has the catch-all category entitled 'Miscellaneous' to accommodate anything that does not easily fall into his other categories. However, foreign news still compares well at 18.3 per cent with Dale's figures of 20 per cent in his X reel and 22 per cent in his Y reel. And war occupies 10.5 per cent of screen time in Handel's survey compared with 9 per cent and 12 per cent respectively in Dale. The correlation is strong enough to suggest that foreign news and war coverage appeared consistently and regularly throughout the American newsreels in the decade from 1930.

Unfortunately there is little in the way of a systematic and thorough analysis of the content of British newsreels during the same period which would enable one to see whether the same trends and emphases were repeated. There are however two minor surveys which were conducted by *World Film News* for July and September 1936.

Table 4: British Newsreel Analysis for July 1936[19]

NEWSREEL	Total no. of items spotted by WFN	Sport	Royalty	Military	Foreign	Empire
British Movietone News	88	28	9	4	17	6
British Paramount News	49	11	8	2	7	4
Gaumont British News	61	22	8	4	14	2
Pathé Gazette	25	12	7	–	1	–
Universal News	85	21	11	9	7	1
Total	308	94	43	19	46	13

Table 5: British Newsreel Analysis for September 1936[20]

NEWSREEL	Total no. of items spotted by WFN	Sport	Royalty	Military	Foreign	Empire
Movietone	91	22	5	6	19	1
Paramount	52	8	7	5	13	3
Gaumont	88	20	8	5	26	1
Pathé	58	14	5	4	13	3
Universal	68	17	4	9	15	1
Total	357	81	29	29	86	9

Several points can be made about the *World Film News* surveys. Both the topics 'Royalty' and 'Empire' are items that one would not have expected to find in the content analyses of

American newsreels. It is also obvious that these two surveys are by no means as exhaustive in their classifications as their American counterparts. Yet for all that, the preponderance of sport as the number one subject compares exactly with the American reels, as does the prevalence of foreign items, within which *World Film News* included the Spanish Civil War.

A more recent survey, conducted by the Slade Film History Register, attempted to look briefly at two British newsreels, British Paramount and British Movietonews, to ascertain how many stories they issued relating specifically to Germany or the Germans between 1933 and 1939. The results are equally as revealing in determining how much newsreel time was given over to foreign affairs coverage.

Table 6: Stories relating to Germany or Germans, 1933–1939[21]

	BRITISH PARAMOUNT NEWS			BRITISH MOVIETONEWS		
	'News-type items'	Other	Total	'News-type items'	Other	Total
1933	20	11	31	20	10	30
1934	12	7	19	11	8	19
1935	18	16	34	21	11	32
1936	16	22	38	16	8	24
1937	26	15	41	11	5	16
1938	43	12	55	43	9	52
1939	29	5	34	16	1	17
Total	164	88	252	138	52	190

Unlike the surveys already cited, the Slade analysis introduced a qualitative factor into the proceedings, by dividing the coverage on Germany into serious news, what it termed 'News-type items', and anything else relating to Germany. It estimated that there were approximately 1,248 stories per year for each of the two newsreels, given two newsreel issues per week, with an average of twelve stories per issue. From such a total it is evident that there were a low number of stories per annum reflecting hard news on Germany or the Germans, the greatest total being forty-three stories out of 1,248, which was reached in 1938, the year of the Munich crisis. However as a proportion of all stories relating to German issues, the percentage of serious items is high, reaching approximately sixty-five per cent for Paramount and seventy per cent for Movietone.

At the quantitative level the Spanish Civil War was comparatively well covered. During the period from 27 July 1936, when the first story on Spain appeared in Gaumont British issue 269, to 3 April 1939, when issue 549 covered the entry of Franco's troops into Madrid, there were altogether 280 newsreel releases from this company. The Spanish Civil War was reported in seventy-seven of these 280 releases. Movietone first carried a report on the war in its release for 23 July 1936. From that point until 3 April 1939, Movietone carried sixty-six reports on Spain out of some 281 issues. Pathé carried sixty-four stories on Spain between 3 August 1936 and the same date in 1939, out of a possible 278 releases.

The first report to appear in British Paramount's coverage did so on 6 August 1936, in issue 568, and from that point up to issue 845 for 3 April 1939, there was a mention of the Spanish Civil War in sixty-seven out of a possible 277 newsreel releases. Universal had the lowest count of all five newsreel companies with just thirty-nine Spanish stories out of 281 issues beginning with issue 630 for 23 July 1936, and ending with issue 911 for April 1939.

The claims of the American and British critics, then, are by no means justified. To suggest that the newsreels were exclusively trivial in content is unfair. Sport may well have been the most popular newsreel topic by far. But a good deal of time was also given to foreign affairs and to war in particular.

CENSORSHIP

By 1936, film censorship had been in operation in Britain for many years. The Cinematograph Act of 1909 had provided the legal basis for the censorship of films, although it had in fact been instituted to protect cinema audiences against the risk of fire. For the Act empowered the Home Secretary to put into effect regulations for the exhibition of inflammable film provided there were adequate safeguards. Henceforth such film could only be exhibited in premises which were appropriately licensed for that purpose. The licences were to be dispensed by local authorities who were in turn empowered to delegate the authority to local justices, watch committees and to borough, urban or rural district councils.

'Subject to the Home Secretary's regulations, the licensing authority may attach conditions to the granting of a licence and it has been ruled by High Court decisions that these conditions may relate to matters other than the safety of the audience.'[1] So it was that the local authorities found themselves in the position of acting as the final arbiter and censor of films which were to be shown in their areas.

The British Board of Film Censors was not actually set up until 1912, and even then it was founded and maintained by the film trade itself. Although the submission of films to the Board of Censors was at first voluntary, with no mandatory obligations on the part of the film renters, by 1933 it had become an unwritten law among the renters that only certificated films would go on release into the cinemas. It was the Board's job to send to licensing authorities a statement of the films it had reviewed, passed and classified under one of its various headings such as 'U' or 'A'.

In 1929, J. R. Clynes, then Home Secretary, issued a Home Office circular containing model rules for the guidance of local authorities, as part of a plan to evolve a common policy for local licensing authorities. The circular had been based upon the experience of the London County Council, and certain other authorities, with regard to their experiences of film approval. It acknowledged the work of the Board of Film Censors and stipulated that no film which had not been passed as suitable by the Board should be shown without the consent of the local council concerned and that the Board's classification of films should be adhered to.[2]

From the very beginnings of censorship, the newsreels were exempt from the conditions appertaining to most films and were not subject, officially, to a review by the Board of Film Censors. When the Board had been set up in 1912 they had decided for several reasons that newsreels should not come under their aegis. First of all the Board was more concerned with fictional and feature films, and by that time the newsreels were only just becoming recognized as a regular part of the cinema programme. It has also been suggested that 'the tradition of a free press' was applied to the newsreels, thereby swaying the Board's decision not to interfere with their presentation of the news.[3] But it is more likely that the speed necessarily involved in the printing and distribution of newsreel film to cinemas probably played the greatest part in determining what the Board would decide. It is noticeable also that the LCC included in its regulations on censorship for 1921 an exception for material which included 'photographs of current events'. This exemption had apparently been included in the conditions imposed by other councils throughout the preceding decade, and was subsequently incorporated in the successive drafts of the Home Office model conditions and eventually absorbed in the licensing regulations of the two hundred or more licensing authorities.[4]

Yet this ability to proceed without a censor's certificate did not make, as one might at first suppose, either the newsreel companies or their product more independent in outlook. For as Neville March Hunnings noted, it simply left the newsreels 'in a more exposed position, for they were completely unprotected by the law (as indeed they still are).'[5] It also left the newsreel companies open to criticism and pressure from any quarter, in particular from that most notorious and nebulous of sources, public opinion. The newsreels were a feather for every wind that blew, and the years prior to 1935, and immediately after, reveal just that. The film trade for its part showed little interest in protecting what might be termed the freedom of the cinema's press. In fact the situation was quite the opposite, for the Cinematograph Exhibitors' Association went out of its way to oppose the introduction of what it called 'propaganda' on the cinema screen. And, as far as the CEA was concerned, propaganda was a word which embraced any form of controversial statement or opinion, whether reported or performed.[6] It is difficult to see how the newsreel organizations could fail to get into trouble when such limited terms of reference were applied.

Before 1935 the public criticism of newsreels was mostly concerned with the depiction of violence and what Warwickshire County Council called 'harrowing pictures of fatal accidents'.[7] Today one tends to get the impression that the public outcry against the depiction of violence on the screen is a postwar phenomenon, enhanced by the arrival of television. But there is enough evidence to suggest that it was as prevalent during the 1930s as it is now. One good example turned up in *The Times* for Friday, 1 December 1933, in a piece entitled 'Horror in News Films' and read: 'There is now being shown in this country an American newsreel which ends with a shot of one of the lynched kidnappers of a certain Mr Hart hanging from a tree surrounded by a howling mob.' *The Times* columnist was evidently most worried about the effects of this film upon the undoubtedly vast cinemagoing audience, for he continues, 'this is the latest and most horrifying manifestation of a growing tendency to sacrifice all decency to sensationalism in the presentation of news on the screen.' He concludes: 'It is greatly to be hoped that before long steps will be taken to safeguard the public from the exhibition of such scenes.'[8]

The morality of what should or should not have been shown on the cinema screen does not concern us here, but what is of utmost interest is the response that such outcries elicited from the newsreel companies. This particular newsreel was withdrawn from the cinemas and in a statement circulated to all the press, an official of British Paramount News, the offending company, said:

In view of the public resentment at the showing of this newsreel we have decided to withdraw the whole shot. I would make it clear that there has been no question of representation from official sources, nor at the time it was withdrawn did we know that it was intended to ask a question about it in the House of Commons. We are servants of the public and we withdraw it as a gesture to their opinion.[9]

Such overt acts of self-censorship were not enough to stave off the mounting criticism, particularly from the local authorities. Early in 1934, Warwickshire County Council wrote to the Film Censorship Consultative Committee at the Home Office demanding that newsreels should be censored. Later that year the same County Council passed a resolution:

That this Council views with concern the offence to public feeling, and the harmful effect upon children, likely to be caused by the exhibition in news films of incidents of harrowing scenes of loss of life and of suffering, such as have lately been shown in connection with a fatal aeroplane accident, a liner disaster, and more recently an assassination, and urges the Secretary of State to take such action, or to bring such pressure to bear, as will prevent in the future the introduction into news films of such incidents.[10]

In August 1934, a twinfold action came from the Film Censorship Consultative Committee, which declared that it was considering the question raised by Warwickshire, and from the British

Board of Film Censors, which stated in its annual report for 1933 that it was considering the definition of the term newsreel, for purposes of censorship. Birmingham actually went so far as to include newsreels in censorship in November of that year, and the LCC came up with a definition of the term newsreel as being 'any exhibition of films (known in the trade as "Topicals" or "Locals") of actual events, recorded in the press at the time or about the time of exhibition, whether exhibited with or without sound effects or commentary.'[11]

Thus 1934 proved to be a bad year for the newsreels, as far as public and local authority disquiet at their depiction of violence was concerned. Finally the Government felt compelled to step in, and on 24 October 1934 the Home Office issued circular 676417/6 under the title *Revision of Model Conditions*.[12] Obviously the circular was a sop to public opinion and to the pressure which had emanated from the local authorities to include the newsreels under film censorship. For it reported that 'in recent months a number of newsreels have been the subject of criticism on account of the objectionable nature of the incidents depicted in them.' For the most part the circular concerned itself, not unexpectedly, with the depiction of violence and with the question of what constituted a proper interpretation of the phrase 'photographs of current events', in order that licensing authorities could consider the desirability of adopting the revised model conditions to licences granted by them. It went on:

There may be a great difference between the effects produced on the screen and by a description in a newspaper, and it is necessary, in order that the susceptibilities of the public may not be offended, that this fact be taken into account in the presentation of pictures and commentary at cinematograph exhibitions. It should be borne in mind that the first of the model conditions which prohibits the exhibition of films likely to be offensive to public feelings, applies to newsreels as well as to other films.

Yet for all the public and local authority clamour, this circular seems to be as far as the government felt compelled to go, in order to be seen to have acted over the matter of violence in the newsreels. The Government never felt the necessity to interfere with the newsreel companies over this issue, nor to impose censorship on them. However a different attitude obtained with regard to points of political controversy.

In the first instance complaints over the introduction of what was called propaganda into the newsreels came from politicians, who objected to the reporting of speeches by political leaders. In 1933, for example, Herbert Morrison maintained that 'At the LCC I have called attention to items included in a news film two weeks running in London cinemas which appeared to me to encourage Fascist mob militarism.'[13] Similarly Ernest Bevin, who was at the time the General Secretary of the Transport Workers Union, 'protested against the use of newsreels for propaganda purposes and instanced a film report of Lloyd George in which the latter accused the Allied Powers of breaking their pledge to Germany about disarmament.'[14] Of course all that these men were worried about was the appearance in newsreels of other people expressing political opinions with which they did not agree. However the newsreels still had to tread warily, and eventually the General Council of the Cinematograph Exhibitors' Association reached such a stage of fright that it only reluctantly felt able to 'give permission' to the newsreel companies to include in their issues speeches by cabinet ministers.[15]

But what proved to be far more important was the number of actual instances where Government interfered in what should or should not be shown to audiences because of political overtures from one source or another. *Kinematograph Weekly*, a cinema trade magazine, cited several examples of political interference of this sort. One such example concerned the newsreel coverage of violent demonstrations and rioting which occurred in the Place de la Concorde in Paris on 6 February 1934. Since the rioting had been part of a right-wing attempt to overthrow the Third Republic, the French Government requested that the French newsreels should not show their material on the events. But British Paramount News had also covered the proceedings and the film, as they stated, was 'already in our hands the day after the events in Paris, having been brought out of France before the French Government's censorship had taken effect (and was), subsequently the subject of diplomatic representations. As a result the pictures were not released until two days later.'[16] Of course, to cause a delay in the exhibition of newsreel material was not quite so reprehensible as outright requests for suppression, which once again emanated from the French Government over British newsreel coverage of the assassination of King Alexander of Serbia in Marseilles on 9 October 1934. For apart from the diplomatic affront and disgrace involved in having a visiting monarch killed on French soil, the French disarray was compounded by the fact that Louis Barthou, their Foreign Minister, had been murdered along with King Alexander. Hence the French call for outright suppression of the material relating to these events.

Paramount went ahead and showed their film. But the row caused by the exhibition of these pictures in British cinemas led to a debate in the House of Commons on 1 November 1934. Capt Cunningham Reid, the Unionist Member of Parliament for St Marylebone, opened with a question asking the Home Secretary, Sir J. Gilmour, whether he was contemplating the imposition of censorship upon cinema newsreels. The Home Secretary replied: 'No sir, but I have thought it my duty to see representatives of this branch of the industry and to point out that it rests with them so to handle their material as to make it unnecessary for the Government to consider the imposition of any censorship on newsreels.'[17]

The fact was that the Home Office was little worried about what the newsreels showed, unless of course they reflected opinions bearing upon matters which the Government might consider to be 'touchy'. And from 1935 onwards the British Government of the day was becoming increasingly worried about the general events in Europe, as a result of which their interest in the newsreels' reflection of those events became that much more acute. As Norman Hulbert, who was an MP as well as managing director of the largest news theatre circuit in Britain, went on to put it, 'There was no Government control, although sometimes a hint was given that it was not desirable to publish a certain item, and it was usual to respect their wishes on such occasions.'[18]

The British Board of Film Censors, for its part, was not averse to cutting politically sensitive items from other films. A *March of Time* release called 'Threat to Gib', which showed the threatened grip by the Fascists on the Mediterranean owing to the situation in Spain, was banned. Although the *March of Time* was a newsreel, it was in fact a monthly newsreel compilation and therefore did come under the Board's jurisdiction. In November 1937, Joris

Ivens's documentary *Spanish Earth* was cut because it contained a suggestion, and only a suggestion, that Germany and Italy were intervening in Spain. Another film, made under the title *Britain's Dilemma* and shown in the United States with that title, which dealt with the events of 'the retreat' from the League, Manchuria, Abyssinia, Spain and China, and stopped short at Czechoslovakia, was released in Britain after a number of cuts and retitled *Britain and Peace*. Munich in fact proved to be the breaking point for the newsreels, and as Neville March Hunnings has commented, 'between Munich and the outbreak of war, exhibitors, councils and Government all took a more restrictive attitude over the whole field of censorship.'[19]

This restrictive attitude manifested itself most strongly in connection with a British Paramount story on the Munich crisis. During the crisis four out of the five newsreels showing in London played down the Czech point of view, but British Paramount, with the independently minded G. T. Cummins in charge, gave it a good deal of screen time. Paramount invited Wickham Steed and A. J. Cummings to speak during the reel. The issue was withdrawn on 22 September, the very day of its release. A telegram was allegedly sent by Paramount to its theatres saying: 'Please delete Wickham Steed and A. J. Cummings from today's Paramount News. We have been officially requested to do so.'[20] Paramount was reported later to have denied that they had been officially requested to do so and said they had done it at their own discretion. However on 23 November, Geoffrey Mander, the Liberal MP for East Wolverhampton, asked in the House of Commons 'Why representations were recently made by His Majesty's Government to the American Embassy for the withdrawal from a Paramount newsreel of items contributed by Mr Wickham Steed and Mr A. J. Cummings?' Sir John Simon, the Chancellor of the Exchequer, spoke in reply:

His Majesty's Government considered that certain passages in the newsreel referred to, which was being shown at the time of the Prime Minister's conversations with Herr Hitler at Godesberg, might have a prejudicial effect upon the negotiations. The Ambassador of the United States, I understand, thought it right to communicate this consideration to a member of the Hays organisation which customarily deals with matters of this kind and which brought it to the attention of Paramount who from a sense of public duty in the general interest, decided to make certain excisions from the newsreel. . . . I am glad that the ambassador and ourselves were in complete accord.[21]

If indeed this account accurately reflects the truth of the operation, and there is little reason to believe that it does not, then it gives a good idea of the tortuous yet effective way in which the Government had set about securing the excisions it desired whilst at the same time ensuring that it appeared to 'keep its hands clean'. They must have informed the American Ambassador, Joseph P. Kennedy, of the offending items, who in turn would have informed the Hays office, presumably in America for they did not have an office in this country. The Hays organization must in turn have conveyed the feelings of all concerned to the head office of American Paramount, who finally got back to the offices of British Paramount in London in order to effect the cuts.

Understandably Sir John Simon's argument that the British Government and the American Ambassador just happened to find themselves in complete accord over this matter did not convince. Furthermore, as Dingle Foot put it so succinctly in a Commons debate on 7 December:

Are we seriously asked by a Minister of the Crown to believe that the conversations which were taking place on that day or maybe the next between the Prime Minister and Herr Hitler would really have been affected by the news film displayed at a London cinema? I do not believe any member of the House will believe it for a moment.[22]

Geoffrey Mander had remained unconvinced from the start of the affair, for on 1 December he had broached the subject in the House with the Prime Minister, in an interchange which revealed that either Neville Chamberlain had not been informed of the progress on this issue or that he was an expert prevaricator.

Mr Mander:
In what instances in addition to the case of the Paramount newsreel has action been taken to ask for the removal of parts of cinema films on political grounds?

Mr Chamberlain:
I am not aware of any instances in which the removal of parts of cinema films has been asked for by the government on political grounds.

Mander:
Then there is no precedent for the request recently made to the American Ambassador to take action on such lines?

Chamberlain:
No such request has been made.

Mander:
But is it not the case that the Chancellor of the Exchequer said quite clearly last week that he had got in touch with the American Ambassador and asked for the removal of such items?

Chamberlain:
No sir. [N.B. *The Times* reports this as: Mr Chamberlain was understood to reply in the negative.]

Mr H. Morrison:
Will the Prime Minister inquire and make certain whether the headquarters of his own political party do not take a hand in this unofficial censorship?

Mander:
Do I understand the Prime Minister to say that the government exercised no pressure of any kind whatsoever to ask the American Ambassador to get these items withdrawn?

Chamberlain:
The attention of the American Ambassador was drawn to certain items and he was asked to look into the matter.

Sounds of Opposition laughter.[23]

What is of far more importance, however, is to examine the excisions that were actually made in order to determine whether the Government might have wished to cut any items and to establish whether they were detrimental. The story was issued as part of Paramount's release for 22 September entitled 'Europe's Fateful Hour'.[24] It included frontier scenes from the Sudetenland, shots of refugees in Germany and Prague, shots of Germany's new defences on the Rhine, a view of Godesberg preparing for the meeting of Hitler and Chamberlain and, finally, film of demonstrations in London. In the course of this narrative of events Paramount introduced Wickham Steed as the former editor of *The Times* and a friend of President Masaryk and then the commentary went on:

British Paramount News, seeking still further independent and informed opinion, interviewed the famous foreign affairs journalist, Mr A. J. Cummings; and for the man-in-the-street's viewpoint sought the popular broadcasting taxi-driver, Mr Herbert Hodge.

Such an array of people brought together for the purposes of an interview on a topic of current affairs is now commonplace in broadcasting, provided of course some time is allotted for the opinions of the Government under criticism. But the technique as applied to this newsreel was unique in its day and thereby that much more open to attack, as indeed were the opinions expressed by the speakers, each of whom was highly critical of Government policy, all the more so in fact since nobody actually spoke on the Government's behalf. Wickham Steed began with a straight-forward speech which ran:

Has England surrendered? Who is 'England'? The Government or Parliament or the people? The British Parliament has not surrendered for it has not been convened, and still less have the British people. Our Government, together with that of France, is trying to make a present to Hitler, for use against us when he may think the time has come, of the three million men and thousands of aeroplanes he would need to overcome Czechoslovak resistance. Hitler doesn't want to fight. Oh, no. He only wants to get without fighting more than he would be able to get by fighting. And we seem to be helping him to get it. And all this because British and French ministers feared to take a risk when they could have taken it successfully and believed they could diminish the risk by helping Hitler, when he was at his wit's end, instead of standing up to him.

It is possible to ascertain from the script for this story in the Paramount archives that, even as it stood and before it was excised completely, Wickham Steed's speech had been shorn of a concluding paragraph in a piece of self-censorship by Paramount. Perhaps Paramount felt his intended final words went too far:

There may still be a chance of averting the worst if we encourage the Czechs to stand firm and make our Government understand that we repudiate its policy of surrendering our vital interests and besmirching our good name.

After Wickham Steed's speech there then followed a dialogue between Hodge and Cummings:

Hodge:
Well, Mr Cummings, what do you think of the news? Everybody's saying to me that England has surrendered to Hitler. Do you think that's right?

Cummings:
Well, beyond a doubt, Hitler has won an overwhelming diplomatic triumph for German domination of Europe. Nothing in future will stop him but a mass WAR.

Hodge:
I think most of us, although we want peace, er, with all our hearts, we would be prepared to go to war if it was a case of either going to war or allowing Hitler to dominate Europe.

Cummings:
The fact is our statesmen have been guilty of what I think is a piece of yellow diplomacy. If in good time we had made a joint declaration with France and with Russia making clear our intentions, and stating emphatically and in expressed terms that we would prevent the invasion of Czechoslovakia, I'm certain that Hitler would not have faced that formidable combination. If we were not prepared to go to the extreme limit we should certainly not have engaged in a game of bluff with the finest poker player in Europe.

Hodge:
What worries me about it all, Mr Cummings, is whether we've simply postponed war for another year or two, against a much stronger Hitler of the future.

Cummings:
I'm afraid we've only postponed war and, frankly, I am very fearful about what is yet in store for millions of young men of military age in all the countries of Europe.

These then were the speeches which were cut from the Paramount release. They are indeed harshly critical of the Government's policy, though they displayed great foresight, and one can understand why many people might not have wanted them to be shown in cinemas throughout the country. Perhaps Paramount might have got away without any cuts if they had thought to include a Government spokesman. But it is more than likely that Tom Cummins, Paramount's editor-in-chief, knew that the only way to attempt such an innovation as political commentators was by means of a *fait accompli*. Nor can one disguise the fact that the successful attempts to delete these items amounted in fact to political censorship of a supposedly free medium of communication. In their stead the three speakers were replaced by a new story entitled 'Premier flies for peace' in which Neville Chamberlain said:

A peaceful solution of the Czechoslovak problem is an essential preliminary to a better understanding between the British and the German peoples, and that, in its turn, is an indispensable foundation of European peace. European peace is what I am aiming at, and I hope that this journey may open the way to get it.

Geoffrey Mander recounted the nature of the excisions to the House when for a third time, on 7 December, he raised the whole matter of censorship and the restriction of liberty. This time, however, he also tabled a motion:

That this House, attaching the utmost importance to the maintenance undiminished of British democratic traditions of the liberty of expression of opinion, both in the press and in public meetings and also in other media such as cinema films, would greatly deplore any action by the Government of the day which tended to set up any form of political censorship or which exercised pressure direct or indirect.[25]

Besides the example of the Paramount newsreel, he went on to mention other instances of what he believed to be political interference on films such as 'Nazi Conquest No. 1. (Austria)', 'Inside Nazi Germany', 'Croix de Feu', and another one called 'Crisis in Algeria', which purported to show the possibility of a North African *coup*, perpetrated by a Fascist state. The main point of Mander's long speech was encapsulated in his request to the House to observe:

That in all the examples I have given, in every case where cuts have been made, nothing anti-Government, nothing anti-Fascist is permitted, but anything that is favourable to the policy the Government is pursuing is allowed to go forward. . . . I do not say by any means that it is always done at the direct instigation of the Government but I do believe there is pressure by Government departments or by their friends at times. It is widely alleged in the press and elsewhere that the Conservative Central Office is not wholly disinterested in or without knowledge of what is going on.[26]

But despite a heated debate and strong endorsements of Mander's sentiments from other members, including Archibald Sinclair, Dingle Foot, Philip Noel Baker and Wedgwood Benn, an amendment to his motion from a Mr Beechman, which added that the House 'is fully satisfied that His Majesty's Government have maintained these traditions unimpaired' finally won the day, and in effect proved the death knell for the concern over censorship in the Commons.

There were subsequent nominal questions raised in the House throughout 1939, but the feelings which had built up to the debate in December 1938 proved altogether the highest point of concern among MPs at the manipulation of the newsreels. Of course within a short time the newsreels found themselves in the midst of a Second World War, during which, as one might expect, they were strictly regulated as to what they could and could not show and when anyway they became part of an overall propaganda machine under official control.

In the meantime the County Councils Association reared its head again with a further proposal for censorship of newsreels over a week old, which had been instigated by yet another request from Warwickshire County Council, along with one from Hertfordshire, 'drawing attention to the fact that scenes of war, sudden death and violence were included from time to time in newsreels.'[27]

The spectre of censorship or public and governmental pressure haunted the 1930s. The newsreels simply had to learn to live with it. On a more general level it is possible to see the years from 1933 to 1939 as leading quite logically and cumulatively towards the kind of government control that manifested itself during the Second World War. The pressures of public opinion took their toll in the early years and sufficiently sapped the strength of the newsreel companies as well as reducing their capacity for an independent, informed opinion, if indeed they ever had one. The local county councils helped and the government of the day finally broke it.

Before the Civil War, Spain was sporadically covered by the British newsreels and rarely seen on the cinema screen. Film reportage dealt only fleetingly with the more important events of the country's history during the first thirty-five years of this century. Furthermore, these were mainly the years of the silent cinema, when the newsreels had to depend on a visual presentation of events. They were allowed little in the way of comment, since all that they had for further exposition were captions placed at the beginning of a story, and occasionally throughout its run, which conveyed no more than a bare description of the proceedings.

For all such drawbacks, a survey and subsequent viewing of the more relevant Gaumont Graphic issues reveals that this silent forerunner to the Gaumont British News was one newsreel which did capture, albeit infrequently and erratically, some of the highlights of Spanish history. As early as 8 October 1917, Gaumont Graphic released a story under the title 'Barcelona authorities prepare for trouble'. The year 1917 was indeed an eventful one for all shades of political opinion in Barcelona. The people of Catalonia had always desired some sort of separate recognition and autonomy. After 1901 the most effective political force for a while in Catalonia proved to be a conservative alliance known as the Lliga Regionalista, whose national representative was Francisco Cambo, later to become a millionaire industrialist. And in 1907 the Lliga endorsed a campaign for Catalan Home Rule with a Catalan parliament. But the Catalan question might never have exerted such a powerful influence over Spanish affairs at the turn of the century had it not also been for the fact that Barcelona had become the most industrialized city in Spain. In the words of one historian: 'The goals of middle-class Catalans were to wrest regional autonomy from the centralised Spanish parliamentary system, protect and advance the region's economic interests and encourage the modernisation of Spain.'[1] To this end the leaders of the Catalan Lliga, along with some small liberal groups, called an independent assembly to meet in Barcelona on 19 July 1917.

Also in 1917, the two most powerful trade unions in Spain, the Anarchist CNT and the Socialist UGT, combined in a revolutionary general strike. The UGT issued a strike manifesto on 12 August, and although support from the CNT, who did not actually sign the manifesto, was erratic, a general strike did spread from Barcelona to the rest of the country. Yet both the efforts of the Catalan Lliga and the trade unions in Barcelona ultimately came to nothing. Cambo felt his hand was being forced by a general strike which he denounced as 'a stupidity'[2] and he failed to carry a majority of the middle-classes with him in his attempt to force concessions from the central government in Madrid. For their part, the trade unions could not rally broad support, particularly from the Army, and the strike died down after concerted action by the police and the military. Ultimately, the result was that the government of Catalonia remained in the grasp of the established cliques in Madrid.

This was the point at which Gaumont came in, and their story reflected the ultimate show of strength by the combined armed forces with the ending of the strike. In fact by the time that Gaumont Graphic actually got round to releasing their story on Barcelona, most of the events in Spain had quietened down. However, Gaumont must at least be given the credit for being in the right place with their cameras, if not at the right time.

By 1921 Spain was heavily committed to a strong military policy in Morocco, and the Graphic covered their fortunes twice in that year. The first of the two reports, shown on 21 April 1921, contained film of 'Spanish troops encamped at Sidi Dais' in Morocco. The second, on 30 September, helped to foster the perennial image of Spain with a story on 'Bull fights in Spain to raise funds for wounded from Morocco'. It also contained shots from Morocco itself of General Silvestre, who later in the year was prompted by King Alfonso XIII into a rash military action which led to the defeat at Anual. Gaumont, however, appear not to have covered the defeat itself, when Silvestre's entire command of twenty thousand men was caught by the Riff tribesmen under Abd el Krim and almost annihilated.

The crisis brought about by the Catalan and Moroccan questions led in part to the emergence of the dictator General Primo de Rivera in 1923. If the machinations and intricacies of how he took control in Spain were beyond the powers of presentation of Gaumont, at least on 8 September 1923 they heralded his arrival with a story entitled 'Revolution in Spain'.

But with the advent of sound recording on film, Gaumont, along with other newsreel companies, eventually extended their horizons. This technological advance did not necessarily mean an immediate increase in depth of news reporting, for there was still little room for editorial comment. The period from 1929 to 1932 was 'the changeover period' when 'sound technology was limited by the fact that only one track existed on which speeches, commentary, sound effects and music would have to fight for a place.'[3] The professional newsreel commentators did not really arrive on the scene until 1935. And during the changeover period, the newsreels evidently felt the presence of sound to be such a new and engaging phenomenon in itself that it mattered very little what was actually said or spoken.

So it was that the important events which took place in Spain on 14 April 1931, when a Republic was declared, were somewhat disappointingly covered on film. For a while the Gaumont company maintained the silent Graphic as well as the new Sound News, and in fact it was on their silent newsreel that they released a story called 'Spain: New Republic'. At the same time, British Paramount News had a sound story entitled 'Nation votes for Republic on Polling Day as King Alfonso abdicates'. However, Paramount's report contains little more than a series of title cards to convey the gist of the narration. The opening title sets the scene with the headline 'Alfonso abdicates', followed by 'Madrid. First pictures from Spain where scenes of wild disorder mark polling day. Nation votes for Republic.' The accompanying film shows shots of people milling through the streets of Madrid, smiling and looking towards the camera; then there follows a scene of men looking at lists pinned up on a wall, complemented by a view of crowds at the polls with voting slips in their hands.

The generally harmonious picture is broken by the next caption:

'Riot. At the Puerta del Sol, Royal Police still loyal to the King clash with Republican crowds.' Film of people retreating before mounted policemen serves to convey some sense of the strong feelings aroused by the declaration of a Republic, as do shots of police on foot, and armed with long batons, confronting and harassing civilians. The departing King Alfonso is brought into the fray after a title announcing 'Dethroned. Ex-King Alfonso, with his English Queen and family, brings to an end the reign of the Bourbons.' The newsreel footage which follows this title must have been culled from the Paramount stock-shot library, for it shows Alfonso in better times, on horseback and reviewing a contingent of troops. This in turn is succeeded by the caption 'Spanish Reds riot. Fire and pillage. Mobs terrorise capital and wreck holy buildings as seething unrest sweeps country.' There are then shots of mobs collecting firewood, looting houses and churches, and starting fires in the streets.

The story is concluded by 'The new Republican leader, Senor Alcala Zamora, in an exclusive interview with Paramount Sound News.' Alcala Zamora, a middle-of-the-road Catholic who turned to the ideals of a Republic late in the day, addresses the camera and there is a sound recording of his speech. But the novelty is all because he speaks in Spanish. Understandably, in view both of the technical problems and the fact that there is no commentator on the story, there is no attempt to translate or even to convey the gist of his remarks. Throughout this report the soundtrack is totally naturalistic in character, with little more than the sounds of voices in the street and the occasional shouts and yells.

A week after the story on the proclamation of the new Republic, Paramount took up the King's departure in their issue for 23 April with a piece entitled 'Alfonso in England'. In an attempt to capitalize upon British interest in Alfonso's English Queen, Paramount showed film of their arrival in London as 'sympathetic crowds give exiled monarch a royal welcome.' In contrast the report also contained headlines stating: 'Citizens of a new regime. In Madrid, Republican throngs congregate to pay homage to the memory of Pablo Iglesias, the founder of Spanish Socialism.' This was accompanied by film of crowds being addressed by a speaker, who remains unidentified, and the story closes with the crowd marching and singing.

The succeeding years, from 1931 to 1935, proved a traumatic period in the political history of the Second Republic in Spain, but they seem to have escaped the notice of the British newsreels. Universal News did attempt to arouse interest in the miners' riots in Asturias with a report released on 8 October 1934, apparently within a couple of days of the riots and subsequent fighting. It is not surprising, therefore, that the story turned out to be made up entirely of footage taken from their stock-shot library and was not even film of Asturias at all. And it is little wonder that the company felt the necessity to slip it into their 'News in Brief' section of the newsreel. The historian Kenneth Watkins has suggested that 'It was the Asturian events which brought home and highlighted the Spanish situation for politically interested sections of the British people.'[4] The Left in Britain were deeply affected by the harsh measures taken to suppress the uprising and Members of Parliament, among them Ellen Wilkinson, visited Spain in an attempt to assess the situation for themselves. Mrs Leah Manning, who went as part of an official delegation, wrote a book on her experiences there in which she commented: 'Such a campaign of hate as was described to us would have done credit to the Allied and German propaganda machines from 1914–1918.'[5] But to judge from the newsreel response alone, one would not have thought that 'The event which had received the most publicity outside Spain, during the preceding years (i.e. before the Civil War) had been the Asturian revolt in October 1934.'[6] It might have been the case that the newsreel companies were not allowed into the area to film the riots. In any event Universal were notably forthcoming in putting at least some impression of Asturias before the British cinemagoing public in October 1934, even though their story was woefully inadequate.

Yet if the newsreel coverage of Spain during this period was so scant as to preclude any investigation to find out whether the newsreel companies were holding to any particular 'line' on Spanish affairs, at least it is possible to determine, from their other European coverage, what events generally were taking the newsreels' interest at the time. From this one can ascertain what messages they wished to put forward. And such a survey, however brief, is essential in order to evaluate whether, by the advent of the Civil War, there were in evidence any pre-ordained ideas that could be superimposed upon the film reports which were to come out of the Civil War.

At the outset of the 1930s the British newsreels were much concerned with political moves on the European front towards disarmament. At its simplest this manifested itself with such clips as one from a British Movietone story, released on 18 September 1930, in a report entitled 'Foreign Secretary at Geneva: Mr Henderson talks to you from the Home of the League of Nations.' Henderson appears and says, in part: 'Friends, here we are at Geneva once again dealing with the great question of world peace and doing everything humanly possible to prevent future war.'

At the time Arthur Henderson was part of a preparatory commission, set up by the League, to pave the way for a fully-fledged commission on disarmament. Such an extract could only have been seen as reflecting his personal optimism at the outcome of the preparations, but within a short time such hopes and aspirations for the prospect of world peace became commonplace on the newsreel screen. Another Movietone story, for 13 July 1931, was called 'If the Nations of the World Could See and Speak to Each Other There Would Be No More War'. It contained speeches made by the three party leaders from the stage of the Albert Hall in which they all urged world disarmament. Ramsay MacDonald spoke of creating 'that state of disarmament which it is our conviction is the essential ingredient of peace' and of getting 'the Nations of the World to join in and reduce this enormous, disgraceful burden of armaments.' Stanley Baldwin spoke of 'the Will to Peace' existing 'throughout Europe among the statesmen' and of his conviction that 'the cause of Peace is going to be aided by international disarmament.' Lloyd George stated: 'You will never disarm, you will never effect real disarmament until you renounce war, not merely on a scroll, but in the hearts of men.'

Such hopes for world peace received a severe international setback when on 18 September 1931 the Japanese invaded Manchuria. But within a short time the League achieved its Disarmament Conference, and Movietone could once again spotlight Arthur Henderson speaking from Geneva. He was no longer Foreign Secretary but he was president of the conference and in that capacity he declared in Movietone's issue of 4 February 1932:

Ladies and Gentlemen, I greet you from the city of Geneva, where I have had the honour of opening the first World Conference on International Disarmament. I am not unmindful of the many difficulties and pitfalls in our path, but the difficulties and the pitfalls must be faced with courage.

However the problems which were soon to confront both politicians and newsreels alike over hopes of disarmament began to place a great strain upon their desire for peace. The international situation grew steadily worse after Hitler came to power in Germany in January 1933, and was exacerbated by his determination to rearm in defiance of the Treaty of Versailles, which in October of that year led him to withdraw from the Disarmament Conference.

By 1935 the newsreels were beginning to change their outlook, reflecting the growing concern over international events. This showed itself most clearly in a Movietone release with the title 'Is there to be an Armaments Race?' on 7 March 1935. The commentary ran:

At the new home of the League of Nations in Geneva, the chief news is a nation's army. It is announced that Britain will spend more on armaments; why? Because the whole world is arming. Japan demands parity on the sea with Britain and the United States: she wishes to complement her great military strength by greater sea power. Germany is building aeroplanes, commercial craft, but perhaps convertible: her right to rearm has been tacitly recognised. With mighty masses of manpower, Soviet Russia parades a Red Army, second to none in her history. Aeroplanes for Italy, thousands of them, lined up in spectacular array. Mussolini has fostered an airforce which challenges comparison with the finest in the world. France maintains her military strength, trains artillery, and mechanises her powerful army. France demands security and will not disarm. And Britain, long content with dominance on the sea, contemplates bigger estimates for all three services. For the army, still the small professional body of tradition, successors to the old contemptibles. For the royal airforce, becoming more and more important to Imperial defence, and for the navy, also an increase. Already the United States have faced the same problem but have taken the course which seems now to lie before Britain, an increase in armaments to preserve some defensive ratio with the offensive power of other nations.

This Movietone story was released three days after the 'Statement Relating to Defence' had been issued as a White Paper. A. J. P. Taylor is categorical that the latter document 'announced that the British Government had ceased to rely on collective security and were now going to rely on the older security of armed force.'[7] Movietone's newsreel report was just as unequivocal in its vindication of the British Government's standpoint with regard to rearmament. The opening lines to the commentary suggest that Britain was being compelled to prepare herself militarily because the other nations of the world were now doing so. The use of the terms 'Imperial defence' and 'defensive ratio' lays strong emphasis, however, on the point that Britain should not be seen as a potential aggressor. And the review which scans the rearmament by the world powers leads quite logically, although somewhat apologetically, into a final rejoinder stating Britain's case.

The spirit of peace exists by implication, although throughout the story the visual accompaniment is of a decidedly aggressive character, not resting simply within the realms of military preparedness, but pointing most of all to armaments in action. The reasons for this could well have been threefold. First, the shots of military action would contrast vividly with the commentary's insistence that Britain was rearming for the purpose of maintaining the peace by acting as a deterrent. The final shot of a ship and planes against a tranquil sunset would appear to reinforce such a message. Secondly, it could be argued that by showing military action the newsreel was attempting to rekindle a hatred of war in cinema audiences, and thereby strengthen the message that Britain should go to any lengths to prevent future conflict. It would not have been necessary to instil hatred of war in an audience since many of them would have endured the First World War. Finally, it should not be forgotten that the newsreel might well have been using plenty of action simply to attract audience attention, and so it drew upon the same visual iconography of war that had always met with great success in every realm of the film industry. Certainly this was the case by the time of the Abyssinian War.

British Paramount News opened their coverage of the Abyssinian War with a story released on 7 October 1935, within a matter of days of the fighting. They were able to do so only because the first-hand footage shot by their own cameramen is nondescript film of Italians embarking from the port of Naples and of Abyssinian troops on manoeuvres. There is battle footage in this release which purports to be of Italian and Abyssinian soldiers in action. Yet in fact this material comprised 'Special trick war material from America', as their library entries readily admit.

Paramount wished to emphasize the destructive capacity of modern warfare and obviously felt they did not yet have enough newsreel material from Abyssinia to do so. Ironically, the newsreel way to point out to an audience the dangers and horrors of war was to show as much dramatic and warlike footage as they could lay their hands upon, a method which belied their occasional worries about offending the public's susceptibilities through the exhibition of such film. The trick material in question included:

1. General top view of soldiers advancing over No-Mans Land. (Film that looks suspiciously as though it has been culled from a feature film.)
2. Big close-up of tank into camera, over barbed wire, and shell exploding at side of tank.
3. Air view of planes bombing, smoke coming from ground.
4. Long shot of house blown to pieces.
5. Close-up of *English* and *German* planes colliding in mid air.
6. Front view of soldiers advancing; shell explodes in their midst; some get killed.
7. Close-up of explosion covering the whole of the screen.
8. Big general view of soldiers advancing; firing of machine gun from behind ruins; smoke and aeroplane flying close to ground, machine-gunning soldiers.
9. Close-up map of Abyssinia.

There are several other interesting features about this story. Most of all, it is noticeable that the newsreel begins by generating an obvious sense of distance. After an opening credit that states quite simply 'War', vividly superimposed over the flames from an explosion, the camera cuts to establishing shots of Mussolini and Rome. A siren sounds, then people are seen in the streets of Rome excitedly reading newspapers with headlines of war, to be followed in turn by a view of church bells ringing. The next montage takes the audience to Naples where troops embark, waving and carrying a banner of Mussolini. Crown Prince Humbert and a band of officers bid them farewell.

Then the story cuts to Addis Ababa, where after another establishing shot of the Emperor there follows an unusual array of film which consists of warriors dancing frenziedly in the streets, only to fall to the ground in a trance, whereupon they put their swords to their own throats in acts of mock suicide. The commentator explains that this depicts a tribal custom whereby they pledge to offer up their lives for the Emperor. But when it is followed a few feet later by shots of uniformed but bootless Abyssinian troops marching on rough terrain, there can be little doubt that the cameraman must have been treating the audience to a sight rarely seen, and indeed not expected, of a traditional European army.

The point is brought home in the succeeding shots, which present a general view of row upon row of modern Italian aeroplanes. After showing Count Ciano, then Bruno and Vittorio Mussolini, the film breaks into the montage of trick war material.

So far the review has traversed the ground from an exultant Rome to an alien Addis Ababa and a make-believe battlefront, only to come to rest finally in London where Ramsay MacDonald, the former Prime Minister, proceeds to deliver the following speech to the newsreel camera:

It is war and war is horrible and it is dangerous as well. But I can assure you all that the action this nation has taken, has been to the good. Every effort will be made to stop it.

The contrast between a warlike Italy, a wartorn Abyssinia, and a peacefully inspired Britain is admirably and succinctly drawn by means of simple editing and an effective juxtaposition of what the newsreel considers to be the issues at stake.

Somewhat similar motives appear to have been at the heart of the newsreel coverage of Spain during the first half of 1936. The image presented by the newsreels immediately before the start of the Civil War is typified by several Paramount and Universal stories. From these, one gets the distinct impression that Spain was for the most part considered to be an exotic, faraway place with manners and customs very different from those in Britain, and that politically it was seen as potentially unstable and volatile. For instance Paramount's issue for 30 April has a story from

Seville in which the opening titles recount that 'Senor Barrio accompanies Catalonian President to Bullfight'. The film shows Martinez Barrio, the speaker of the Cortes and a native of Seville, taking Companys, President of the Generalitat of Catalonia, to a bullfight in his home town. It soon becomes obvious, however, that this story is concentrating its attention upon shots which perpetuate the popular image of Spain as a place of bullfights and matadors. Of the sixteen shots that make up the story, only four isolate the politicians involved, and the rest cover the decorations adorning the parade, people dressed in national costume on horseback, matadors and the bullfight itself. The off-stage commentator's voice fleetingly mentions the politicians and then goes on to describe the bullfight to the accompaniment of Spanish music and the roar of the crowd.

Paramount's issue for 15 June concerned itself even less with politics, containing as it did a story entitled 'Bees rout rheumatics'. After a caption jovially announcing 'Five stings and you're cured', it goes on to recount that a professor in Madrid was demonstrating before the cameras his new treatment for rheumatics. This amounted to a series of stings on the afflicted parts of the patient's anatomy, a treatment which reportedly 'claims amazing results'. Such an item at that date must have helped to engender the feeling that Spain was somewhat far removed from what might ordinarily be expected to go on in Great Britain and that it was largely remote from the British way of life.

During the first six months of 1936, however, Spanish politics were not entirely absent from the British newsreel screen. On 16 February 1936, Spain went to the polls and the Popular Front, a group comprising the parties of the Left, was returned with the largest number of votes and the greatest number of seats in the Cortes. But from the moment of the election a wave of violence overtook the country, resulting in riots and murder. Paramount reported the election result but in a manner which emphasized the attendant violence. For their story on 20 February noted that 'Riots follow election which gave the parties of the Left a clear majority.' The story contained footage of people outside polling booths, people voting and victorious politicians on a balcony acknowledging the cheers of their supporters. But the final shots show evidence of skirmishes between crowds and the police, with civilians running before mounted policemen and policemen on foot flailing people in the crowd with truncheons. The report mentioned that there were 'Three killed and scores injured' in the fracas which was being shown. To this extent the newsreels suddenly found themselves at least partially in line with the newspapers, for 'throughout the entire first six months of the year the British press was regularly reporting details of the class clashes, which were an almost daily occurrence.'[8]

All five British newsreels made a point of emphasizing the unstable nature of Spanish politics during these opening six months of 1936, whenever they mentioned Spanish politics, that is. Universal News perhaps best exemplified the mood they wished to convey in two stories. The first was entitled 'Spain celebrates' and was shown as part of the release for 4 May 1936. The commentary made the blunder of thinking that Manuel Azana, the President of the Republic, and Diego Martinez Barrio, the Speaker of the Cortes, were one and the same person as it stated:

Spain celebrates the fifth anniversary of the Spanish Republic. No government has yet been successful enough to have any anniversary celebration. However, Manuel Azana Diego Martinez Barrio the, for the moment, President of the Republic, reviews the army and hopes they will discriminate between friend and enemy. What is called a political outburst did take place, but the part of our Spanish operators' film showing the President in difficulties was confiscated by the police, and the camera operators themselves nearly got confiscated too. To be President of Spain just now requires bags of courage. Political and physical intimidation are continually being attempted by those who are agin the government, and there are always lots of those everywhere.

It is not surprising that Universal were confused as to who was the right and proper President of the Spanish Republic, since in fact Azana was not elected to the position until 10 May, some six days after Universal's report first appeared. However it had become apparent since 26 April, when special elections for presidential candidates were held, that he would be the choice. And there was certainly no reason why his name should have been confused with that of the Speaker of the Cortes. Everything had been completely sorted out, however, by the time Universal released their report on Azana taking office. This time he was afforded his correct name, indeed his full name. But the implications with regard to the Spanish political situation remained the same, as Universal's release for 18 May commented:

Spain at last gets some order out of chaos. Her new President drives to the Cortes, Parliament House, to take the oath of allegiance to the Republic. But he is so closely guarded that not even the camera is allowed to get within shooting range. Don Manuel Azana y Diaz is duly sworn in and then reviews the Madrid garrison troops from the balcony, a very high balcony, the higher the better, because even a new President can't be expected to agree with some old Spanish customs.

On the whole, the image of Spain as presented by the British newsreels before the advent of the Civil War was only a rudimentary one. It has been suggested that 'in the years preceding the Civil War, British opinion was being wooed for the cause of Left and Right in Spain', beginning with such events as the Asturian revolt, and that 'This conditioning paved the way for the more ready acceptance of the partisan propaganda of the years 1936–1939.'[9] Be that as it may, the British newsreels had played little if any part in such a wooing, though there had been a modest amount of conditioning over what to expect from the general political situation in Spain. Thus far the British newsreels had simply sketched in some very rough outlines of the story. The Civil War was to change all that.

The Civil War broke out on 17 July 1936 with the rising of the garrison at Melilla in Spanish Morocco. By that evening the insurrection under Colonel Segui was complete and the city was under martial law. On the same day there were risings at Tetuan, under Colonel Saenz de Buruaga, and Ceuta, under Colonel Yague. By the early morning of 18 July the insurrection had spread to the mainland of Spain with General Queipo de Llano leading the rebellious troops in Seville, while fighting also took place at Cadiz, Jerez, Algeciras, La Linea, Cordoba, Granada, Huelva and Malaga. The next day, 19 July, saw Moorish troops from the Army of Africa landing at Cadiz, and in the North of Spain the rebels achieved victories at Pamplona, Burgos, Saragossa and Valladolid.

The first week of the war had profound repercussions upon both sides in the fighting. On 18 July the Prime Minister, Casares Quiroga, resigned his office, whereupon President Azana invited Martinez Barrio to form a government. But the attempts of Martinez Barrio and General Miaja, his new Minister of War, to treat with the rebels came to nothing, and during the evening of that same day Azana and Martinez Barrio called together the Socialist leaders Largo Caballero and Prieto for discussions. A new government was formed under Giral, a former Minister of Marine. The morning of 19 July saw a decision to distribute arms to the people. By 20 July risings in Madrid and Barcelona had been subdued. Four days later the Nationalists, for their part, had established a junta at Burgos under the presidency of General Cabanellas and comprising those leaders of the rebellion on the mainland. They included Generals Mola, Saliquet, Ponte and Davila. In fact the real power lay with the actual Nationalist commanders in the field, where General Mola was in charge of the

Nationalist territories in the North of Spain, from El Ferrol to Saragossa and from the Pyrenees to Avila, in Nationalist Andalusia where General Queipo de Llano held sway, and in Morocco and the Canary Islands where General Franco was in command.

The Gaumont British Newsreel managed to get its first coverage of the hostilities on to the cinema screen in a story entitled 'Spanish Revolution' released in issue 269 for 27 July. The report began with the fighting on the mainland and chose to ignore the initial uprisings in Morocco. Gaumont's first pictures of the fighting immediately took pride of place in the overall issue and occupied the opening slot in a collection of five items. The story took up 116 feet of film out of a total of 717 feet devoted to this particular newsreel.

The visual emphasis of the story concentrated on the dramatic nature of the conflict, with shots of destruction and devastation. The commentary, written by Ted Emmett, is interesting for several reasons. The main contrast he wishes to draw is revealed when he states that 'Gaumont British News tells a graphic story of bloodshed and violence in the one-time lazy south.' Ted Emmett's message is one of peaceful tranquillity torn asunder by war and is melodramatically reinforced by such statements as 'The land of smiling tomorrow is grim today' and 'Through the streets of Madrid naked murder is stalking, the ever-present spectre.'

Emmett invites the audience to identify with the situation by describing Seville, Saragossa and San Sebastian as 'places known so well to tourists in times of peace' (though it is debatable how well known they were at that time to what was predominantly a working class cinema audience), and then confronts them with 'pictures which unfold the cataclysm that has taken toll already of 20,000 lives.' Lest the audience should fail to grasp 'the tragedy of civil war', Emmett employs an array of visual symbols sufficiently commonplace to evoke a response when he states that 'churches and cathedrals burn, public and private buildings are sacked and pillaged as by the army of an invader.' But then he deliberately distances this war 'in a country divided against itself' when he shows that 'Even young girls and women are armed with rifles and revolvers' and as he concludes 'Death walks in sunny Spain.'

What is perhaps most noticeable about Gaumont's first report is that nowhere does the newsreel go any way towards trying to explain the causes of the fighting. Showing some of the 'First of the actual pictures from Spain in revolt' seems to be its main aim. There is no attempt at all to evaluate the political situation which might have been seen to cause the military rebellion. In fact the report does not even elaborate upon who was in rebellion, but states quite simply that 'In the rising of the Fascists against the Government, brother raises his rifle against brother.' 'Fascists' and 'Government' are the terms which suffice to describe the multitude of warring parties, both religious and political. What the report does do, however, is assess the destructive nature of civil war in human and personal terms; and the British audience, for its part, is invited to sympathize with the plight of the Spaniards.

This was very much the attitude which all the newsreel companies took in their opening stories on the Civil War, with varying degrees of success. Suddenly forgetting the picture of Spain it had begun to draw in the preceding months, Universal's first report on 23 July commented that 'Barely two months ago it was thought that Spain was in for a period of quiet prosperity with the election of Senor Azana as President, but it was not to be as recent events have shown.' Universal had managed to get a story into its issue for 23 July by the simple expedient of drawing its film material from the library of stock shots on Spain which they had accumulated. Their second report for 30 July did however contain some first-hand film material, including shots of Fal Conde, a leading Carlist, with 'rebel troops marching through Pamplona, accompanied by women of the Fascist movement.'

In many ways the most interesting and certainly the most ambitious opening report on the rebellion was put out by Movietone in a story called 'Spanish Turmoil'. That too had been released as early as 23 July and depended largely upon library footage. But at least it attempted to put the proceedings in Spain into some kind of context. The commentary was read by Eric Dunstan and recounted:

All is turmoil in turbulent Spain, and the cost of political anarchy is death and destruction. This unhappy country, reft into two almost equal camps, illustrates all the tragedies of civil war under modern conditions. Innocent people lose their lives; property of law-abiding citizens is wrecked; and half the combatants fight half-heartedly for one cause or the other because they are forced to take sides.

The outbreak started in Spanish Morocco among men of the Foreign Legion, here seen on ceremonial parade under the walls of Tetuan. Commanded by prominent military officers, presumably sent from Spain because their loyalty was suspect by the Socialist-Communist Government, the troops rapidly took charge of Morocco and crossed over the straits to carry the conflict into Spain.

Here all soon became confusion with no certainty which side particular troops were espousing. Scenes like this were typical in every city, but in one instance police would be searching Fascists for arms and in the next it would be Communists whose movements were under suspicion.

And against cities where a known hostile element was in charge, troops of one side or the other would march and direct an intimidating bombardment. Such is the fruit of anarchy, of a people divided against itself.

To describe the Government in Spain as being 'Socialist-Communist' was certainly a mistake. The administrations of both Casares Quiroga, who had resigned on 18 July, and Giral, who had finally taken over, were composed entirely of middle-class liberals from Republican parties.[1] The Socialists, Communists and Anarchists had agreed to support the latter administration, with the arrival of hostilities, and overcome their differences. But not until 4 September, when Giral resigned and Largo Caballero, the Socialist leader, took office as Premier, did Communists join a western government for the first time. However, at least Movietone's report had avoided the pronounced moralizing which had concluded Pathé's opening coverage of the events in Spain. Pathé's story, with film from Pathé Journal of France, for its release of 3 August, had ended on the words:

And while we watch this grim struggle let us be thankful that we live in a country where men are free to express their political opinions without being shot, where internal strife is a thing unknown. While we here live under the protection of the Law, young Spain learns to shoot.

Gaumont's second report in issue 270 also brought Britain more forcefully into the fray. For this story highlighted the beginning of a stream of refugees from Spain to such havens of safety as Marseilles and Gibraltar. Once again it was placed in a prominent position in the release, this time as the concluding item in a run of six stories, and it comprised some 156 feet of film, only being beaten for length by a story on George Bernard Shaw reaching the age of eighty.

Here Emmett's commentary notes that 'English and Americans are numbered among those who have escaped with their lives and belongings' and in a truly patriotic tone adds that they have arrived at the makeshift stopover in Gibraltar, 'thankful once again for the reassuring sight of a British bluejacket'. He elaborates on this theme by stating: 'Overland, refugees pour into Gibraltar, making a temporary camp by the wayside under the benevolent eye of the Rock of Gibraltar's British police.' Evidently Emmett wished Britain to be seen by the cinemagoing public as a bastion of stability and order. But he does not stop there and goes on to describe how Britain is playing a role, albeit a small one, as the arbiter of peace and justice. For he describes an incident in which 'Submarines loyal to the Spanish Government have occupied the Straits of Gibraltar. The submarine C3 has been sunk by aerial bombing, but wild shooting between the combatants brought a stern reply from the British warships.'

The Spanish Government had indeed assembled a fleet in the Gibraltar waters, which by 19 July consisted also of the battleship *Jaime Primero*, dispatched from Vigo, and the *Libertad* and the *Cervantes*, dispatched from El Ferrol. Their express aim was to prevent General Franco transporting the Army of Africa across the straits. In fact an earlier draft of Emmett's script acknowledged the plan by noting that the Spanish submarines were 'patrolling to hold up the passage of rebel troops from Morocco'. But this latter sentence was finally deleted in the spoken commentary, and Emmett chose instead to make great play out of the intervention of the British warships.[2]

The rest of Gaumont's second report on Spain charted the advances of the first campaigns by showing scenes from the fighting around Guadalajara and in the Guadarrama mountains. On 19 July Mola had sent Colonel Garcia Escamez to relieve Guadalajara, but he had only reached a point some twenty miles from the city before it fell to Republican forces sent from Madrid. After some military engagements Garcia Escamez withdrew to take up a position in the Somosierra Pass of the Guadarrama

Mountains. On 21 July another Nationalist force under Colonel Serrador also set out for the Guadarrama and for the Alta de Leon Pass. The subsequent engagements for both these passes proved to be the first set battles of the war, and all the newsreels included coverage from the Guadarrama Mountains and the Somosierra Pass in particular. Throughout these issues it is the internal nature and strife of the Civil War that is stressed. Emmett's commentary for the second Gaumont report points this out by concluding: 'Women and young girls are among those who have shared with their menfolk the privilege of shedding their blood. This is the price of a new Spain.' Similarly in the fifth Gaumont report, Emmett shows 'men and women, boys and girls, going into action in the battle of Somosierra, the battle for the key to Madrid.'

The composition and preoccupations of these opening Gaumont stories were matched by similar coverage in their British Paramount counterparts, the first of which did not reach the cinemas until 6 August. Although the location for Paramount issue 568 is actually Barcelona much the same story is told. Visually the attention is focused upon general shots of blazing buildings and furniture burning in the streets. In fact much of the material showing destruction in the city as well as many of the shots purporting to reveal 'Graphic pictures of fighting' were culled from the British Paramount stock-shot library, as their library entries make clear. They were certainly not shots taken at the time of the uprising in Barcelona. It is not surprising that Paramount failed to get first-hand footage of the insurrection in Barcelona, for it began as early as 19 July, when the newsreel companies could hardly have been prepared, and was for the most part quelled by the evening of 20 July. They did, however, arrive in time to secure film of civilians being issued with rifles, an act which Luis Companys, the President of Catalonia, had at first refused to sanction until the CNT, the Anarcho-Syndicalist Trades Union, had taken matters very much into their own hands by raiding arms depots. Paramount also secured film of foreign warships in Barcelona harbour. There is a United States warship with American nationals on board and in the process of being ferried from the shore with their belongings. Similarly they obtained film for the end of the story of 'Insurgent forces at Somosierra'. But a long intervening passage, a montage of war scenes including howitzers firing and cavalry charging, is faked from material taken earlier than the events it is meant to depict. It is used to emphasize the carnage of war along with shots of dead horses and wounded soldiers.

If Paramount were a little slow off the mark in obtaining first-hand film material, they more than made up for their tardiness in their two subsequent issues. The release for 10 August centred upon Toledo, where the Nationalist forces under Colonel Moscardo, after an initially successful uprising, were driven back into the fortress of the Alcazar by the militias which had descended upon the city from Madrid. One week later, on 17 August, in issue 571, Paramount went even further afield, securing film from many locations. The story contained shots of Government warships shelling the Nationalist stronghold of Algeciras, which had been in revolt since 18 July and which had been successfully augmented by units of Moors from the Army of Africa, before the Republican fleet had put into effect its blockade of the sea route. Paramount would appear to have been mistaken, however, in calling the Government cruiser the *Jaime Primero*, since the latter was in fact a battleship and by 9 August it was on its way to Ibiza as part of an expeditionary force. Gaumont covered the same incident and simply referred to Algeciras being 'shelled by Spanish war-ships'. The rest of Paramount's story of 17 August included scenes of General Mola at the headquarters of the Nationalist junta in Burgos. Unlike Gaumont, Paramount had at least singled out some of the leading personalities in the war so far, for this story went on to spotlight Largo Caballero in Madrid. The report concluded with film of incidents at Villa Franca, Tolosa, Gainza, Madrid and, once again, Toledo.

Gibraltar had appeared fleetingly at the beginning of the report with a general view of the Rock and a long view with a pan over yachts and warships in the harbour. It was to appear more extensively in the subsequent issue, with a story on refugees having their papers vetted by a British 'bobby' at the gate of a refugee camp, while an armed British soldier in a kilt stands guard nearby. The camera traverses a row of refugee tents and takes in some posed shots of Sir Charles Harrington, the Governor of Gibraltar, as he inspects the facilities. Soup is being served to hungry refugees and their children. Once more Britain was seen to be the saviour of the situation and, not for the first time, the Rock of Gibraltar took on a symbolic significance. This story then went on to chart the advances in the war itself with film of the Nationalist troops rejoicing after the capture of Tolosa, the former Basque capital, which had been effected on 11 August under the command of Colonel Latorr.

What is most interesting about Paramount's opening coverage of the Civil War is their willingness to use stories of more than just general interest. It was Paramount who drew attention in issue 573 for 24 August to the German battleships which had anchored off Alicante, a Republican stronghold, 'as a warning to Spain that there must be no further bloodshed of German Nazis in Spain.' On the same day of release Gaumont's issue 277 and Movietone's issue 377 chose instead to spotlight the celebration of the Feast of the Assumption in Seville on 15 August. Franco and Queipo de Llano were present at the ceremony, during which they replaced the flag of the Republic with the Monarchist flag. Gaumont covered the event and 'a religious procession through the streets followed.' Emmett pointed out: 'This is the first demonstration of this character that has taken place in Seville for many years.' The natural inference to be drawn was that the Republic was irreligious and had consequently prevented any such ceremonies from taking place in previous years. Emmett then underlined his remark by stressing the unruly nature of the Republic. To do this he showed film which spotlighted the heavy damage that had been done to the British Consulate in Algeciras by Government forces.

Paramount were also quick in acknowledging that the Insurgent forces contained a large contingent of Moorish troops. This they did in a story entitled 'Moors aid Rebels' which was released on 31 August with film of General Cabanellas reviewing a unit of the Army of Africa at Burgos. Gaumont showed similar film on 3 September, backed up by a statement to the effect that 'General Cabanellas, head of the Provisional Government, is confident of victory as fresh contingents of Moors from across the water march towards Madrid.' Gaumont may have been slower sometimes than Paramount in making use of a story but they were certainly ahead of the rest in injecting comment. At the time, for instance, all that Movietone would say with regard to the outcome of the rebellion was that 'There's still nothing decisive to report from Spain.'

Yet whether or not the war in Spain was believed to be near to an immediate end, the newsreel companies had thus far spared very little by way of expense or manpower in their coverage of the events. Of course, next to the Abyssinian War, the hostilities in Spain were the first of any magnitude to put to use the full might of sound recording on film. And certainly the Spanish Civil War was the first European war experienced since the arrival of sound film, which might go some way towards explaining the volume of film expended upon it. In the opening two months of the war, the amount of film shot by the newsreel companies was considerable, even if one takes into account the fact that Gaumont had access to some of the material taken by Movietone cameramen through its deal with Fox Movietone of America, and that Pathé might utilize the footage shot by Pathé Journal of France or Arcos of the Soviet Union. Cameramen had been placed with the Republican forces and the Insurgent troops and film had been received from the main campaigns of action; from the Sierras and Aragon in July, and in August, northwards from Seville where Franco and the Army of Africa fought and against San Sebastian and Irun where Mola led the Army of the North.

But it is noticeable, even within the opening two months, that the way the newsreels used their material varied somewhat from company to company. There was generally little comment of a political nature, for instance, from Paramount but simply a narrative of events which, as befitted a company dedicated to a policy of anonymity for its commentators, kept to a formula of descriptive reportage. Pathé's commentaries also adhered to simple reportage. This was in complete contrast to Gaumont's commentator, Ted Emmett, whose opinionated, florid and literary style was full of subjective responses to the situation.

Yet for all Paramount's commendable intentions in attempting to avoid comment and controversy in their reporting of the news, it is, ironically, Emmett's unashamed efforts to formulate opinions and mould public response which provide the better insight into the newsreels' messages and intentions. For there is evidence to suggest that even at this comparatively early stage the newsreels were beginning to realize their potential as a tool of propaganda and as a formative element in the creation of public opinion on Spain. Gaumont British News were well equipped for this purpose, since their editing machinery was very much in the hands of one man, Emmett. Of course Emmett was by no means in complete command and anything he might wish to say would undoubtedly have passed before the eyes of the producer-in-chief at the very least. But for all that his control was such that not only did he write and read the commentaries on all stories but he also helped to edit the film coming in from the cameramen. This helped to ensure a continuity of storyline through the whole of any one particular issue, as well as from one story to the next. Such continuity was noticeably lacking in the work put out by Gaumont's British rivals. Perhaps the only competitor to such an integrated technique was *The March of Time*, which was a monthly release so that more time and effort could be allocated to its compilation. It will be seen that Emmett's conception of the impact a release might make was exceptionally acute, not only by virtue of its overall appearance, but also with regard to the position that one story might occupy in relation to another. The results he achieved were highly refined and effective.

The first newsreel release on Spain from Gaumont which was seen to be consciously propagandist in tone was issue 274. It was shown on 13 August and the particular story was entitled 'The Blonde Amazon'. In it a British schoolteacher by the name of Phyllis Gwatkin Williams, who had happened to be in Spain at the outbreak of the war, spoke of her experiences.

This story is interesting because it reveals both a bias in news reporting in favour of the rebel, Insurgent forces and an anti-war message. The first point was appreciated even at the time of the newsreel's release. The October edition of *World Film News*, for example, had a headline boldly proclaiming 'Newsreels show political bias. Editing of Spanish Civil War scenes discloses partisan views.' In the editorial which followed Brian Crosthwaite wrote:

The Gaumont British newsreel in its issue of August 13 has, I think, made a new and very dangerous departure from the rule of impartiality, which we are led to believe they have imposed on themselves, in its presentation of a witness of the Spanish rebellion. The lady interviewed, described for us as 'The Blonde Amazon', was looked after by Government troops and recounts the stories with which they regaled her . . . of burning four fascists in a car, executing seventy officers with a machine gun, and so on. She herself had seen a church burned down in front of her hotel; and she tells how the women-fighters were the worst of all.

Now we have no right to doubt this particular lady's word; but it must be pointed out that although she was selected from some hundreds of refugees from Spain, many of whom have an entirely different story to tell, she was not a witness at first hand of the most important part of her story and had apparently no knowledge of Spain to give any importance to her account.

The choosing of an unreliable but sensational witness is deplorable but perhaps understandable. The Gaumont British Newsreel editor has however gone to considerable pains to give verisimilitude to her story by cutting in, at the appropriate and telling moments, shots of a car burning, a church burning, fierce-looking civilians, their fists raised in salute, women fighting and the noise of machine guns, which in conjunction with the interview has become straight anti-Government atrocity propaganda. This method of cutting to stock shots is the normal method of giving reality to the fiction film; but when it is used to give reality to what is only a witness's statement in a newsreel film which we are in the habit of accepting as objective it becomes deadly dangerous.[3]

Crosthwaite's analysis of the visual components of this story is very accurate. After the opening credits announcing the 'Exclusive GB News interview with mystery woman of the Spanish Revolution', the first shot is a posed view of Miss Williams standing in the midst of a band of armed Spaniards. She is holding a gun in one hand and a bayonet in the other. Since she is not stated to have participated in any action, and it is not explained where she was based in Spain, one can only assume that a cameraman set up the opening shot for effect. Nor can it be the case that this shot was taken from a photograph, for after a momentary stillness, it breaks into movement. It is possible that this opening shot was faked after she had returned to Britain, but it was rare indeed for such extremes of deception in the newsreels by 1936. What is most likely is that Gaumont followed up this one person's movements after she had returned to this country. For then the camera cuts to Miss Williams coming down her garden path and sitting down on a garden seat. She proceeds to narrate the course of events as described by Crosthwaite. Her narrative is entirely personal in character and highly impressionistic.

At the same time her story is enhanced by a series of visuals, drawn from the Gaumont stock-shot library. It begins with a shot of troops giving the Republican salute, then advancing down the street towards the camera and waving their arms and bayonets in the air. It is noticeable that they advance at random and the general impression is one of confusion. Even in the ensuing shots of uniformed troops climbing on to trucks, they do so haphazardly and without any obvious discipline being exercised. Most of the armed men, however, appear in civilian garb, generally in working men's overalls.

These shots are followed by views of burning buildings, a close-up of some girls practising the actions of loading a rifle, then a long shot of a blazing church, a close-up of the same leading into a pan across to people cheering and once again giving the Republican salute. This sequence ends with a view of the church. The final montage is of civilians firing rifles, highlighting a girl shooting, and a shot of people advancing in a crouched manner along a boulevard and taking cover behind trees on the pavement. The last shot is a close-up of Miss Williams as she proclaims: 'If people could realize how terrible war is, they'd do everything they can to prevent it.'

It is not entirely true to say that the civilians in the piece are 'fierce-looking' in character. Indeed those giving the Republican salute look to be quite happy to do so for the camera. However most of them appear to be armed, and in one shot they are evidently seen to be leading another civilian in captivity, with his arms raised and under rifle sight, to what can only be conjectured to be a fifth columnist's fate. The uniformed troops who come into camera are certainly seen to be ill-disciplined and contrast strongly with the presentation in other stories of the Nationalist forces. To take only one example, British Paramount issue 571 has shots of General Mola inspecting a contingent of his army at Burgos where it is obvious that his regulars form ranks in an orderly and military fashion. They appear well disciplined and smartly dressed as befits a professional army. But then it should not be forgotten that, after all, the Nationalist forces were made up of the bulk of Spain's standing, professional army as it existed before the onset of the war. And if the presentation of the Republican soldiers in the Blonde Amazon story is such that it becomes a problem to tell the difference between civilians and soldiers, this again only reflects the truth. For at the outset of the Civil War the Republican army was indeed a ragbag, and as Movietone put it in one of their earlier stories, 'The Government troops are difficult to distinguish.'

However the crowds in this story are shown to be anarchistic by nature, with no mention whatsoever of the constructive side to the Republic's attempts to mould a social revolution. The crowds appear to be gloating over the burning of a church. In fact the anti-religious character of the Republic became a recurrent image, in direct contrast to the presentation of the Nationalists as deeply religious people, perhaps best shown in Gaumont's story on the Feast of the Assumption at Seville. Paramount issue 571 for once takes the theme even further by showing 'Red Government fighters ranging themselves before the Statue of Christ and His Angels in Madrid' and proceeding to fire at and then desecrate the broken remains. This action takes place to the accompaniment of a commentator stating: 'You are now about to witness an event that shocked the world.' And the Universal News for 24 August put the matter at its simplest by saying 'To be religious is to declare oneself a rebel', completely ignoring, for example, the mass of Basque Catholics on the Republican side.

There can be no doubt that the Republicans committed many acts of desecration and infamy, indeed many atrocities. But what is lacking in these accounts, most of all, is a sense of balance. It will be seen that when the newsreels had evidence of Nationalist atrocities, such as the massacre at Badajoz, they failed to use it.

It is emphasized very forcefully that women were part and parcel of the Republican forces and on one occasion Miss Williams states that they were 'the worst of all'. The newsreels had already noted that because of the very nature of civil war women were fighting on both sides of the warring armies in Spain. But the recurrent motif which typifies the depiction of Nationalist womanhood is best seen in Paramount issue 572, where there is a shot of triumphant Nationalist troops at Tolosa. For there is a procession led by a woman beautifully dressed in traditional Spanish garb, mantilla and all, with the Spanish Monarchist flag draped over her shoulder.

All in all, despite the fact that the Nationalists constituted a rebel, Insurgent army, it takes little effort to conclude that the imagery surrounding it is of a traditional, conservative Spain, fighting to preserve its heritage. While the duly elected Republican Government is presented as maintaining an undisciplined army bent upon destruction and upheaval. It would appear also that Crosthwaite's claim about the Blonde Amazon story amounting to little more than 'straight anti-Government propaganda' is essentially correct, though not always for the reasons he put forward. It is not so much a case that what was shown of the Republic was wrong, it is more a matter that what was shown to British cinema audiences consisted of no more than a one-sided presentation. They were not told the whole story. Indeed there is no mention at all of what was going on in Nationalist Spain.

Crosthwaite's editorial went on from a detailed investigation of the Blonde Amazon story to some general criticisms of the newsreel reporting on the Civil War. He claimed that 'in recent newsreel issues about Spain the pro-Rebel bias has been too obvious to escape notice' and, more specifically, that 'the Rothermere-controlled British Movietone News blatantly uses the terms "Red" and "Anti-Red"' to depict the warring factions. And certainly Movietone's depiction of the Republican side in the fighting was particularly misleading and emotionally charged. Phrases like 'exultant young Reds', 'the trail of Communist arson' and 'Red militiamen' abound in the opening Movietone stories and seem calculated, in their contexts, to capitalize upon the highly emotive connotations of the terms used. They culminated in Movietone's story for 10 September which begins with the sentence, 'The hammer and sickle is in the ascendant at Madrid'. And that description came about simply because two Communists had just joined Largo Caballero's first Cabinet.

However, all the newsreel companies were just as capable, at least in the early stages of the fighting, of referring to the combatants by such simplistic labels as 'Reds' and 'Fascists', neither of which did justice to the multiplicity of interests involved. In presenting the Blonde Amazon to the cinema audience, the Gaumont commentator, for instance, had made a point of emphasizing that she was 'neither Red nor Rebel'. And whilst the Republican Government at the time might not have been happy with being called 'Red', the Franco forces were certainly not pleased with being described as 'Rebels'. They complained often about the use of the word in the press and elsewhere. Within a comparatively short space of time it is noticeable that most newsreel companies came to settle for the use of 'Rebel', 'Insurgent' or 'Nationalist' on the one hand and 'Government' or 'Republican' on the other.[4] In this instance, it would appear that the problems involved in settling upon an appropriate terminology stemmed not so much from bias as from a basic inability to find the correct words to describe the plethora of warring parties on both sides. The American news media, who were less interested in this European conflict than Britain, employed the same kind of polyglot phraseology, as was revealed in a Boake Carter radio broadcast for the Columbia Broadcasting System which ran in part:

Hello everyone, Philco Radio Times, Boake Carter speaking. Well, death, fire and pestilence and starvation, those four horsemen of war galloped over the smouldering ruins of the once beautiful Madrid today with a vengeance. And behind them, stretched the shadows of two mailed fists to set the nerves of Europe aquiver again with anxious expectancy and fighting with the most desperate bitterness yet seen in the Spanish Civil War. The armies of the Fascist leader, General Francisco Franco, flung themselves again and again against the Loyalist defenders and with equal bitter stubbornness the Loyalists refused to give way.[5]

Carter's account was broadcast on 18 November 1936. One day later the real leader of the official Fascist Party in Spain, Jose Antonio Primo de Rivera, was shot by the Republicans in Alicante. It is not likely that he or his possible successors to the leadership of the Falange, Fernandez Cuesta and Serrano Suner, both of whom languished in Republican prisons, would have regarded Franco, who was not even a member of the Falange, as the leader of the Fascist Party. Nor indeed did Franco himself at the time, and within the next four months Manuel Hedilla took over the leadership.

After his remarks on biased terminology, Crosthwaite's editorial went on with its general comments about newsreel reporting. In a patronizing fashion that was typical of contributors to *World Film News*, he feared lest 'Shots of unkempt militia-men contrasted with Mola's smart regulars, backed by a carefully worded and tendentious commentary, impel the innocent middle-classes to side with the better dressed.' Although very badly expressed, the basis of his fears was founded in reality. Similarly he notes: 'when the film uses its subtle technique of assertion by implication, the cumulative effect of atrocities and desecrations (nearly always by Government forces) becomes terrific.' As has already been seen, stories with churches burning, shooting of fifth columnists, and worse, do appear regularly at this early stage of the war. But only when aerial bombing of Republican cities came to play a large part in the war is there any hint of criticism in the British newsreels of Nationalist infamy. And even then new forces were present in the formation of British opinion which accounted for the change more readily than did sheer antipathy towards Franco's pilots. During this early part of the war, a newsreel could so easily invoke fear of offending public opinion at scenes of horror (always a ready stand-by) when sequences of Nationalist atrocities were available. That way any such material was prevented from reaching the cinema screen. Such a course of action was followed, for instance, when cameraman René Brutin secured some dramatic footage of the destruction of Badajoz. Colonel Yague took the town on 14 August and a terrible onslaught followed, during which his legionaries and Moroccans wreaked havoc. Brutin shot film of the carnage and still photographs from his material were reproduced at the time; but his film material never reached the screen since the newsreel company concerned, Pathé Gazette, simply removed it.[6]

There was one final point emerging out of the Blonde Amazon story which Brian Crosthwaite failed to take up. For the anti-war message inherent in this particular story had far-reaching implications with regard to the formation of public opinion on Spain by the newsreels.

The very last words spoken by Miss Williams on the soundtrack are: 'If people could realise how terrible war is, they'd do everything they can to prevent it.' Clearly it was the intention of the newsreel production team to leave an anti-war impression in the minds of the viewers, and this was made all the more evident by the fact that this was the last story out of five items contained in this issue. The bias reflected in the coverage of this story really takes second place to the point that the scenes of the Civil War, the scenes of women fighting, of churches burning, were all being used first and foremost to generate a hatred of war. For this was by no means the first time that the British public had been exposed to such sentiments, and indeed there is every reason to believe that such coverage of the Spanish Civil War was made to fit very nicely into a strong campaign that the British newsreels had conducted so far, and were to conduct for some time to come, to keep Britain out of any potentially warlike situation. Furthermore, this story did have a particular message for British viewers alone during the month of August 1936, since it was during that month that the British Government laid down a policy in pursuit of non-intervention. The Blonde Amazon story can only be clearly understood in the context of such a policy.

The Blonde Amazon story was highly unusual in its construction. Generally, Ted Emmett would act as commentator and host throughout the full length of any one Gaumont story. Certainly on occasions he would cut into a story extracts and speeches from prominent politicans or personalities to back up the point he wished to make. But invariably he would introduce the extract, slip in the speech to be added, then return to his own comments for further elaboration, finally rounding off the report with his own conclusion. But here, after introducing Miss Williams to the camera, Emmett retired from the story, allowing a complete outsider, presented as a neutral observer ('neither Red nor Rebel, but a British schoolmistress'), to take over the commentating entirely and come to her own conclusion. Never had Emmett been seen to delegate so much responsibility, and this departure from the old formula was not to be repeated throughout the rest of the Civil War. Evidently at this moment Gaumont did not wish to be seen to be interfering at all with what was presented as the 'ordinary' person-in-the-street's point of view. Yet it is also interesting to note that such a radical departure in Gaumont's news presentation came at a time when, perhaps by force of circumstance, they felt unable to comment upon the British political response to the Civil War in Spain.

By 7 August Britain, along with Belgium, Holland, Poland, Russia and Czechoslovakia, had accepted in principle a French draft declaration of non-intervention whereby there would be no trafficking, either directly or indirectly, of war material or aircraft with either side in Spain. The great fear was, of course, that the events there might lead to a general European war and 'there was no politician in England prepared to argue that the country should actually involve itself on one side or another in the conflict.'[7] Throughout the rest of August there was a great deal of diplomatic activity to ensure that Germany, Italy and Russia should adhere to the idea of a non-intervention agreement, and to this end Anthony Eden, the Foreign Secretary, attempted to form a commission to supervise its working. The first meeting of the Non-Intervention Committee was set to take place at the Foreign Office in London on 9 September.

For some reason not one of the newsreels reported any of this, not even the fact that as early as 3 August the British Government had immediately accepted the French idea of non-intervention on its initial presentation. The diplomatic activity in August was apparently ignored, and although the Non-Intervention Committee met on 9 September, in London of all places, there was no mention of it in any of the British newsreels. The omission is difficult to account for. The British press covered its every move, and *The Times* contained the complete official communiqués issued by the Committee, as well as one from Lord Plymouth stating the reasons for Britain's response:

The chief concern of the United Kingdom Government in consenting to the establishment in London of the Committee (for non-intervention) had been to prevent the civil war from spreading beyond the Spanish frontiers and to secure a measure of cooperation among the Powers in what threatened to become a most dangerous international situation.[8]

Yet in 1936 the newsreels seemed strangely reluctant to report such opinions openly or to report the activities of the Non-Intervention Committee, perhaps because during this time the apparent diplomatic successes at the conference table were being so blatantly disregarded in reality. Movietone in fact virtually implied as much in the one newsreel story they released in 1936 which did make mention of non-intervention. Their story on Spain for 12 October concluded by saying:

When will it end? We may well ask. Russia now proposes to renounce non-intervention on the supposition of help given to the Rebels by Italy, Germany and Portugal. So the struggle may be prolonged yet for many months.

And in August 1936 Gaumont obviously felt that a story such as the Blonde Amazon was sufficient to endorse the common feeling against war in general and against British involvement in Spain by implication.

The next Gaumont story, after the Blonde Amazon, that was seen to display an avowal of peace appeared with issue 277. This report began with a story on the war that covered Seville, where Franco and Queipo de Llano were unveiling the monarchist flag, then moved to Algeciras to show damage done to the British Consulate there, and ended in Madrid where 'all the hospitals are full of wounded'. It noted that 'Madame Azana, the wife of the President, has organised and equipped a special building for the reception of emergency cases', and concluded with shots of special armoured trains which were in use on the Talavera front, before the collapse of that city and its capture by General Yague on 4 September.

What is most notable about the item is the place it holds within the release. The opening and closing stories were generally held by the newsreel industry to be the positions most likely to capture the public's imagination, or to leave it with the most enduring images of the incidents portrayed. This particular item is given first position, and is followed by a story entitled 'I Hate War' which contains a speech to that effect by President Roosevelt. In fact Roosevelt is recounting his personal horror of war originating in his own experiences in Europe during the First World War. Nowhere does he make any explicit reference to the Spanish situation, though probably Spain was at the forefront of his mind. For on 5 August his Secretary of State, Cordell Hull, had made it known that the American Government would adhere to a strict policy of non-intervention. Indeed America's position was so avowedly neutral that she did not even take part in the Non-Intervention Committee.

To make matters more explicit, the introductory speech overlaid by the Gaumont commentator announced: 'While Europe is disturbed, President Roosevelt talks of peace.' For the British audience, Ted Emmett did an excellent job of tying Roosevelt's speech directly in with the opening story on Spain. By the simple use of juxtaposition, Emmett used the second story to build upon and enhance the latent message contained in the first item.

It is a trick Emmett put to even greater effect in issue 278, which was released on 27 August. For this issue contains six stories amounting to some 672 feet of film. Of these six stories, the last three refer directly or indirectly to Spain: item four contains thirty-two feet of film in a story entitled 'First British Ambulance leaves for Spain'; item five contains eighty-two feet of film in a piece called 'Spanish Civil War Eighth Edition. Captain Juber with Government troops at Azaila'; and item six, the final story, draws Spain into a report entitled 'Wonderful Britain', which lasts for 274 feet.

The fourth and fifth stories, referring directly to Spain, draw a simple contrast between Britain intent upon furthering the cause of peace, and Spain at war. Emmett describes the short scene with the British ambulance as 'The Mayor of Holborn wishes God Speed to the British Ambulance Unit leaving London' and then in turn endorses the action on behalf of Gaumont by adding 'With a handshake the brave adventure of these ambulance men has started, and we too wish them the best of luck.' Then he cuts immediately to a battlefront in Spain with the words, 'In Spain itself life goes on as has by now become normal. Cavalry advancing means the evacuation of towns and villages by those of the civilian population not engaged in the fighting.' The remainder of the story is somewhat short in comparison to earlier reports on Spain, as Emmett narrates that 'On the Saragossa front our cameraman has followed the troops commanded by Captain Juber.' In conclusion he states that 'These pictures were obtained in Azaila when an action was in progress against the rebels,' but characteristically he does not fail to add that the action depicted is 'one of the many life and death struggles which are the daily experience of Spain in this year of grace.'

The real effect of the contrast between Britain and Spain is felt in the final story, with the title 'Wonderful Britain', for this begins with the words 'At this time when the agony of Spain streaks like a jagged scar across the face of Europe, it is well to pause and reflect upon the position of the world today.' This introduction serves as an excuse for a fleeting mention of Abyssinia, 'so recently wracked with the torments of awful war', and then 'From Abyssinia our review takes us to Palestine, where racial factions clash unhappily day by day, where riot and slaughter crowd an all-too-complete programme of misery and despair.' The commentary is accompanied by the appropriate stock shots of mayhem and destruction, only to be brought to an abrupt end by further library shots of a tranquil Britain over which Emmett adds in a suitably patriotic tone: 'In a spirit not of boastfulness but rather of gratitude we turn from these fitful scenes to fortunate Britain, still, with its tradition of sanity, the rock of steadying influences amid the eddying stream of world affairs.'

By this point, on the face of it, the contrast between Spain and Britain has been lost. But the two previous stories have proved to be of immense use, for in showing Britain coming to the aid of Spain in plight, and then showing Spain ravaged by war, Emmett is able to proceed to a stirring eulogy on Britain at peace. The recurrent image of Britain as a 'rock', akin to earlier newsreel stories, is amply expanded in this report, which goes on to recount a domestic tale of trade recovery and increased prestige:

Britain's industries have shaken off the chains that kept them fettered in the aftermath of the World War. They have risen from the Slough of Despond which clogged the wheels of progress in the Depression of the last decade. Trade returns are steadily improving. Weekly and monthly the official statistics form a heartening accompaniment to the efforts alike of the small merchant and the big boss of giant industry to better times. Our railways today stand second to none. Shipbuilding yards, for many years hushed in the inertia of unemployment, have been given a lead by the triumphant completion of the *Queen Mary*, now unquestionably supreme upon the merchant lanes of the sea.

Frequently overlooked but never to be forgotten is the vital factor of British justice, the fairest in the world, the physician of civil life whose equity and incorruptibility has never been called into question. This honesty in the courts of evil and wrongdoing is a sure fortress against the social hatred that fosters revolution. The Army, the Navy and the Air Force of this country have proved a sure protector and deterrent in the unrest that has prevailed abroad.

Britain is taking her stand in the belief that a strong defence is a guarantee of peace. Statesmen who may have drawn upon themselves criticism from time to time, have none the less worked unremittingly for peace at home and abroad. As we look back we realise that their efforts have brought this country safely through the innumerable crises that have beset it in the past few years.

And above all we look to the head of this great nation whose example and courage have won the admiration and envious respect of other nations less happy. Every member of the Royal Family works unselfishly and without stint in the cause of social service. The aim and the achievement of Queen Mary and the royal dukes and duchesses has been less to rule than to serve the country of which they stand head. For the King, already in the short time since his accession, has proved a worthy successor to his great father and to his grandfather, Edward the Peacemaker. Long may he continue to lead Britain from the chaos of world affairs closer to the days of lasting peace, prosperity and happiness.

Such sentiments must stand well in comparison with the overtly patriotic newsreels and documentary shorts made during the Second World War, at a time when film-makers were openly proclaiming that their 'first object is the putting across, in the best possible film terms, of any message of morale, information or propaganda which Government departments and other official bodies might from time to time think desirable.'[9] Of course in the case of this Gaumont newsreel, released in late August 1936, there is no evidence of any government pressure to produce such a story, as there would be in time of war. But then there would not need to be with such an eloquent spokesman as Ted Emmett in charge of production. Nor can it be chance alone that prompted Gaumont to produce such a story at a time when British statesmen were pursuing a course of action to ensure that this country was not drawn into a general European war as a result of the turmoil in Spain. Gaumont evidently felt that they had a part to play in leading public opinion. They revealed the tragedy of the war in Spain with all its repercussions for Spanish society, then they showed a peaceful Britain in the midst of increasing prosperity. The implication was that this country was in danger of losing 'its tradition of sanity' and its position as 'the rock of steadying influences' if it pursued any policy other than the one which the Government was advocating at the time.

After the initial voluminous coverage of the Civil War by all the newsreels during the first month and a half, by contrast the end of August and the beginning of September were comparatively quiet. The story was no longer 'hot' in newsreel terms, and therefore Gaumont, for instance, carried no report at all in its issue for 31 August. This was for only the second time in a run of eleven consecutive issues; nor did it do so on 7 September, a week later.

Paramount, for its part, had failed to carry stories on Spain in only two out of a possible eight issues during August, but during September it made no mention whatsoever in five out of eight releases.

On the military front the beginning of September proved disastrous for the Republic, and the newsreels naturally tended to reflect that fact. But since the war was obviously nowhere nearer an end they were compelled to cover it campaign by campaign, and such a task necessarily lent itself to exaggeration in order to sustain audience interest. This was shown in Gaumont issue 280, which began with the words 'Our cameraman at Irun and Saragossa has sent back dramatic pictures of the fighting in the key areas of the Spanish Civil War; the fate of these towns determines the fate of Spain.' Certainly both towns were important, but not that much so.

At the same time General Mola, with the Army of the North, was conducting a campaign against the Basque provinces of Guipuzcoa with the aim of securing Irun and San Sebastian, thereby cutting off the Basque corridor with France. The Nationalists had begun a sea bombardment of San Sebastian on 17 August and Paramount first showed film of its damaged harbour in the release for 24 August, then followed this up with footage of the land fighting around the city in its issue for 31 August. Gaumont's release for 3 September commented: 'At San Sebastian Government troops are seen raiding a farmhouse where the occupants, suspected of Rebel activities, are captured, searched and taken away. Not far away towns and villages are blazing under the incendiary bombs of air-raiders.' But San Sebastian did not actually fall until 13 September, and in the meantime the newsreels' centre of attention had turned to Irun, which fell on 4 September. Three days afterwards, bearing witness to the speed with which the newsreel despatches were now reaching the cinema screen, Paramount acknowledged the Nationalist victory in a story entitled 'Rebels take Irun'. The report further highlighted the growing importance in this war of aerial bombardment, with shots of Nationalist planes attacking the city. Gaumont chose to emphasize the devastation as Emmett recounted that it was 'Once a proud city, now a smoking ruin'. He elaborated on this theme by showing:

Refugees fleeing into the safety of France, over the international bridge and across the river; from the inferno of gun-fire dealing death and mutilation, into the sanctity of a neutral land; that is the best that can be offered to the wretched peoples of Spain today. That proud city is a mass of debris, a mournful monument to the savagery of war, its heartbreak and desolation. Once again we give you a burning example of war's futility.

Yet if the military advances and setbacks were the major preoccupations of the newsreel companies, simply because they provided the most visually captivating and dramatic film material, the political repercussions for the Republic and the Nationalists alike during the month of September were not entirely ignored. On 12 September the Nationalist junta voted for the war to be conducted under a single command and Franco was elected as the General at the head of this command, though this was not made public. But the newsreels had already singled Franco out for attention. On 14 September, for instance, Gaumont's release contained a short story in which Franco was recognized as 'the leader of the uprising' and in which he went on to speak 'fervently for the microphone'. Somewhat flippantly Emmett noted that Franco spoke 'unfortunately, in Spanish' and no effort was made to translate anything he said into English. On this occasion Gaumont had in fact used the film made available to them by Movietone. And Movietone used its own film for a report, also on 14 September, in which they did translate what Franco had said during the course of a commentary from Leslie Mitchell which ran in part:

If the Rebels win, General Franco will become a world figure, so whatever your sympathies this little talk from him should be of interest.
The General is doing his best to tell you in an unfamiliar tongue that Patriotism, Religion and Family Life are his creed. And he concludes with the words 'Viva Espana'—Long Live Spain.

Similarly the change in Republican leadership which had taken place on 4 September was recognized by Gaumont in issue 284, which commented that 'After the capture of Irun by the Rebels, the Government was replaced by its Socialist counterpart.' Largo Caballero's new government was predominantly Socialist and comprised six Socialists, two Communists, two members of the

Republican Left and one each from the Republican Union and the Catalan Esquerra. But Emmett also invested it with an aura of instability as he went on to note that 'already a plot against the life of its head, Senor Largo Caballero, has been unearthed.'

But political personalities were not considered to be the most engaging form of cinema news. Whereas in July and August stories on Spain had consistently occupied key positions in the newsreels, with a length approaching as much as 230 feet on something like the Blonde Amazon, by September reports from Spain appeared only in the less valuable middle ground. Indeed, Gaumont's coverage of Franco's accession to military command was relegated to a section entitled 'Roving Camera Reports' which consisted of four or five snippets and was tantamount to the briefest mention possible. In this slot it ran to barely thirty-two feet. The Spanish Civil War was dying as far as its news-bearing potential was concerned and might actually have done so, were it not for the fact that a new story broke on the siege of the Alcazar at Toledo. Mention of it appeared in all the newsreels on 21 September.

Gaumont's story for that date in issue 285 began by drawing a contrast between the Republican defeats at Irun and San Sebastian. The Basques had surrendered San Sebastian to the Nationalists with little opposition and had actually gone so far as to shoot a band of Anarchists who wished to destroy the city before the enemy arrived. Emmett's commentary underlined the point:

Shelled by the Insurgent army's artillery and bombed by its planes, captured Irun presents a sorry spectacle. San Sebastian too has fallen, but the holiday resort known to so many foreign visitors as a gay and beautiful place has not shared the fate of Irun.

The commentary elaborates further as 'the Carlist troops, entering in triumph, were greeted with wild cheering by the civilian population.' It then proceeds to add: 'From the Government side came reports of a tragedy so overwhelming as to defy description. The historic fortress of the Alcazar, beleaguered for two months, has been mined and blown to pieces.' The visual shift from a city in ruins, to a city saved from destruction amid joyous celebrations, and back finally to a city besieged and mined, is effectively complete. But what is also interesting to note is the mention of the aerial bombing of Irun. For Gaumont's next issue on 24 September took up the matter of aerial warfare in greater detail, stating that 'Aeroplanes continually combing the key roads to Madrid set fire to fields of wheat and rendered homeless and desolate many innocent victims.' Clearly aerial warfare was becoming recognized as a new force to be reckoned with, and as Movietone's story on the same date put it: 'Reports say that it is aerial supremacy that is giving the Rebels their advantage.'

But the newsreel accounts said little about whose aeroplanes were flying for the Rebels. Italian Capronis, flying for Franco, had for instance been instrumental in the bombing of Irun. And Gaumont had actually shown film of them doing so, though without ever going so far as to identify them as such.

The newsreel policy throughout 1936 on foreign intervention in Spain was very similar to its policy regarding the existence of the Non-Intervention Committee: the less said the better. And if it was possible to get away without saying anything at all, then nobody could be offended. Over foreign intervention the newsreels appear to have endorsed the government line, which was officially to ignore the facts, despite the evidence put forward by press and politicians:

Government spokesmen in France and Britain who were committed to supporting non-intervention were very unwilling to admit the facts of German and Italian intervention. Question time in the House of Commons often became heated and prolonged as members of the Opposition attempted to wring from the Government an admission that intervention was taking place which would prove that the official policy of non-intervention was a failure. Reports of equipment and men sent into Spain which appeared continually in the press were officially ignored until the facts themselves became too self-evident.[10]

In the case of the newsreels, even when the facts over foreign intervention were self-evident, they were simply not acknowledged in 1936. And, after all, the facts about Italian intervention had been learned very early on in the war: 'The first public knowledge of intervention came on July 30 when three Italian planes made forced landings in French Morocco on their way to join General Franco.'[11]

The *News Chronicle* and the *Manchester Guardian* were just two of the British newspapers which reported the facts about German intervention. For example, during the first weeks of the Civil War, a *News Chronicle* journalist who was based in Lisbon witnessed eight hundred tons of arms and oil being unloaded from the German ship *Kamerun*. The war materials were then sent on by train into Spain.[12] Furthermore, the *Manchester Guardian* estimated that by the end of 1936 there were approximately fourteen thousand members of the Condor Legion in Spain, comprising technicians, pilots and signals detachments.[13] Their figures were based upon estimates given to them by Anthony Crossley, the Conservative Member of Parliament, who visited Nationalist Spain in December 1936.

Indeed the facts about foreign intervention were officially recognized with the publication in London, in October 1936, of the findings of the Committee of Inquiry into Breaches of International Law in Spain. For the committee reported evidence of German intervention from British subjects who had been in Spain during the month of August. Some time later documentary filmmakers like Ivor Montagu were to produce filmed interrogations of German and Italian prisoners of war captured by the Republican forces. The Progressive Film Institute was to release these under the titles *Prisoners Prove Intervention in Spain* and *Testimony of Non-Intervention*.[14]

But in the autumn of 1936 the most the newsreels were willing to show of any kind of foreign 'intervention' was the provision by the Russians of food and essential supplies for the Republican side. Movietone in its release for 16 November and the Pathé Gazette in its release for 23 November both carried stories on the subject of Russian provisions for Spain. Both reports concerned the same incident, the loading with food on the Odessa quayside of the freighter *Kuban*, destined for Barcelona. Movietone's report began, however, by heralding 'A significant arrival in Moscow' and proceeded to describe the arrival of the new Spanish Republican Ambassador, Marcelino Pascua, in Moscow where he was to meet Molotov and 'to cement the friendly relations existing between the two Governments'. The story concluded, 'Russian eggs and Russian wheat for the Spanish Government's loyal supporters.' Pathé commented that 'Russia continues to give all the help she can to the Spanish Government.'

The siege of the Alcazar at Toledo continued to command the

better part of the newsreels' attention in the second half of September, just as it did for Franco. Professor Hugh Thomas has advanced two reasons why Franco determined on 21 September to postpone the advance upon Madrid in order to break the Republican siege of the Alcazar. He considers that 'the lure of the Toledo arms factory was probably the determining cause of the Nationalist diversion' but to Franco 'the spiritual (or propaganda) advantage of relieving Moscardo' was equally very important.[15] The military factor might well have been the prime cause, but to judge from the amount of film produced by the newsreel companies on the relief, Franco's latter purpose was thoroughly vindicated. For the siege, which had begun on 20 July, and the subsequent relief, which ended after more than two months on 27 September, were well and truly suited to the sensational and dramatic treatment afforded by the cinema.

Paramount, for instance, had not released a report on Spain since 7 September, then on 21 September it issued a story as 'the survivors of the fortress garrison still hold out after sixty-three days' siege' and immediately followed this up with a piece on the mining of the Alcazar. Gaumont followed the events even more closely. A short piece in issue 284 recounted that 'the Government called upon miners to sling dynamite among the Rebel defenders'; their next issue noted, 'The historic fortress of the Alcazar, beleaguered for two months, has been mined and blown to pieces.' The subsequent coverage expressed surprise that 'Even after the fortress of the Alcazar was shattered by mines, surviving defenders returned a spasmodic rifle fire. From the courtyard of the old Santa Cruz convent comes one of the constant stream of victims mortally wounded.' This last story also revealed how important a part the Alcazar had begun to play in Republican thinking. On 20 September, Largo Caballero arrived in Toledo and demanded of his officers that the Alcazar be captured within twenty-four hours. Gaumont filmed his arrival and announced that 'The Prime Minister, Senor Largo Caballero, who has personally taken charge, toured the destroyed area while refugees fled to what little safety is still left in Spain.'

In the event the Nationalist General Varela relieved the city on 28 September. But neither Gaumont nor Paramount showed anything of the relief until they had secured footage of Franco actually touring the captured city. The reason for this is probably explained in the Paramount release for 5 October. For here, apart from showing 'The first pictures of the survivors as the Insurgents take the city', there was also a short piece announcing that General Franco had now been proclaimed 'Head of Government', an event which had occurred at a meeting of the Nationalist junta in Salamanca on 29 September. In fact by the time that a decree was issued in Nationalist Spain on 1 October, Franco was being installed in Burgos as the Head of State, but such niceties escaped the eye of Paramount as much as they seem to have eluded the junta, who thought that they had agreed to Franco only being made Head of the Government.[16]

Gaumont also announced 'The Relief of Toledo' in their issue for 5 October, in an exciting story which allowed Ted Emmett to display his undoubted expertise as commentator and editor. It ran:

On the road to Toledo our cameraman secured these vivid pictures of the Insurgents' advance to relieve their comrades besieged in the Alcazar fortress for seventy-one days. The wreckage of an occasional aeroplane, grim though it is, pales into insignificance as the awful ruin of the Alcazar comes into view. Cautiously the Rebel troops advance, expecting every corner to send a whistling messenger of death. The historic siege of the Alcazar is ended. General Franco, accompanied by gaunt and bearded General Moscardo, who commanded the beleaguered garrison, walks in grim silence through the shattered streets. Amid the ruins, haggard inhabitants of the city siege eat and exercise after many weeks of imprisonment and semi-starvation. General Franco spoke with great emotion to the troops who had scarcely strength enough to stand to attention. In a story of the horrors that war inevitably brings, this has been the most terrible of all.

This report shows just how effective Gaumont's presentations could sometimes be. Paramount, for example, had chosen to show their film in three consecutive stories, each of which displayed footage relevant to the most recent developments in both the siege and the relief. Gaumont pursued the same course, though they also rounded off the whole incident with a long story entitled 'The Relief of Toledo', some 147 feet in length, which was given pride of place at the opening of the release and which attempted to lead the audience through the final stages of the ordeal in one all-embracing story. It also appears from the visual montage in the Gaumont story that Franco was present in person at the actual relief, which was not the case, thereby giving his role greater symbolic value. Inadvertently the film also bears witness to the important part played by the Army of Africa in this campaign, since the shots of the 'Insurgents' advance to relieve their comrades' centre upon Moorish troops.

The siege of the Alcazar had a great emotional impact outside Spain, as well as within the Nationalist and Republican camps. The newsreels show this, but so also does the fact that the siege inspired feature film producers in the commercial cinema to consider using it as the basis for fictional scenarios. In December 1936, 20th Century-Fox announced that they had scheduled for production a film titled *The Siege of the Alcazar*, and producer Darryl F. Zanuck, was reported as saying that, 'Its heroism has thrilled the world.' As it happened the project was shelved, but not before Ivor Montagu was prompted to write an open letter to Mr Zanuck in the pages of *World Film News* where he pointed out 'the dangers of one-sided treatment'.[17] One film that was finally produced came from Italy in 1939 entitled *L'Assedio dell' Alcazar*, directed by Augusto Genina. For all its attempts at historical veracity, this film understandably vindicates the cause of the Nationalist defenders.[18]

The Alcazar at Toledo had not been the only Insurgent garrison under siege throughout September. Colonel Aranda, along with a contingent of Asaltos, Falangists and Civil Guards, had been pinned down in Oviedo by Asturian miners since 20 July. But Oviedo's relief on 16 October merited simply a short report in Gaumont issue 295. At this point of time only a single, solitary Nationalist garrison, defending a monastery near Cordoba, remained inside Republican territory, and so Franco's forces turned in earnest upon Madrid. The newsreel companies evidently felt that the capture of the capital was imminent. Paramount showed shots of Franco and his forces closing in upon the city, then cut to scenes within the city itself showing Largo Caballero and numerous shots of lorries loaded with cannon, and buses filled with troops, as they set out for the front. On 2 November, Paramount's release again had footage on Madrid but highlighted the work of a Scottish Ambulance Unit, ferrying casualties to a hospital on what was to prove to be its last trip before being bombed.

Gaumont too highlighted the plight of the city. A Roving Camera Report for 5 November noted: 'Madrid becomes once more the centre of world interest as Government forces prepare to make a last stand against the encircling Insurgent forces. Trenches built around the city are filled with militia, awaiting the decisive hour in Spanish history.' And such reports were essentially correct. Madrid was very much in danger of being overrun and the government of Largo Caballero determined to leave on 6 November for Valencia, a move which seemed to confirm suspicions that the city would fall. As a result Gaumont's newsreel for 9 November went so far as to announce 'The Fall of Madrid'. Obviously Gaumont believed this event to be such a foregone conclusion that they intended to make a scoop of it. Yet for all their haste, they were careful enough not to commit themselves too far on this story. There was always the danger that if they put forth an uncompromising story on the fall of Madrid, and it proved to be wrong or hopelessly premature, then their credibility as news-gatherers would suffer. The opening title proclaimed 'The Fall of Madrid', but after that the succeeding montage of commentary and film was subtly constructed by Emmett in such a way that nobody openly reiterated the point. The commentary ran:

Madrid, the capital city of the country of despair. The Rebels have achieved their big coup in the story of wracked and tortured Spain. Bombed from the skies and shelled almost without pause, the lot of civilians is more easily imagined than described. The Government's War Minister and Premier, Largo Caballero, has fled from Madrid while only a few of his troops remained to put up a weak resistance against the forces of General Franco. Foreign Legionaires and Moors advanced to print another chapter in the history of unhappy Spain.

Only at one point in the script does Emmett actually make an incorrect statement. Ministers, civil servants and politicians had indeed left the city, but there is no evidence of any Republican troops leaving as well. On the contrary, the city's Republican forces had been supplemented at the end of October by Russian tanks, aircraft and their crews. And within two days of Largo Caballero's departure on 6 November, the first units of the newly formed International Brigade arrived in the city. Neither of these factors was mentioned since the British newsreels appeared to be maintaining a strict silence about acknowledging the presence of foreign troops on either side, apart from the Moorish troops that constituted the Army of Africa. But where this Gaumont story does mislead is in the juxtaposition of commentary and accompanying film. At the point where the script mentions 'a weak resistance against the forces of General Franco', for instance, there are shots of General Franco walking up some steps into a building. These shots are actually of Franco at Burgos and had been first used in Gaumont's release for 20 August. In their new context, the visual montage makes it look very much as though Franco is entering a building in Madrid, after capturing the city, and it is left for the audience to draw this inference without the commentary ever explicitly stating such a fact.

So it was that when Madrid did not fall, Gaumont simply resorted to stories on the defence of the city, such as GB issue 300 which stated that 'many of the inhabitants have fled, but those remaining bend every muscle and sinew to resist the invader. Round Madrid the circle of death closes, spare a moment to pity them.' Or stories such as GB issue 302, which recounted: 'Insurgent troops encircling the capital concentrate their efforts on one big push with all the forces at their disposal. General Varela seems to be happy and confident as he discusses the plan of campaign.' Clearly Gaumont appeared in no way embarrassed by their mistake despite the fact that it had been noticed. *World Film News* for December 1936 commented:

An incredible blunder was made by all the newsreels in their issues dated November 9; apparently suffering from a surfeit of 'intelligent anticipation' they announced the fall of Madrid and some even included shots purporting to show the entry of Franco's troops into the city.

The newsreels had entirely miscalculated the capacity of the Government forces to defend the Capital. This is not the first time that their information about Spain has been inaccurate and ill-informed. Maybe it will teach them a lesson.[19]

World Film News had also made a mistake, however, in their condemnation. For Paramount had not been party to the blunder. In fact, since their report on the Scottish Ambulance Unit on 2 November, Paramount had made no mention of Spain. It did

not do so until 16 November, where there was reference to
Spaniards convalescing in Moscow as part of a compilation entitled
'Where Stands Peace?' in issue 597.

The sub-title to this story was 'Nations arm and ally' and it
covered three locations: Vienna, Warsaw and Moscow. It began
with the visit of Count Ciano, the Italian Foreign Minister, to
Vienna. He is dressed in a Fascist uniform and proceeds to inspect
Austrian troops, finally addressing them with the Fascist salute.
The story then cuts to Warsaw where Marshal Ritz Smigly and
President Machisky take the salute before a parade of Polish
soldiers. The commentary states that 'Marshal Ritz Smigly,
newly appointed Head of the Army, co-operates with President
Machisky to increase the country's forces to nearly 300,000.' The
reason given for such an action is: 'A buffer state between Germany
and Russia, two formidable nations unfriendly to each other,
Poland treads warily', though the commentator notes that 'Ritz
Smigly has the army and people behind him in his determination
that in any event, Polish independence shall be preserved.' The
final location is Moscow, where once again the visual emphasis is
on a huge military parade at which the salute is taken by Stalin
and Voroshilov. The occasion is the nineteenth anniversary of the
Russian Revolution and the script notes: 'A million and a half
troops pass through the Red Square, Moscow, watched with
interest by many foreign military attachés, a British representative
among them.' At this point passing reference is made to a band
of convalescent Spanish soldiers, in Republican uniform, watching
the proceedings and applauding, while the commentator adds that
'Spaniards, who had fought in their Civil War, a woman included,
are given front seats.'

The final shots are of the parade with tanks advancing towards
the camera, the crowd cheering and a concluding view of planes
flying overhead. But the real point of this story, which visually
depends upon an assemblage of military power, is aptly summarized in the concluding sentence of the commentary: 'As in 1914,
Europe stands upon a sword hilt; everywhere the nations are on
the march; one thing is plain, no ordinary citizen in any country
wants war.'

The role of Britain in this European context was spelt out very
clearly a week later by Paramount with a speech by Stanley

Baldwin entitled 'Premier takes stock, finds Britain best', during the course of which he said:

In many countries abroad we see fear and suspicion, economic and industrial depression, the destruction of liberty and freedom, conscription on an increasing scale, violence and disturbance, and in Spain we witness the climax in the terrible horrors of Civil War. Contrast these conditions with the peace and prosperity of our own country. For five years we have enjoyed a steady industrial recovery which is still continuing. In the first nine months of this year, employment increased by well over half a million. We have steered clear of Fascism, Communism, dictatorship. We have shown the world that Democratic government, constitutional methods and ordered liberty are not inconsistent with progress and prosperity.

All the newsreel companies carried this speech in their issues for 23 November. The line that these newsreels had put forward with regard to the Spanish Civil War, the implications of that War for the rest of Europe, and finally the role of Britain throughout the turmoil, are here manifested in a speech from the Prime Minister of the day. The contrast is complete: Spain in chaos as a result of strife and devastation, Europe on the verge of rearming, and Britain in the midst of 'peace and prosperity'—with the obvious corollary that in order to sustain such a tranquil state of affairs this country should stay out of any potential altercations. It is 'Wonderful Britain' all over again, and the opinions of the newsreels are seen to be vindicated by the leading figure in the Establishment. Indeed even the setting for Baldwin's speech was made comfortably reassuring, for the Prime Minister was sitting at his desk in a traditional oak-panelled study. The speech itself was delivered straight at the camera, and although Baldwin's delivery is unexciting and by no means impressive, at least it is put across with calm and confidence in a thoroughly straightforward, if somewhat deadpan, manner.

Even at the time of this speech by Baldwin, the Establishment itself was in danger of being undermined by the Abdication Crisis, and it is perhaps worthwhile digressing from the Spanish Civil War at this point in order to see how inherently conservative the newsreels could be in their coverage of events. For the newsreels' answer to such a threat as the Abdication Crisis was simply not to report it, until the moment at which they could also announce something positive, such as to herald a new King. As *World Film News* put it: 'With the entire British Press "ostriching", it was too much to expect the infinitely more cowardly newsreels to take an independent line.'[20] *World Film News* did a survey of newsreel coverage on the Crisis and considered:

So badly had the newsreels got the jitters over the Constitutional Crisis that even when King Edward VIII abdicated, their specials were contemptible. None of them had the courage to face up to the issues involved and the attempt to use the Queen Mary angle plus stock shots of the new King to cover up their cowardice, impressed nobody.

But the main gist of their argument was summarized in the conclusion:

The Crisis has clearly demonstrated that the newsreels are dependent upon and fearful of the magic word authority and that they are unable to fulfil their responsibilities to the public on an issue of domestic importance. When will one of the newsreels have the courage to break through?

In the heat of their invective *World Film News* had once again failed to avail themselves of all the facts. The brief analysis of the newsreel response was accurate as far as it went. But Paramount, with the independently minded Tom Cummins at its head, had actually prepared a story entitled 'The King: Crisis' to go out in its issue for 7 December. It included shots of Mrs Simpson and a title which described her as 'the American society woman, whom it is rumoured that the King intends to marry.' In the final event they did not fully utilize the story and the Paramount library entry states, quite simply: 'This story had to be withdrawn.' No reason for the withdrawal is given in their records, but then it is not likely that Paramount would ever have gone so far as to record in their papers the reason why they might wish to withdraw such a story from circulation. Nor is it possible to ascertain from other sources precisely why the story was cut, as is the case when Paramount were compelled to excise the story they released on the Munich crisis. It is possible that pressure was exerted by the Government in one form or another, but such overt acts of censorship were rare.[21] A further possible explanation is that the inherently conservative nature of the newsreel establishment precluded the coverage of incidents which could in any way be construed as controversial.[22]

Nor did such an attitude necessarily hide any political undertones, sometimes it stemmed from a fear, possibly mistaken, that criticism and controversy in newsreel content would alienate the large cinemagoing audience. Ironically it was *World Film News* which pinpointed the dilemma inherent in the attitude of the men it continually castigated, when, a few months later, it commented:

On May 25 (1937), four men walked into the shining new offices of British Movietone News in London's Soho Square. They were: R. S. Howard, Editor of Gaumont British News; Cecil Snape of Universal; Louis Behr of Pathé; and G. T. Cummins of Paramount. Inside they were met by Gerald Sanger, Movietone's Production Chief, for a hush-hush heart-to-heart. Within a few minutes they had reached complete agreement. The Wedding of the Duke of Windsor was barred from every screen in Britain. Britain's cinema addicts had lost the year's biggest story after the Coronation. The trade had lost the chance to pack every movie house in the country solid, for days on end.

So quickly did the newsreels' Big Five make their decision, that at first there were rumours of hands being forced by Goverment pressure, or interference from powerful vested interests. Later information showed that they had acted entirely off their own bat. What underlying reasons led to the anti-Windsor policy?[23]

This comment highlights two main factors in newsreel thinking. It shows the way in which the newsreel companies could close ranks, on their own initiative, to prevent any coverage of matters they considered to be potentially controversial. For if the five largest newsreel companies did not cover an event then there were very few other newsreel companies to do so. And it reveals the sort of problems the newsreel companies encountered with regard to their decisions on what they should or should not cover. As newsreel men they appreciated that there was a certain amount to be gained by capitalizing upon events which were very much in the public imagination. Yet they had to balance their natural response with their belief that coverage of controversial matters could in the long run be detrimental to their standing as gatherers and purveyors of the news. As *The Factual Film* put it some years later:

The cinema manager is said 'not to want politics' on the screen being, as a business man, concerned to exhibit what the largest possible section of the public will pay for, rather than what might cause, through its immediate and pressing importance, expressions of conflicting reactions among the audience.[24]

The marriage of the Duke of Windsor might not in itself have been construed as 'politics', but it certainly had profound political ramifications. As far as the newsreel companies were concerned there had evidently been enough 'expressions of conflicting reactions'. They were not prepared to rekindle public feelings on the Duke of Windsor's marriage to Mrs Simpson, for the very same reason they had chosen not to exacerbate the situation by giving coverage to their relationship in the first place. They obviously thought that to issue newsreel coverage on these matters of intense public debate meant that their editorial comments might well be taken up and used by one side or the other. They chose to play it safe, once again.

The British Press reacted in much the same way as the newsreels. Indeed British wholesale newsagents even went to the lengths of cutting out most references to King Edward VIII and Mrs Simpson from American magazines in 1936 in order to ensure that there was no coverage.[25] Yet the true irony in the press response was that whereas the newsreels were vilified for their reaction, by the likes of *World Film News*, the press were applauded for taking a somewhat similar stand. *The Report on the British Press*, published in 1938, for instance, had the following to say:

The biggest recent example was the Simpson crisis leading up to the abdication of King Edward VIII. The entire British Press was aware of most of the relevant facts long before a line on the subject appeared in the papers. It has sometimes been suggested that an official ban was enforced, but, if anything, the reverse was the case, as there were hints that there would be advantages in gradually accustoming the British public to the existence of the then Mrs Simpson. So far as Ministers were concerned, a request from a Fleet Street quarter for a lead before the crisis broke met with no satisfaction. When Mrs Simpson obtained her divorce decree the Press agreed on a common method of treatment, which gave some prominence to the event without explaining its significance to the uninitiated. Between the decree nisi and the actual breaking of the crisis, when overseas papers were already full of speculation, it gradually became apparent that some publicity was inevitable. Fleet Street hung back, no newspaper being anxious to act in isolation, and some at least awaiting a lead from *The Times*. It was obvious that any newspaper which came out with the story alone might be disastrously affected by an official denial if the affair could be settled behind the scenes. It was also evident that many readers would receive the news with a resentment which might prove dangerous to the newspaper concerned, as well as to the State. So it happened that the vast majority of British citizens remained, almost until the end, in total ignorance of matters which were to bring about a change in their allegiance, not because the Press did not know, and not because the Press was muzzled by an outside agency, but because the sense of responsibility of proprietors and editors, coupled with their fears of the dangers involved to their papers, were greater than their appetite for what could have been the greatest 'scoop' in history. It is significant that in this crisis, failing a clear lead from the King, from the Government, or from the Church, Fleet Street eventually relied on the remarks of a Yorkshire bishop, rather cryptically reported in the northern Press, as an occasion for raising the issue. There has been, and no doubt will be, much disagreement whether Fleet Street acted wisely in showing so much restraint, but the fact that restraint was, without exception, shown, whatever the reasons, is at least evidence of the falsehood of the common belief that there are London papers which will sacrifice anything for the sake of sensational news.[26]

The pressures and process of decision making would appear to have been exactly the same for the press as they were for the newsreels. The outcome was that the press reported very little until the matter was virtually settled and the newsreels reported even less, in effect only that there was a new King.

It was the self-same consensus of silence that had been apparent on certain occasions in the newsreel coverage of the first six months of the Spanish Civil War. Only there it had manifested itself with regard to such matters as foreign intervention and the Non-Intervention Committee.

Little was to change in the concluding weeks of 1936, yet the difference between the newsreel products of the respective companies was admirably exemplified in the final weeks of the year.

Gaumont, for instance, continued to play upon the sense of personal plight and social devastation inherent in the Civil War, highlighting the effects of aerial bombing in its commentary for 7 December:

Madrid in a state of siege shows the effect of constant bombing by Insurgent planes that fly over the Spanish capital by day and night.

Ancient buildings, palaces, galleries containing priceless art treasures, all these bear witness to the marksmanship of the Rebel bombers. Citizens walk among the ruins which only a short while ago were normal stately buildings like those we know in London and our own big cities. Now there is food shortage, petrol shortage, leaking gas and burst mains. This, in short, is Civil War.

The story is succinct, makes its point concisely, and once again draws out a comparison between Madrid at war and London at peace. But as so often with Gaumont stories, it is notable for its omissions. There is no mention of the fact that most of the bombing of Madrid was being carried out by the German Condor Legion, which had been assembled in Seville over a month earlier on 6 November. It was the Condor Legion that from 16 November to 19 November systematically bombed the city both by day and night in order to assess the reaction of the civilian population. This bombing concentrated on the densely populated areas where most panic would ensue, and one thousand people were killed in the raids. Nor did Gaumont mention that it was the International Brigade which greatly contributed to the survival of Madrid from land assault during the same period.

Gaumont's issue 303 had displayed somewhat similar omissions. On 17 November the Nationalists announced a blockade of Republican harbours. The main objective was to prevent war material reaching the Republican forces, and to this end Franco maintained that his blockade would extend so far as to attack foreign ships found in Republican harbours. Such an action had important international implications, especially for Britain,where the Government announced on 23 November that legislation would be introduced which would prevent the carriage of arms to Spain in British ships from any port. On the same day Gaumont released its issue 303 which commented that:

While the siege of Madrid was engaging the attention of all land forces in Spain, the world switched over its focus to the navy. With General Franco's threatened blockade of certain ports held by the Government, cruisers and smaller vessels of the Loyalist fleet left Malaga to play their part. In the meantime all ships of foreign nationality have been warned to keep clear of such harbours as Barcelona. In Bilbao, Government ships are in action, surprising a group of boats transporting ammunition and confiscating the welcome spoils of war.

To judge from this story alone one would have little idea of the international implications of Franco's blockade, apart from the warning to steer clear of Republican harbours. In fact Britain was placed in a difficult spot by Franco's announcement, for British ships were entitled by international law to transport arms to Spain from foreign ports. If such ships were in Spanish territorial waters, they came under Spanish law, but until actually reaching the point of demarcation they were able to call on the British navy for assistance in the case of interference. The Nationalists' declaration stated that they would prevent arms reaching the Republic and, short of challenging the legality of such an act, the only alternative for the British Government lay in granting Franco belligerent rights. The British Government wished to grant such a recognition. The French did not. The outcome was that Britain proposed to prohibit the transport of arms in British ships from all ports. But Gaumont had turned their story on Franco's blockade into a purely foreign affair, concerning only internal Spanish matters.

Movietone were beginning to show a somewhat different attitude. In a long story which they released in issue 394, Sir Malcolm Campbell made one of his occasional appearances before the Movietone cameras with a story entitled 'Preparedness: The grim fate of Madrid brings home the moral of air-raid danger.' The complete commentary ran:

Spain has been out of our thoughts lately, but when I saw the last films which we received from Madrid, I felt that the fate of that unhappy city bore such a moral for us as to justify me in referring to them.

The lesson which we should learn is that most of the damage in Madrid has been caused by aerial bombardment. The terrible havoc which the bombing plane can effect can hardly be realised by the people in this country. What would happen to London in the event of an aerial attack?

I am not a scare-monger, but I regard it as a public duty to draw attention to realities. In pursuance of this policy, and realising the necessity that the public should be safeguarded in the event of a sudden attack from the air, I began the construction of a bomb-proof dug-out myself some months ago. Not because I expected a bomb to fall in our locality, but because example is better than precept and somebody had to start the ball rolling in this direction.

We dug down to a depth of 14 feet and here you see us building the concrete walls. All this entailed a tremendous amount of work, and as the weeks pass we have eventually constructed the roof, which consists of three feet of reinforced concrete, doubly strengthened with steel girders.

The next step was to start piling on the earth. Altogether we shall have 14 feet of soil on top, interspersed with layers of armour plate. This shelter will, I think, resist most types of explosive bombs, but there is another danger, and that is Gas. All the air, which passes through three intakes, is filtered by means of special chemicals, and is circulated through the rooms by electric fans.

As the air pressure inside the building will be greater than atmospheric pressure there is no chance of gas seeping in through the doorway. You can see from these interior shots how normal life could be, under such conditions. A 50-volt electric light plant is installed to provide current for the fans and the necessary illumination.

The building is now nearly finished and, I think, has already provided an example to others. I hope these pictures will not mar your Christmas festivities, but we shall have to take real steps to grapple with this menace from the skies, in the immediate future.

Universal, by comparison, had followed up Gaumont's idea from earlier in the year and its issue 666, for 26 November, contained an interview with Mr Reginald H. Rose, who had just returned home after serving in the Government forces defending Madrid and who was invited to tell his story. What followed was an inadvertently comical account of how Mr Rose had joined up in order to find out what was really going on; of how at first he had been thought to be a spy and had confidently expected to be shot; of how finally he had advanced to corporal and then lieutenant. His final words were: 'I realized that Madrid couldn't hold out much longer and I decided to clear out.'

Pathé and Paramount, meanwhile, were still making a point of showing the blossoming relationship between Republican Spain and the Soviet Union. Pathé did so in its issue for 19 November with two stories, both fifty feet long, neatly juxtaposed to emphasize the point they wished to make. The first story, called 'The Destructive War in Spain', was made up of material from Pathé Journal; the item which immediately followed was entitled 'Moscow's Demonstration in support of the Spanish Government' and was culled from film material provided by Arcos.

Paramount's story in issue 600 for 26 November continued the theme it had first elaborated upon in earlier reports which showed the arrival of the Russian Ambassador in Madrid and Spanish soldiers recuperating in Moscow. For this new story followed the arrival of a Spanish delegation in Moscow where they were fêted and greeted by Kalinin, the President of the Soviet Executive Council. The accompanying commentary stated that the delegation was in Moscow for a meeting of the Communist United Front.

Paramount's next report on Spain, in issue 605 for 14 December, made noticeable advances in the coverage thus far of the Civil War, though not without the inevitable amount of compromise. It began with film of the Spanish Parliament meeting at Valencia for its first session since leaving Madrid. After a general view of the Benicarlo Palace it spotlighted individual politicians. Among those singled out are Hernandez, the Minister of Education, Galarza, the Minister of the Interior, Alvarez del Vayo, the Foreign Secretary, Largo Caballero, the Premier, and President Azana. There follow interior shots of the cabinet ministers talking together and then the film cuts to a shot of the Parliament meeting in assembly with close-ups of Martinez Barrio delivering a speech, which is greeted with applause. The commentator narrates the events as they appear but also adds that the Cabinet has rejected an Anglo-French offer to mediate in the war. The offer referred to had been made on 4 December to Germany, Italy, Portugal and Russia. The intention was that an armistice should be put into operation, a commission sent to Spain, a plebiscite called, and a government set up composed of men who had kept out of the Civil War. But by 11 December the mediation proposal had been rejected by the Nationalists, as well as by the Republicans, a point not mentioned in Paramount's report, and the plan was dropped.

Paramount had failed to state, however, that there were at the time two other Franco-British moves being suggested. One was for controlling breaches of the Non-Intervention Agreement by placing observers at Spanish ports and frontiers. The other was to stop volunteers going to Spain. Both suggestions had come from the British representative at the Non-Intervention Committee, Lord Plymouth. Since Paramount had so far made no mention of the existence of the Non-Intervention Committee, it could not now report two of the recommendations being put forward for its consideration. Instead it chose to mention the mediation proposal put forward outside of the Committee by the British and French Governments. Furthermore, it reported this suggestion within a story on Spain itself and proceeded to show the consequences within that country of their Government's rejection of the idea, without mentioning that the Nationalists had also rejected such mediation. For after the shots of the meeting of the Spanish Cortes, the story cuts to reveal more footage of 'terror-stricken' refugees pouring into Valencia. Although it is never explicitly stated as such, the montage of film and commentary is constructed so that a British audience could not have failed to infer that the Republican Government had neglected its duty to protect the people of Spain from further hardship. The Anglo-French initiative might have failed as well, but at least Britain is seen as having performed honourably in the circumstances by putting forward the mediation plan. The fact that the plan had first been proposed to Eden by Delbos, the French Foreign Secretary, is conveniently forgotten.

All newsreel editions for 28 December 1936 brought with them their companies' annual 'Review of the Year'. Rather than deal with the events of the year chronologically, Gaumont chose to group the happenings under general headings such as 'Home Affairs', 'Sport', 'Disaster', and 'Foreign Affairs', in their issue 313. The largest section was 'Foreign Affairs', given 234 feet of film out of a total of 873 feet allotted to the entire release. Yet Spain took up one short sentence, with Emmett's script reiterating the gist of his message throughout the year. He said: 'Then Spain, unhappy Spain, the lazy, sunny garden of Europe, locked itself in the death struggle between brother and brother.' Despite the brevity of such an insert, the piece still showed Gaumont's sense of economy and production prowess. As the *World Film News* critic said of the release: 'One shot of a weeping mother with her children conveys all the horror of the Spanish Civil War better than a whole battery.'[27]

Paramount by comparison in issue 609 chose to devote ninety-six feet of film to their Spanish story alone, preferring to follow the year through chronologically and culling numerous shots from their stock-shot library. These included Moroccan troops marching into Burgos, with close-ups of Franco and Mola, then faded to

Madrid to show the populace there, with shots of Largo Caballero and his ministers. Another fade took the viewer back to the events of the Alcazar at Toledo, and the story concluded with an assemblage of Irun burning, a woman fleeing with her belongings, mothers and babies, and a final shot of dead bodies. All in all the Review of Spain amounted to a catalogue of Republican defeats, or so it appeared. The shortcomings inherent in Paramount's montage of events were the same ones they had manifested throughout the year. They were more than capable of obtaining an impressive array of newsreel film, but they were not so good at knowing how to use it to best advantage. The criticism levelled at them by the *World Film News* critic was typical: 'Paramount has most of the stock faults, the formal dullness, a commentator who keeps going most of the time, with most of the facts, at most of the speed of which he is capable, and a half-hearted use of natural sound.'

Movietone, like Gaumont, had classified its events under general headings and was praised for having achieved 'a measured, stately progress'. It was inevitably compared with Gaumont since they shared many of the same foreign pictures supplied by Movietonews of America, and there the comment was that 'It is obvious Movietone have not even made the best use of the material available to them.' Universal was criticized for still not possessing a sound unit of its own and for therefore having no natural sound, though commentator R. E. Jeffrey was singled out as having made a 'noble effort' to overcome such difficulties. And the Pathé Gazette was attacked for almost everything it did.

As the *World Film News* critic went on to say: 'The Annual Review is the year's best test of the production ability of a newsreel . . . the Production Departments have months for planning, weeks for cutting and re-recording, days for commenting and final publishing.' After assessing the material from all five newsreel companies, the writer came to the conclusion that 'the 1936 batch of Reviews leads to no new conclusions but instead piles up further proof of a fact that through this year has become more and more widely accepted, that in production Gaumont British News looks down upon its competitors from a mountain top.'

The reason for this production success stemmed simply from the fact that at Gaumont the entire make-up of the reel, at the cutting, commentating, and re-recording stages, was under the control of its commentator, and this co-ordination brought a unity that was noticeably lacking in its competitors' product. *World Film News* put the points of difference succinctly when it said: 'The old system, as it still hobbles along today, implies that the editor should first completely cut each story silent, like a slice of dry bread, then hand the job on to the sound man, who spreads the butter, then leave it to the commentator to add the jam.' Such a system of production was employed at Paramount, which explains why they were never able to capitalize upon their worthwhile and sometimes unusual news film of the Civil War. But if the various newsreel companies were at odds on how best to achieve the most effective methods of production, at least they were in complete agreement on what they were to say. Throughout the latter half of 1936 the message they put forward on Spain was that Civil War was tearing down the foundations of private and social life. By comparison Britain was stable and gaining in prosperity, and every effort must be made to ensure it continued to do so by not allowing it to get involved in the affray.

17 General Primo de Rivera talks to a band of Spanish officers in Morocco.
Is the second on the left an early shot of Franco? (Gaumont Graphic,
April 1921)

23 As churches burn . . .

24 . . . Nationalist sympathisers are led off to a fifth-columnist's fate

25 The women who joined the Republican ranks 'were the worst of all'
26 A newsreel story on British prisoners of war in Spain shows them being given cigarettes (Gaumont British Issue 339 for 29 March 1937) . . .

27 ...and being served with food 'of which there is no scarcity'
28 Later stories commented that the British prisoners 'looked strangely criminal with their cropped hair'

29 'In the fighting line our cameraman is on the spot . . .'
30 . . . 'securing the first sound-film interview from the trenches' (Gaumont Issue 339)

31 and 32 Roosevelt carves a turkey at a Thanksgiving Day ceremony (see page 182) (Gaumont Issue 517 for 12 December 1938)

In November 1936, Tom Cummins, the editor-in-chief at British Paramount, could justifiably claim that 'our men are attached to the military commanders of both the Government and Insurgent forces, the better to secure a complete picture of the present conflict in Spain.'[1] Yet during the opening months of 1937 it is obvious that the amount of film expended on Spain decreases by comparison with the coverage in the first six months of the war, so much so that by June it was noticed that 'for most reels Spain is now in the oblivion class, with cameramen recalled.'[2] The actual campaigns were little covered, in all probability because the events they depicted were fast becoming predictable and repetitive. There was constant reference to the fact that 'still the sorry story of war drags on' and to 'this long drawn-out story of fratricide'. Gaumont in particular paid scant attention to the hostilities, simply noting that 'attack and defence pursue their dogged course . . . day after day in this interminable war.'

The newsreel depiction of the Spanish protagonists was very quickly settled at the outset of the year and reinforced later. A Paramount release for 11 January slipped in a short piece set in Santiago where 'The Historic Spanish City inaugurates a Holy Year'. Santiago de Compostella in Galicia had always been a place of worship for Christian pilgrims wishing to visit the shrine of St James, and this report of a 'Carlist Religious Ceremony' in the city simply showed how a sense of normality was returning, at least to that part of Spain held by the Nationalists. The story highlights the inauguration, with the Archbishop approaching the door of the cathedral and knocking down a wall which had been ceremonially bricked up for the occasion. It is ironic that this particular Archbishop was chosen, since later he proved himself to be something of a dissident cleric in Franco's Spain by retorting to

a vengeful Falangist speech that 'There have been enough crimes.'[3]
However the image of a religiously devout Nationalist Spain was
taken up and used again by Paramount on 1 April when they
commented upon the celebration of Holy Week in Seville and
added that 'Under Franco, the populace revert to the splendour of
old times.' By contrast, the Republican populace was shown to be
in a desperate state. Occasionally there was room to show that 'in
their spare time the defending troops amuse themselves with
fireworks' but the ever-present image of Republican Spain, as in
Gaumont issue 354, noted that they were 'pursuing their normal
course, a course of grim reality divorced from any kind of gaiety'.
As far as the newsreels were concerned the Republic was hard-
pressed and in dire extremes.

If the internal situation failed to engage the attention of the
British newsreels, the same could not be said during this period of
the international implications of the Civil War. As Movietone's
release for 14 January put it: 'In Madrid, the war of attrition
continues. But the world's attention has been directed rather to
the effect of the Civil War on international politics.' Indeed 1937
was to be the year of revelations all round as far as the newsreels
were concerned. That same Movietone release, for instance, also
included a statement to the effect that 'Besides help in volunteers
and munitions, each side has been enlisting the sympathies of
foreign nations.' Nothing more was said about the volunteers for
the moment; but at least now there was some reference, albeit
veiled, to the presence of foreign troops in Spain.

All the newsreels that year began with stories in their issues for
7 January on the Anglo-Italian Mediterranean Pact. They showed
film of Sir Eric Drummond, the British Ambassador, and Count
Ciano, the Italian Foreign Minister, meeting in Rome and signing
the Pact. Gaumont in its issue 316 went on to add that 'By this
Pact Italy assures Britain that she has no intentions of flirting
with Franco for islands in the Mediterranean which are of importance to Britain.' This agreement did achieve some success in
drawing Britain and Italy to the conference table, a necessary act
in view of the fact that, the previous November, Count Ciano had
proposed to Franco that Italy would continue to send aid, if he in
turn supported Italy with her Mediterranean policy. But the
Anglo-Italian Pact signed on 2 January 1937 proved to be no

more than 'a gentleman's agreement', for the detailed negotiations, which it was expected would follow, did not materialize until 1938. Each party went about officially 'assuring the other that it did not intend to change the status quo in the Mediterranean',[4] but the guaranteed freedom of passage through the Mediterranean suffered a severe setback later in the year when Italian submarines began to hit at neutral shipping.

In the prevailing climate of appeasement of Mussolini at the beginning of the year, Emmett thought better than to include the word 'dishonourable' before 'intentions of flirting with Franco' in his report, as an earlier draft of his script had intended. Furthermore, Emmett showed great foresight, albeit unwittingly, in not including in his final script a sentence which he had drafted and which read, 'It is an international burying of the hatchet laid bare by Abyssinia.'

But it was Universal's coverage of the event which advanced the most forthright opinions and which also took the opportunity to bring into the open the matter of foreign intervention in Spain. R. E. Jeffrey recounted this revealing story in issue 678:

We find it rather difficult to explain the real rights of this piece of diplomacy. The picture shows Sir Eric Drummond, British Ambassador in Italy, signing the Anglo-Italian Agreement at Rome. The Agreement guarantees, as far as Agreements can, that each country shall respect the other's rights in the Mediterranean.

Almost immediately upon this signing by Britain and Count Ciano for Italy, came the announcement that 10,500 Italians have been landed in Spain to support the Rebel cause. While this was happening, the Non-Intervention Committee had been politely awaiting Italian and German replies to the suggestion that the supply of volunteers for Spain be stopped. For the man in the street, it's all very difficult.

The script had originally described the 10,500 Italians as 'alleged volunteers' but that phrase had been dropped for the final commentary. However, the story had made notable advances to the extent that it discussed Italian troops and the existence of the Non-Intervention Committee at all.

During January and February, Gaumont released only three stories directly referring to the Civil War, but they too revealed a change. The first report on 14 January in a story about Madrid in ruins went through the now customary array of 'Shattered buildings, railway stations wrecked beyond recognition and evacuation of women and children.' But, more important, it was preceded by a short story entitled 'Gas Masks' which stated that: 'Production has already begun in the new Government respirator factory in Blackburn and soon they will be turning them out at the rate of half a million a week.' The commentary went on to explain that 'Mr Geoffrey Lloyd, Under Secretary for Home Affairs, said that in the event of war gas masks would be issued free by the Government.' As it turned out it was not until September 1938, during the Czech Crisis, that thirty-eight million gas masks were distributed to regional centres throughout Britain. But this story, which was carried by all the newsreels on 14 January, shows quite forcefully two distinct factors. First of all it reveals just how much 'Fear of gas attack from the air was an acute element in the apprehension before 1939.'[5] And it also shows that there was increased 'apprehension at the renewed possibility of general war',[6] resulting from the conflict in Spain. Universal's coverage of the first Government gas mask factory, in issue 680, also went on to show film of a mock air-raid being staged in Hull, during the course of which gas masks were tested. It commented: 'This is the first mass public demonstration of its kind seen in this country.' Of course Movietone, who had used the example of Spain as a warning about air-raids and gas attacks in December 1936, once again brought Sir Malcolm Campbell before their cameras for a story in which he recounted that 'Respirators for all is a timely answer to the danger of air-raids'. Like Gaumont, Movietone made the further implications of their story clear by putting the report on Gas Masks before a story on 'The Spanish Civil War and its complications', which contained their first reference to foreign intervention in Spain.

It is noticeable that within six months of the outbreak of the Spanish Civil War, the points of comparison had changed considerably. At the outset the contrast was between Spain caught up in the turmoil of Civil War and stable, peaceful Britain. Now Britain is plainly seen to be engaging in preparations for war, an unspecified war as yet, but the fear is evident none the less. There had been a change in the newsreel content which accurately reflected the position that Spain had come to occupy in international affairs. Paramount's story in November 1936 entitled 'Where Stands Peace?' had shown other European nations rearming. Now, in

Gaumont's issue 328 for 18 February 1937, there was a story showing Britain continuing the process.

Gaumont's issue 328 had a penultimate story on the Fall of
Malaga. Malaga fell to the Nationalists under the command of the
Duke of Seville on 8 February and there followed a wholesale
slaughter of Republican sympathisers. Gaumont reacted in the
same way that Pathé had responded over the massacres at
Badajoz, by not showing them for fear of offending the audience.
As the commentary put it: 'Many scenes of dead and wounded we
have omitted because they are too horrible. These of a ruined
beauty spot and holiday resort, these are more than enough.' This
report was immediately followed by 'Britain re-arms', the final
story to the issue, in a commanding slot, and some 219 feet in
length, the longest story in the whole release.

The item begins in something of an apologetic tone, stating that
'Parliament has decided that Britain shall spend one thousand
five hundred millions on arms in the next five years. Not directed
against any one country, said the Chancellor, but because of our
vast responsibilities in all parts of the world, and as a measure for
the preservation of peace.' The situation has changed somewhat
from Gaumont's story of the previous August on 'Wonderful
Britain', where Britain was seen to be serving her best interests by
concentrating on her industrial growth and remaining aloof from
what the rest of Europe was doing. Now Britain is seen to be
drawn into the European fray and compelled to prepare herself
for all contingencies.

The opening apologia quickly gives way to the domestic implications of Britain's international commitments. The commentary
continues: 'This means no remission in taxation but it gives
security. Even more than that, it will reduce the figures of unemployment.' The introduction into the story of a potential pallia-
tive in the form of increased employment is elaborated further as
Emmett adds that 'More ships mean more men at work, building,
supplying them with every class of material needed on a modern
man of war.'

Emmett's narrative goes on in the same vein:

The Navy's Air Arm will be developed. We already have the Queen
Bee, the bombing plane that flies without a pilot. Increases here mean
more men at work, aircraft factories will be going at full pressure and

security will bring prosperity. Operational and training centres will be extended for the Royal Air Force, at Speke near Liverpool they have already begun work on the site for a new aircraft factory. This again means more work, more wages for more men. Home and Empire coastal defences will be strengthened and modernised, and the accumulation of essential supplies like oil will be given storage in protected areas. Mechanization of the Army will go forward at record speed, motor car factories will work full pressure, more men at work, more employment. Territorials will be equipped with Regular Army weapons and this will bring much-needed work to many factories. Every aeroplane, every tank means more work and more safety. Even if it means an increase in taxation, what a great insurance.

The script concludes on a typically patriotic note by adding: 'It is a life policy. Even if it does mean an increase it also means security, more employment, and the preservation of peace for this great country of ours, this British Empire.' The message was simple and straightforward: Britain still wanted to preserve peace, but to do so, she should rearm in order to remain secure. Spain might not have been the main cause of this thinking, but in the context of this newsreel release it was certainly seen to be a motivating factor.

During the opening months of 1937, Paramount were also extending their horizons beyond the immediate environs of Spain, only they found their answer further afield. Their issue for 21 January contained a story under the title 'U.S. Ban too late to catch Spanish cargo'. The story begins in New York and shows a ship being loaded with arms for Spain. The newsreel cameraman follows the ship as it leaves port, then aerial shots take up the story as it heads out for sea, pursued by a coastguard vessel which eventually turns away as it reaches the three-mile limit. The incident depicted is that of the events surrounding the sailing of the *Mar Cantabrico*, which on 28 December 1936 had been granted a licence to ship aircraft engines to the Spanish Government through Robert Cuse, acting for the Comintern. The United States Government proceeded to hurry through Congress an Embargo Act in order to prevent such shipments, but it was not passed until 8 January and the *Mar Cantabrico* had sailed on 7 January.

From this point on Paramount finally took up the matter of

Non-Intervention. It is ironic that at the time when Gaumont's reports were seeming to indicate that Britain was becoming more and more embroiled in the international repercussions of the war in Spain, Paramount began covering the attempts at reconciliation through the Non-Intervention Committee. On 20 January Germany and Italy agreed to support an Anglo-French plan to prevent volunteers entering Spain. This proposal had been put forward at the Non-Intervention Committee on 4 December, and reiterated in a Franco-British note on 10 January. A Control Plan was agreed upon whereby there would be observers on the non-Spanish side of Spain's frontiers, as well as patrols of Spanish waters by non-intervention warships. In fact the final scheme was not approved by all parties until 8 March, and for all that Russia, Germany and Italy still managed to supply their respective allies in Spain with military aid. But Paramount's reports showed only the apparent fruits of the Non-Intervention Committee's labours. Their issue for 28 January noted that 'Germany, Italy and Russia agree, with France and Britain, to ban intervention.' Issue 625 for 22 February had a story from Nice which showed the French Mediterranean Fleet at battle practice as 'the Powers put Non-Intervention in Spain into force', and their next release, on 25 February, proudly announced that 'The Non-Intervention Committee appoint 1,000 inspectors as a cordon around Spain to stop arms and volunteers.' This final story showed film of the Spanish–French frontier at Hendaye with gendarmes examining lorries and people as they crossed over into Spain. Clearly the first success achieved by the Non-Intervention Committee at securing a Control Plan was considered to be important by Paramount, important enough to break their long-held silence on the Committee's activities. Yet even this achievement was still being flouted in practice. And it was Universal who once again surpassed themselves in covering this story. Their issue 692 for 25 February contained a cynically inspired report by R. E. Jeffrey, the commentary for which ran:

The nations have agreed that an international fleet shall blockade Spanish ports to stop men and ammunition from being landed. Here is the French fleet.

France is using the opportunity to indulge in manoeuvres, before taking up her position off the Spanish coast on March 6. This agreement between the European nations will, it is hoped, shorten the war on the principle, one supposes, of 'Better late than never'.

There are already about 70,000 foreigners fighting with the Spanish armies, but if you think this blockade is like locking the stable door after the horse has gone, it's no time to mention it.

The French ships will shortly join up with the Russian fleet to patrol the north west of Spain, and everybody surely hopes that the scheme will prove effective and just.

Such events did at least present an alternative to the interminable siege of Madrid. With the exception of reports by Gaumont and Paramount on 4 March, the siege virtually died as a source of potential newsreel interest. Even the stories for 4 March preferred to spend most of the time, after passing reference to the beleaguered city, concentrating their attention upon a British liner, the *Llandovery Castle*, which struck a mine off the Spanish coast but still managed to limp into the French harbour of Port Vendres. After that Paramount for one went to great lengths to seek stories on something else, even, it appears, to reporting stories that were manifestly incorrect. Their issue for 8 March, for example, shows Franco greeting General von Faupel, the newly appointed German Ambassador, at Salamanca. Von Faupel is wearing evening dress and, according to the title, is seen to be 'presenting his credentials' to General Franco. The film might indeed be of the two men together at Salamanca but could not possibly be of their initial meeting, since von Faupel had presented his credentials to Franco some time earlier at Burgos, where he had chosen to dress in the cap and gown of a university professor.

Paramount were intent upon showing that non-intervention was working, for at this point they also prepared two stories, which showed examples of foreigners either in or going to Spain, but in the final outcome they chose not to release either of them for exhibition. The first one contained numerous shots of the Thaelmann Battalion of the International Brigade[7] and the second showed volunteers for Spain.[8] Gaumont were also obviously going through their own deliberations about what should and should not be shown. For they prepared a report for release in issue 338 which showed British prisoners of war in Spain. The story was cut from that release but was used in the next issue[9] for 29 March after some excisions had been made to the script. Emmett's new

script omitted his original reference to British volunteers working for the Spanish Government 'at wages of £5 a week'. He
had circled the phrase and scored it with the word 'out'. Obviously
it might have made it appear to be too attractive a proposition.
Furthermore, in its new context the British prisoners of war story
was suitably played down by putting it alongside 'an interview
from the Spanish trenches'. The commentary then ran:

Mr Anthony Eden, the Foreign Secretary, is again discussing the
question of Non-Intervention in Spain, and our news pictures this week
from the land of civil war include these of British prisoners. Some of the
army of unemployed enrolled for road-making under the Spanish
Government, but they were captured by the Insurgents. Here they are
in a detention camp, being served out with food, of which there is no
scarcity. In the fighting line our cameraman is on the spot, securing the
first sound-film interview from the trenches. And then the deluge.
Taking some of his pictures from a ruined building and some from an
armoured car, our cameraman secured this grim record of an attack on
the village.

The story is notable for several reasons. First of all it acknow-
ledges the existence of 'Non-Intervention', although it does so in a
matter of fact way, as though it had been in existence all the time,
as indeed it had. Nevertheless this was the first time that Gaumont
had mentioned non-intervention. Secondly, it suggests that the
men who went from Britain to fight in Spain were unemployed.[10]
No doubt a certain number of British volunteers were unemployed,
but idealism and ideological commitment must surely have been a
stronger motive in most instances. There is no mention made of
such reasons. Thirdly, this report suggests that they went to Spain
to make roads, when there can be little doubt that as members of
the International Brigade they contributed most of all to the
fighting. Fourthly, the story goes out of its way to show how well
they were looked after in detention by Franco, at the same time
making it obvious that the Nationalist forces were amply supplied
with food. In conclusion it should be noted that only forty-eight
feet of film were expended on the prisoners of war section, whereas
sixty-six feet were used on the succeeding piece which supposedly
heralded the technological advance of a first live interview from
the Spanish trenches. All that the interviewer does with this new

advance is to mention his location and add that a battle is going on for the neighbouring territory.

Gaumont were still displaying their capacity for bias and selectivity when it came to reporting on the British contingent of the International Brigade. This was made all the more evident with a further report on British prisoners which was released on 3 June. For this one Emmett really loaded his terminology by commenting that the prisoners looked 'strangely criminal with their cropped hair'. Again there was an insistence that 'these men were unemployed' and that 'they went to Spain to work on road-making and other such occupations.' There is also film of them in a detention camp being given 'food and a few cigarettes'. For the first time they were at least afforded their proper title as Emmett adds, 'They became part of the International Brigade under the Spanish Government', though he was careful not to mention that they were actually 'fighting', which his first draft had intended. Presumably it would have undermined his point that they were given menial jobs to do.

Meanwhile on 22 March Franco had outlined a new plan of campaign to set General Mola and his Army of the North against the Basques in an attempt to mop up the North of Spain. Mola's army was reorganized and his offensive began on 31 March. Considering how little coverage there was of the actual fighting in Spain at this time, it is unlikely that the war in the North would have received any mention were it not for two factors: the bombing of Guernica and the plight of the Basque refugees, in particular the children.

Guernica was bombed on 26 April and it immediately caused an international outcry. Gaumont released film of the bombed city in their issue of 6 May in a brilliantly edited story, the commentary for which ran:

First pictures from the Basque Republic of the Holy City of Guernica, scene of the most terrible air raid our modern history yet can boast. Hundreds were killed here, men, women and children. Four thousand bombs were dropped out of a blue sky into a hell that raged unchecked for five murderous hours. This was a city and these were homes, like yours.

In fact Emmett's figures greatly underestimate the casualty

toll, which amounted to 1,654 dead, as well as getting the length of the air-raid wrong, for it lasted three hours.[11] But for all that his short report, only fifty-three feet of film, still successfully conveyed the sense of horror felt by many people at this event. His concluding sentence, 'This was a city and these were homes, like yours', forcefully conveys the full implications of aerial bombing to a British audience. But what is perhaps most interesting about Gaumont's report on Guernica is the fact that it acknowledged the aerial bombing at all. After all Guernica had been bombed on 26 April, and Gaumont's report did not appear until 6 May. In the intervening period there had been a welter of press reports putting forward conflicting opinions about what had caused the town's destruction. *The Times* maintained that Guernica had been bombed by aeroplanes. Indeed it went further than that, for on 28 April:

The Times published, as an editorial page article, a report from its Special Correspondent (G. L. Steer) which stated that the planes were part of the Luftwaffe squadrons which were fighting for the Nationalists. The article was accompanied by a strongly worded leader.[12]

Other correspondents who subscribed to the same opinion were Noel Monks of the *Daily Express*, Christopher Holme of Reuters, and Mathieu Corman, who wrote for *Ce Soir* of Paris.[13] All four had been in Guernica itself at some point during the day of 26 April. But several other correspondents had not arrived in Guernica until 29 April, after it had fallen to the Nationalists. These journalists included James Holburn, also of *The Times*, W. P. Carney of the *New York Times*, Georges Botto of the French Havas agency, Max Mossot of the Paris *Journal*, Pierre Hericourt of *Action Francaise*, and Richard Massock of the Associated Press. And 'They were told by the Nationalist press department that Guernica had been either partly or wholly destroyed by the retreating Basques.'[14]

In view of the conflicting reports, Gaumont might well have been expected to accept the opinion that Guernica had been destroyed by retreating Basque incendiarists. After all, Irun had been destroyed in a similar manner and then Gaumont had made great play out of the needless destruction, comparing it to San Sebastian which had been captured relatively intact. Yet in this instance they chose to accept that Guernica had been bombed and they emphasized the destructive capacity of aerial bombing. It should be added, however, that they also chose to join the ranks of 'the various British papers' in which 'responsibility for the attack was never definitely known or apportioned'.[15] Although Gaumont saw Guernica as an undoubted outrage, they never went so far as *The Times* in accusing German planes of the bombing. Indeed they never even explicitly accused the Nationalists of engaging any German planes to fight on their behalf. Over Guernica, Gaumont seem to have chosen to follow a path midway between the reporting of *The Times* and the avowedly partisan reporting of certain other newspapers. Furthermore, Gaumont was the only British newsreel to make any mention whatever of Guernica.

In commenting on Guernica, C. L. Mowat has suggested:

Such events, and the reports on them, produced a crisis of opinion in Great Britain; it is this which gives the Spanish Civil War its tremendous importance in British history in the late thirties. It widened existing divisions, between government and opposition, between right and left (terms hardly used in the political sense in England before this) . . . Division of opinion over the war in newspapers and pamphlets reflected and enlarged the wider cleavage. It led to a changing of sides over peace and war . . . Non-intervention and pacifism crossed over from the opposition to the government: 'no war' became the slogan, not of the left, but of the right.[16]

Certainly there was little evidence of any such 'crisis of opinion' or 'division of opinion' reflected in the newsreels. On the whole they continued to reflect a consensus of pro-Government opinion. They had always supported the Government's call for 'no war', for instance. Yet the bombing of Guernica, in particular, does seem to have reinforced the change of emphasis in the Gaumont response to the Spanish Civil War. It sparked off a further series of reports in Gaumont newsreels, throughout the rest of the year, which put more and more weight on aerial power and warfare. And it is reports like these which help to explain the greatly exaggerated fear of bombing among people in Britain during the period from September 1938 to the outbreak of the Second World War.[17]

Before Guernica there had been but one report from Gaumont during 1937 on such matters. After Guernica such reports proliferated and took on ominous overtones. Gaumont's issue 363,

for example, showed that 'Flying over Henlow, our cameraman
with the Royal Air Force secured pictures of parachute training'
and went on to reveal 'The most spectacular of all air exercises, a
mass formation of flight. Two hundred and fifty planes darkened
the sky and the roar of engines set the earth athrob. It was the
biggest mass flight ever attempted.' Gaumont's issue 378 showed
how '398 Planes test London's Air Defence Plan' in a story noting
that the mock raiders were foiled and that London's Air Defence
Plan 'claims 80% success'. Shortly afterwards Gaumont highlighted Air Ministry and War Office representatives at a mock
air-raid during the rush hour in Berlin. 'At the first warning,' the
story ran, 'houses, offices, shops, buses, cars and trams were all
deserted for bomb and gas-proof shelters.' It concluded by stating:
'Overhead, squadron after squadron of bombers darkened the sky,
playing a duet of death with defending anti-aircraft guns. This is
peacetime make-believe, in war it would be worse than this.' The
same issue, no. 390, complemented Germany's show of strength by
observing Hore Belisha, the British War Minister, as a representative at some French Army manoeuvres. But the film of aerial
power continued right through into the following year with such
pieces as 'Russian Air Display' (3 January) which spotlighted a
mass parachute descent near Moscow, presided over by Stalin, and
with 'Planes by the hundred and men by the score of hundred,
swarming on wings like an army of locusts . . . And when the
descent is accomplished the sky is darkened once again with rank
after rank of bombers.'

Yet if the bombing of Guernica was seen to have profound
long-term implications for the rest of Europe, it was a more
immediate concern for the lot of the Basque children which
expressed itself most in May 1937. France and Russia agreed to
take numbers of evacuated Basque children, as did Britain where a
Basque Children's Relief Committee was set up for the purpose of
receiving 4,000 of their numbers. The matter of the children really
gave the newsreels a cause to follow and they joined the ranks of
'mobilised public opinion' among those 'several ad hoc bodies
which were, in effect, "popular fronts" drawing in members of all
parties'.[18]

Gaumont and Paramount ran stories in their releases for
20 May. Paramount's report, entitled '6,000 children evacuated

from stricken Bilbao', showed the ss *Habana* arriving off La
Rochelle in France under the caption 'The humane work of the
Great Powers saves kiddies from the horrors of siege and war.'
Gaumont noted that 'Hundreds of children have been evacuated
from the danger zone at Bilbao, the city of bombardment and air
raids.' They dismissed the rest of the War by saying: 'As the long
Civil War drags interminably on, the one factor that emerges
triumphant is the dogged endurance of this nation divided against
itself, each side fighting for what it believes to be right.' The
attraction for the newsreels of this story was that they could follow
through the journey of the contingent of children destined to live
in England. So all the newsreel companies had follow-up pieces on
the arrival of the children. The Paramount cameras were at
Southampton to see the *Habana* dock and they chose to have
cameramen go with the children on the final part of their journey
to a camp at Stoneham in Lincolnshire where they were to be
boarded. Gaumont in their story recounted: 'Everything is being
done for their care and comfort but nothing can replace what they
have lost. This is the price of war, paid by those who should know
nothing of its horrors. The heart bleeds for these children. It is a
grim reflection on our own civilisation.'

The campaign to take the city of Bilbao was one of the few
military actions to receive any newsreel attention. That there
were few cameramen still covering the fighting is demonstrated by
Paramount's story, for though they did a News Special on the fall
of Bilbao, which took place on 19 June, in their issue 660, devoting
some 290 feet of film to the event, most of it was in fact drawn from
material they already had in their library. There was a small
amount of first-hand footage, but they also drew upon stock-shot
film from no less than eight previous stories to fill it out. Movietone's issue of the same date, 24 June, also reported on Bilbao and
noted once again that there were Italians to be found among the
victorious forces alongside the Carlists from Navarre and the
Moors from across the Mediterranean. Ivan Scott's script for that
release also contained an interesting little reference to the return
from Spain to Ireland of 'General' O'Duffy's 'Irish Brigade', 633
Irish volunteers who had fought for Franco.

Events which were taking place at sea off the coast of Spain
quickly turned the newsreels away from the land campaign, for

which they were undoubtedly more than grateful. At the time when Britain had agreed to take the Basque children, the British Government had decided to join the French in escorting refugee ships once they were outside territorial waters. In fact the Basque children had been the first to benefit from such protection. And luckily for Gaumont, they had chosen to send one of their cameramen aboard one such ship, which was stopped by an Insurgent warship and ultimately rescued by the British navy. The result was a highly dramatic and engrossing piece of reportage which ran in issue 368 on 8 July:

The Gaumont British News cameraman at Santander secured these amazing pictures of the flight of refugees to the security of France. Their only thought is escape. Some are blind, some are crippled, most are old women and children. Before they leave they are searched carefully for food or valuables, for neither of these must be taken out of the country. The ship that takes them is a French ship, the *Tregastel*, which has had several adventures off the coast of Spain. Their living conditions on board cannot but be wretched but at least they think they are safe.

Out of the silence comes the crash of gunfire as a warning shot across the bows announces the arrival of the Insurgent warship *Almirante Cervera*. Signals are exchanged and the refugee ship stops. But the British patrol ship, H.91 HMS *Bulldog*, appeared on the scene with the French ship *Vauquois*, to preserve the freedom of the high seas. The *Tregastel* is allowed to proceed as the *Almirante Cervera* makes off. The merchant ship on the left of this picture is the *Kellwyn*, skippered by the famous Potato Jones.

And so these luckless people continue their voyage, but long months of hardship and malnutrition have told their tale. The signal is run up for a doctor and the *Vauquois* sends one across in a small boat. And so their journey ended with a safe landing at Pauillac. From the welter of war on sea and land they came safely to France.

Gaumont British had an extraordinary piece of good fortune in securing this story. They could not have done better if they had wanted to make a feature film: an exciting scenario running the gamut of emotions from relief at escaping from Spain, to trepidation at the prospect of being thwarted and captured, to elation at arriving at a haven of peace. Finally, the story had a complete dramatis personae; the best known cruiser the Nationalist fleet could offer in the *Almirante Cervera*, a British ship appropriately called HMS *Bulldog* and Potato Jones, renowned in Britain for his blockade-breaking exploits, thrown in for good measure, though quite what he was doing there is never explained. Furthermore, the story was able to highlight an instance when the British visibly maintained the stance they were taking in the Spanish Civil War, namely the desire to preserve the peace, whilst at the same time protecting the innocent.

Britain's desire 'to preserve the freedom of the high seas' was, however, shortly to receive a severe setback. For in late July Italian fears at the supposed extent of Soviet aid still reaching the Republic caused Mussolini to consider starting a submarine campaign against such shipping. The trouble was that the Russian material was being transported to Spain under the flags of many neutral countries. However, that did not deter Mussolini's submarines from attacking vessels of all countries, Britain and France included, and the submarine campaign increased in intensity throughout August. Mussolini also decided to throw Italian aircraft into the campaign, flying out from their base in Majorca.

Paramount's release for 5 August contained a short story of a 'Spanish ship shelled by two unidentified submarines' off Marseilles. It is strange that the newsreels had difficulty establishing their identity, for in order to shell the Spanish merchantman the Italian submarines would have been compelled to surface. And Mussolini had reportedly given orders that his submarines 'would raise a Spanish flag if they had to surface',[19] so at the very least they might have been thought to be Spanish Nationalist submarines. Another Paramount report on 6 September showed two damaged ships which had managed to reach Falmouth harbour. One was the Spanish Government destroyer, the *Jose Luis Diaz*, and the other a British merchantman, the *Hilda Moller*. Pathé's release for that date recounted:

The Mediterranean was once the playground of Europe, but now events on that sunlit sea are serious enough to bring some of the members of the British Cabinet together for an urgent meeting. The men who control Britain's policy intend to leave no stone unturned and to take all possible steps to deal with the situation.

A British destroyer has been deliberately attacked. A British merchant ship has been torpedoed while on her lawful occasions. So our navy goes into action. Destroyers search the Mediterranean. More ships are being hurried from British waters. To the pirate submarine, depth charges will bring an end to her career.

The British Government had indeed decided to take action, and the outcome was a conference called at Nyon on 10 September. On the first day of the Nyon Anti-Piracy Conference, Britain and France agreed to send fleets to patrol the Mediterranean with the intention of attacking suspicious submarines. An agreement was signed to that effect on 14 September. Paramount's newsreel for 16 September covered the arrival of the delegates at the Conference and singled out Eden, Delbos and Litvinov for recognition. By the time of their next issue on 20 September they were able to release a story entitled 'Piracy patrol starts before Nyon ink dries'. It contained shots of the same three statesmen signing the Agreement as well as shots of HMS *Cairo* leaving Sheerness to take up her duties in the Mediterranean.

Gaumont's report for 20 September began with shots of the Spanish Government destroyer off Falmouth, but added a new twist to the tale by commenting that 'Sixty of the crew came ashore and refused to rejoin the ship, deserters from the war which is destroying Spain.' Then it cut to a view of a British tanker, the *Stanbridge*, 'hit during the same air-raid, a yawning hole in her side shows how near she came to ending her days in Spanish waters.' The story ended at Felixstowe, where 'Forty officers and men with 209 Squadron prepared to leave for Malta. Bad weather delayed them, but they left eventually to take up their duties with the Anti-Piracy Patrol. The Air Force is co-operating with the Navy in the Mediterranean to safeguard merchantmen from attack by submarines. There is also danger in the war zone from bombs that fall promiscuously from the aeroplanes of one side or another. To prevent misunderstanding, HMS *Warspite* has adorned her decks with the red, white and blue of the Union Jack.' Once more this Gaumont story, like Paramount's and Pathé's, had failed to make any mention of precisely who it was in the Mediterranean the British merchantmen had to fear. But then the British Government was still attempting to re-establish friendly relations with Italy, and this became obvious when on 18 September the British and French gave the texts of the Nyon Agreement to Ciano in Rome and invited comments. 'Unidentified submarines' and 'bombs that fall promiscuously' were

phrases calculated to offend nobody. In one respect this story from
Gaumont had made an advance, for it described the Spanish
Civil War as 'a war which has imperilled the peace of Europe for
more than a year.' Such an opinion had been implicit in their
newsreel coverage during 1937 but it had never been quite so
openly acknowledged.

On 16 October, the Non-Intervention Committee met in London
to discuss once again the withdrawal of volunteers from Spain.
Surprisingly Gaumont covered this meeting. This was the first
time that Gaumont had actually shown film of representatives
gathering for a meeting of the Non-Intervention Committee,
although the latter body had been in existence for over a year.
Indeed Gaumont had shot film of the Committee meeting earlier
in 1937, in July, and the film had been put into their library
(library no. 10,316). But it had never actually been used for release.

Paramount also covered the 16 October meeting in a story
entitled 'World Fences for Peace as Franco acts', released on 18
October. But they chose to spend most of the story upon film
which had been sent back to them of Franco holding a youth
parade at Burgos under a title announcing that 'Franco assures
world that Spain will remain Spanish'. This report is in itself
interesting. For in covering the Burgos event the actual shots
chosen by the editor to constitute the final release are those which
isolate and romanticize the Spanish youth. The story picks out a
series of shots of pretty Spanish girls and well-groomed men; as
well as a shot of a Moor on horseback which has a distinct look of
being posed for the camera. All the shots of Franco himself are
taken from below, as he stands on a dais, so that the viewer is
always seen to be looking up at him. This piece occupies the fifth
slot in a sequence of seven items and before it there is a report on
Neville Chamberlain. As the commentator put it, 'In his first talk
since taking office Mr Chamberlain outlines the ideas behind the
National Fitness Campaign.'

Gaumont used the same stories in its issue 397 for the same date
of 18 October, but in a different way that once again reveals the
immense gap in quality of production between these two newsreel
companies. For Emmett chose to open his release with a Non-
Intervention report; he moved from there to Franco at Burgos,
then proceeded to string together shots of Franco, Mussolini, and

Hitler as a prelude to Chamberlain talking about the National Fitness Campaign. The purpose was to draw a comparison in speech-making between the three dictators and the British Prime Minister. The commentary accompanying these shots ran:

Representatives of nine countries met at the Foreign Office to discuss the withdrawal of volunteers from Spain. Incidentally, at the same time, news had reached the League of Nations of a threatened war in Nicaragua. Luckily in that case there's no fear of intervention, because nobody knows where it is.

But on the question of Spain, a great step forward was achieved when Italy agreed through Count Grandi to a partial withdrawal of volunteers. And what of Spain itself? This year 35,000 people took part in the Festival of the Race, at Burgos. A review by General Franco, a study in light and shade, a grim reminder of how the youth of Spain marches in the Valley of the Shadow of Death.

And here we present a comparison in speech-making. General Franco, Signor Mussolini and Herr Hitler show a vivid contrast to Mr Neville Chamberlain. Amid the European turmoil, our Premier speaks to you of the aims of British statesmen.

The comments on the Non-Intervention Committee leave a lot to be desired. For the Committee only met on 16 October and agreement was not reached on the withdrawal of a 'substantial proportion' of volunteers until 4 November, and even then the agreement had to be put to the two Spanish parties concerned. Franco did not agree in principle to the plan until 20 November and the Republic on 1 December. Yet here was Gaumont, on 18 October, showing film of Committee members arriving for the meeting and at the same time proudly proclaiming that agreement had been reached with Count Grandi. But the way this story and the one on Franco at Burgos are used to build up to the final shots of Chamberlain is impressive. The Burgos parade floridly emphasizes that the Spanish youth 'marches in the Valley of the Shadow of Death'. Then the film cuts to shots of Franco, Mussolini and Hitler, each properly afforded his correct title, and each caught at a highly excitable moment, gesticulating furiously, the sequence building up in speed from one dictator to the next. To cut, as the film then does, to a shot of a thoroughly composed and carefully articulate Neville Chamberlain, gives the impression of moving from chaos to tranquillity. This feeling is enhanced by the fact that Chamberlain is situated in a classical context, standing before a marble fireplace in an imposing room. Furthermore, unlike the dictators, Chamberlain delivers his speech in a humble tone, hardly moving, except to raise his arms in an arc from his side to his well-known hands-on-lapels pose and then occasionally to point towards the camera. Unfortunately Chamberlain was not speaking on anything more immediately pressing than the National Fitness Campaign, but at least he is seen to be concerning himself with domestic matters; and the content of the speech is relatively unimportant for the main purpose of this shrewd piece of editing, a contrast in style between the agitated dictators of Europe and the solid respectability of Britain's premier.

The year ended for the Republicans as it had begun, with military defeats. Gijon fell to the Army of the North on 21 October. Paramount and Gaumont noted the defeat in their issues for 28 October. Paramount commented that 'The last Government stronghold in Northern Spain falls to Franco', while Gaumont made great play out of the fact that 'Contrary to popular report there was practically no fighting before the Fall of Gijon. The streets are desolate and almost deserted. It was an Insurgent airman, making a forced landing in what he thought were the Government lines, who discovered that the troops had left. He passed the word through and the army of occupation began to march. Thus another town fell to General Franco.' In part their report was correct. The Republican leaders in the city fled to France on 20 October and twenty-two Republican battalions surrendered. When the Nationalists, led by Colonel Aranda and General Solchaga, entered the city in victory, Asturias had been completely lost to the Government.

That ended the newsreel coverage of Spain for 1937 as far as Paramount were concerned. They released no more Civil War stories that year, and Spain did not even merit a mention in their Review of the Year.

Gaumont, Universal and Pathé all proceeded in November to take a report which contained footage of Mussolini attending a ceremony in Rome in honour of those Italians who had died in the First World War and in Spain. Gaumont duly entered the story as 'Mussolini honours those who died in Spain' in their records (library no. 10,915). But they did not in fact use the story in any of their releases. Universal showed film of 'the ceremony in honour of those militiamen who have fallen with the Italian troops in Spain' as part of issue 765 for 8 November. Pathé also used the film which it took from the LUCE newsreel of Italy as part of a report entitled 'Fighters in a Foreign Land', shown in their issue 91 on 15 November.

Gaumont went on to include Spain in its Review of the Year in issue 417. They openly admitted that 'Throughout the year crisis after crisis hinged upon this Civil War' and further recognized that 'Europe came near to being caught up in the toils of this war.' Then Emmett commented: 'And Britain for the sake of safety decided to spend five hundred millions upon re-armament.' To mention all three factors in the same breath was indeed an admission for Gaumont. But then 1937 had proved to be a year of admissions for Gaumont, as it had for the other newsreels.

Movietone made the point even more clearly in their issue 447a with a commentary from Leslie Mitchell which ran in part:

War clouds our memories of 1937. In contrast to those peaceful Twenties when the League of Nations dominated the international realm, 1937 has seen the glorification of Power Politics, which always carry the threat of war.

So far have we changed in a year that the precautions for safety against air-raid which in 1936, when Sir Malcolm Campbell built his dug-out, seemed laughable, now are recognised as wise and common-place. We become air-raid wardens and conduct anti-air-raid rehearsals, just in case we should have war again.

And we are rearming just as fast as a peace time organisation of industry will allow. It is a rearmament against war, because—we are told—a strong man armed holdeth his goods in peace.

Rearmament has helped to preserve prosperity and to keep men in employment, but—strange circumstances for a time of plenty—stock markets have plunged downwards and America's Wall Street has had the jitters since early in the year.

And the reason has been—the fear of wars. When President Roosevelt, newly inaugurated, calls Shame upon the makers of war, the world applauds but Wall Street dreads the implications of his words.

The fear of another Great War originates in the localised wars which are already raging. The Civil War pursues its ding-dong course in Spain. Franco wins all the North, Bilbao, Santander, Gijon. But Madrid holds out; the capital is still in Government hands.

Bitter fighting around Teruel heralded the advance of 1938. On 15 December the Republic had launched an attack on the town which was defended by a Nationalist garrison under its commander, Colonel Rey D'Harcourt. Franco did not decide until 23 December that he would attempt to relieve his beleaguered comrades and thereby suspend for a while the offensive he had planned for Guadalajara. And the newsreels proceeded to resume their in-depth coverage of the hostilities, with all companies reporting the Teruel offensive. Paramount obviously felt the war might just be near to an end. Its headline for 6 January ran '500,000 Spaniards locked in death fight for Teruel'; then they followed this up with a lead-in title which read: 'Aragon. Is it the turning point? Both sides stake all in bloodiest fight of the Civil War.' Movietone were still less certain about the outcome and their report on 13 January stated quite simply that 'the end of the war seems no nearer.' There was a great deal of confusion about the events surrounding the battle for Teruel. By Christmas Barcelona Radio announced that the town had fallen to the Republican forces besieging it. Meanwhile on 1 January Franco announced the fall of the town to his forces. Gaumont's report for 3 January showed how thoroughly up to date their news service was by spotlighting Teruel as a town 'in which a Franco garrison was besieged' and going on to mention that 'Later reports said that Franco had recaptured Teruel but this was denied by the Government', not forgetting to add their customary rejoinder that 'whichever side is winning battles, Spain is always the loser.' In fact the town did not capitulate to the Republican forces until 8 January, whereupon the besiegers became the besieged until the town was recaptured by Franco on 7 February.

The slow down in both Republican and Nationalist military activities was to a great extent caused by the blizzards which beset that part of the country, a factor which did not escape the attention of Gaumont who made use of it as part of a jokey story on 17 January about 'Snow in different parts of the world'. They commented that 'Snowfall heralds no playtime in the war zones of Spain . . . Round Teruel the men of Franco's army still pursue their desperate hunt for victory, snow for them means only additional hardship . . . It's a pity the snow can't sweep away the war itself.' The Moorish troops in Franco's forces who were not used to such extremes of cold and who lacked winter clothing must have echoed such sentiments.

Throughout January the Nationalists also pursued a relentless campaign of bombing against Republican cities and against Barcelona in particular. The Nationalists had virtual control of the air by this point in the war and proceeded to use it to bomb Republican cities at random. One particularly devastating raid took place upon Barcelona on 28 January. The raid lasted one and a half minutes and left 150 dead. The day before Paramount had released a story in issue 722 which contained headlines that sounded remarkably similar to the events which were to follow the day after. The story was entitled '138 Killed by Franco Planes' Lightning Raid' and the titles proclaimed 'The raid which made Europe gasp. 90 seconds of death and destruction.' A likely explanation is that the first newsreel prints rushed to the West End halls for 27 January referred to another Barcelona air-raid, whereas in the light of the happenings of the day after, Paramount could simply capitalize upon the latest news and augment their old pictures with new titles for release to cinemas in the rest of Britain, which got them later. So it was that they appeared to be keeping right up to the minute with their news coverage, and their library entries recorded the amended titles.

Gaumont continued to use the destructive capacity of aerial bombardment for purposes other than simple reportage. Their release for 3 February contained a long story entitled 'Planes in Peace and War'. It concluded by bringing up 'The question of bombers which bring death to British subjects from the wars of other nations'. This particular part of the story noted: 'Three warplanes belonging to General Franco's Air Force dropped bombs near the London steamer *Thorpeness* and seven of the crew were killed.' The report went on to show film of the burial of the crew members at Tarragona and a tribute being paid at the funeral by Spanish Government troops. Emmett's script pointed out that 'The *Thorpeness* carried on her top deck a Union Jack painted on a tarpaulin 25 feet by 18 feet.' But he failed to add that in all probability the planes had been Italian, for in January there was a sudden outburst of both Italian submarine and aeroplane activity in the Mediterranean. Attempts to sink British merchant ships bringing supplies to the Republic had been made on 15 and 19

January, and on 1 February the British ship *Endymion* was actually sunk. Strong words from Anthony Eden brought an end to the submarine activity, but aerial attacks continued for a while afterwards.

The story on 'Planes in Peace and War' had begun, however, with a piece entitled 'Wellington Bomber' which Emmett used to demonstrate Britain's own potential in the field of aerial bombardment. It was placed at the very beginning of the release and ran:

Latest addition to the ranks of Britain's Air Force is the Wellington Bomber, now undergoing its first trials. It is of Geodetic construction, which means that it has the whole of the interior available for accommodation, free from obstruction from supporting struts and wires. The Wellington is a twin-engined monoplane, with retractable undercarriage, and is capable of carrying a crew of seven. The armament includes three guns, one forward, one amidships and one aft. Particulars of weight, range and speed are on the secret list, but they are said to compare favourably with any in the world.

Aerial bombing continued to occupy the minds of the other newsreels as well. Pathé, for instance, released stories on the *Thorpeness* bombing and Barcelona in their issues for 14 February and 10 March respectively. But since on both occasions they had obviously had no cameramen of their own on the spot, they had been compelled to acquire film of the incidents from the Progressive Film Institute. Movietone had carried a long report on 'The Horror in Barcelona' in its release for 14 February and also included yet another story on 'Air Raid Precautions in Britain'. Leslie Mitchell commented: 'Pictures of actual air-raids take the mockery out of mock air-raids, but the campaign long publicised by this newsreel for informing and training the public makes steady headway.' And they proceeded to show footage of specimen air-raid shelters on view at Caxton Hall.

Universal, meanwhile, had hit upon the idea of sending their commentator R. E. Jeffrey to Spain to see the situation for himself. The trailers for his two stories announced 'A Revelation in Newsreel Journalism' and stated that 'Never before has any newsreel commentator visited a battle front to secure first-hand news for his audience.' The two reports were shown on 14 February and 17 February. Jeffrey made a point of saying: 'I am pro neither side. I am on the side of the people. The side of the people who wish to avoid war.' And he added: 'I went not for the Spanish Government or the Nationalists, but for you.' His comment that 'This war has developed the weapon of propaganda to a high degree' was well exemplified when he went on to show his interview with Franco and his family: 'Senora Franco, a gracious and beautiful woman. General Franco, courteous, and as a father and husband, unassuming and affectionate. Twelve years old, lovable Carmencita, an adoring daughter. I can only speak from what I found. To me they were charming and considerate.'

But more pressing topics soon compelled the newsreels to turn their attention elsewhere. For on 13 March Hitler entered Vienna and incorporated Austria into Germany. By this point Gaumont's opinions on rearmament were so well formed they could be included in any crisis story, whether it be on Spain or Austria. So everything that had so far been said on rearmament as an adjunct to the Spanish Civil War was now switched to the coverage of the Austrian situation. And Gaumont's issue of 17 March, after showing 'the first actual pictures received from Austria following the fall of the Schussnigg Government and the advance of the German troops', went on to recount the by now familiar message:

What of our position in Britain today? Mass meetings have been held in Trafalgar Square and the Prime Minister has made a statement in the House of Commons; both make it clear that Britain's duty is to herself. Britain must be strong and even the present re-armament programme must be speeded up. An appeal to employers and workers of all kinds will be made to co-operate in the time of national emergency.

Shadow factories where the production of aircraft is proceeding must be able to produce at greater speed than hitherto. Production of armaments in all departments must be increased by national effort. Not to take part in war, nor to interfere in the wars of others, but to preserve the peace of our own Empire. These are the guarantees of our national security, our independence, demanding expenditure down to the last shilling if necessary.

Sir Samuel Hoare, the Home Secretary, has called for a million air-raid workers. Here again it is no alarmist call but a wise determination to be prepared. The Home Secretary said that the more disturbed is the continent of Europe, the more urgent it is for us to make every possible preparation against the most dangerous form of modern warfare. If Britain is prepared then air-raid terrors will be less formidable.

British morale and the personnel of the Empire's fighting forces are second to none. Our soldiers and sailors and airmen are unrivalled, but without the implements of war they would be helpless. A nation's fighting strength today depends almost as much upon the skill of the engineer and the scientist, as it does upon those who carry arms. The spirit of Britain, backed by all the weight of armaments that she is capable of producing, will guarantee the safety of our people, not only now, but also in the future. If a sacrifice is called for to provide those armaments, those aeroplanes and guns and tanks and battleships that comprise the grim paraphernalia of war, then let us make that sacrifice. What sacrifice could be too great to make in exchange for security, the safety of our homes and our own people, your safety?

Less than a week after this Gaumont report, the Government took what A. J. P. Taylor considers to be a further significant step in the advance of British rearmament. For on 22 March 'the services were freed from the restriction not to interfere with "normal" trade. Henceforward, for example, manufacturers could be induced to switch their works to making aeroplanes, despite the civilian demand for motor cars.'[20] This, together with the TUC agreement to relax craft restrictions in the engineering industry on 23 March, 'marked the real beginning of a war economy.'[21] The newsreels had done their part in preparing the country for such a Government move.

Spain continued to exercise British statesmen throughout this period, albeit to a lesser degree. The most serious repercussions, as far as the British Government was concerned, arose over the resignation of Anthony Eden as Foreign Secretary. Clearly the agreement between Italy and Great Britain, made in January 1937, had done little to alleviate the tension that had developed between the two countries. The Italian submarine campaign had shown that. Now, in February 1938, Chamberlain was anxious to revive negotiations over the agreement. Eden for his part saw this as an opportunity to ensure that some Italian volunteers were withdrawn from Spain before Anglo-Italian talks should start. Chamberlain did not.

Gaumont's report on Eden's resignation, which occurred on 20 February, stated quite simply that he resigned 'following a difference of opinion with the Premier' and that 'Britain's relations with Italy were the cause of the break.' It added that 'he still

enjoys the high esteem of all his colleagues and the general public.'
Apart from reporting the result of a vote of censure on the
Government in the House of Commons, which was defeated by
330 votes to 168, and noting that 'Parliament stands by the
Premier', Gaumont had nothing more to say about the event.

Paramount went a step further and invited Clement Attlee to
comment upon Eden's resignation in issue 730. The idea of inviting
a politician, and the Leader of the Opposition at that, to comment
upon such a resignation was indeed new and unprecedented.
Paramount must have approached the idea with some trepidation.
And rather than give Attlee the respectable surroundings which
they normally afforded political personages, at least those who
were in power, they chose to record his speech in the open air where
he was obviously disturbed by the sounds of nearby traffic. He was
allowed none of the trappings of authority which had previously
been given to Baldwin and Chamberlain in interviews of this sort.
In the final analysis it made little difference since they withdrew
the story from circulation just a few hours after it was released.
None the less Attlee's speech is in itself highly critical:

Everywhere this will be hailed as a great victory for Signor Mussolini
and throughout the world it will be said that this country has surrendered to the demands of a dictator. They are not prepared to stand
for the League of Nations; they are not prepared to stand for Democracy; they are prepared to make any kind of a deal with the dictatorship
powers. There will be no longer in this country a Government that is
prepared to stand up for international law and right, but a Government
that is prepared to enter into any kind of a deal with aggressive Fascist
powers. This policy is not a policy that would lead to peace, it will not
lead to a settlement of the affairs of Europe. It is essentially a war
policy and it aligns this country with the reactionary forces of the world.
The repercussions of this event will be widespread in the Dominions, in
the Colonies, and throughout the world. It is most noticeable everywhere that the enemies of peace and democracy are rejoicing, and the
friends of this country are depressed.

Attlee's interpretation of the situation proved to be correct, at
least in part, for Hitler and Mussolini claimed that they had
forced Eden from office and many people, particularly in Britain,
believed their boast.[22] In the event the new pact which Chamberlain so dearly wanted was not signed until 16 April. Gaumont

immediately announced in issue 450 that 'after many months of mistrust and misunderstanding between Great Britain and Italy, friendship has been renewed.' At the same time they noted that 'It was hailed as a major contribution towards the settlement of European problems', finally adding: 'France once again will fall into step with Great Britain in the cause of world peace.' But as with the pact of a year earlier, little was solved by this new agreement, apart from the guarantee to maintain the status quo in the Mediterranean, for Britain continued to tolerate the presence of Italian troops in Spain until the war was over. Indeed the one condition to the agreement, which stated that the pact would not come into operation until the Italian volunteers were withdrawn, presumably after a victory for Franco, was dropped later in the year. Britain's duplicity over Spain was now revealed in its true light and the Republican Ambassador, Azcarate, sent a protest to the Foreign Office 'expressing his horror that the public exchange of letters between Italy and Britain should calmly accept Italian troops in Spain till the end of the Civil War, while at the same time Britain was nominally maintaining the Non-Intervention Pact and a plan for the withdrawal of volunteers.'[23] However, by this point Britain was less interested in the internal conflicts of the war in Spain and more interested in trying to detach Mussolini from Hitler.

At the beginning of March Franco had determined upon his next offensive into Aragon. The campaign began on 9 March. The success he achieved was swift and immediate and on 10 March Belchite fell. Paramount reported the victory on 24 March under the title 'Franco Push: End Near?' with film of General Yague as 'the Insurgents drive through towards Barcelona, while the Government fall back before the fiercest onslaught of the year'. In fact it was an army corps of Navarrese under the command of General Solchaga that took the town. But the success of Franco's army in Aragon prompted the newsreels to turn their attention once again to the actual fighting. Gaumont and Paramount did general reports in their respective releases for 3 March. Gaumont noted: 'Insurgent troops sweep on in General Franco's biggest drive since the war began. Night and day the tramp of marching feet echoes among the hills on the Aragon front.' They then singled out the retreating Republicans and mentioned that 'Government defenders have destroyed all bridges that lay in their retreating path but pontoons built by Franco's engineers take their place and the troops press forward over the Ebro river.' Emmett concluded: 'Spain's Government are holding on desperately.' Paramount also highlighted the crossing of the Ebro, which had taken place when General Yague crossed with his troops on 23 March, in a story entitled 'Barcelona faces defeat'. One week later both companies again spotlighted the same story, this time from Luchon in the Pyrenees where refugees were pouring into France.

The war was escalating all the time in favour of Franco. On 25 March General Yague captured Fraga, actually in Catalonia, and then marched on to Lerida where for a week he was thwarted by a division of Republican troops under El Campesino. But Lerida eventually fell on 3 April. Paramount covered both victories in their report for 11 April with a story called 'Lerida. Now Victory?' showing 'graphic pictures of the final stages as Franco's forces race onwards with victory beckoning', along with shots of Franco and Davila, the commander in chief of the Aragon offensive army. The Republic was hard-pressed, and on 13 May Alvarez del Vayo went before the Council of the League of Nations in an attempt to make the members who had agreed to Non-Intervention reconsider their action in view of the fact that it had proved to be ineffective. But Lord Halifax, the new Foreign Secretary, forced a quick vote on the issue and no further action was taken. Gaumont reported upon the events in their release for 16 May. They glossed over Spain almost completely, simply stating: 'Representatives of many nations gathered for discussions on Abyssinia, Spain and China.' Then they ignored any discussion which ensued on Spain to show that 'There were two representatives of Abyssinia in addition to the Emperor himself, who came to hear the views of the British Government in a speech to the Council by Lord Halifax.' But the attempt to mollify Mussolini continued for 'in his speech Lord Halifax pointed out that it was the view of the British Government that each member of the League should choose its own course of action with regard to recognising the Italian conquest.'

The newsreels might choose to ignore Spain at the meeting of the League, but events in Spain itself compelled Halifax to turn his attention towards it when on 2 June, Granollers, a town near

Barcelona, was bombed. The town had no military value and most of the casualties were women and children, amounting to some four or five hundred dead. Paramount's release for 9 June covered the story. Despite a title announcing '400 killed in air-raid', the actual film in the report of the bombed-out market town was markedly restrained in relation to the overall footage which their cameraman had sent back. The shots in the release concentrate for the most part upon film of dead adults with one or two shots of injured children. The footage they did not release contained horrifying shots of headless children, dead babies and row upon row of children's coffins.[24] The newsreels' fears for the susceptibilities of the cinemagoing audience proved to be the strongest motivating factor in preventing this material from being shown, and the true horror of Granollers was kept from the eyes of the British public. But public feeling was aroused over this incident and Halifax felt compelled to send telegrams of protest to Burgos, though little resulted.

By June the rapid advances made by the Nationalists were beginning to slow down. On 15 April Vinaroz had been taken, cutting the Republic in two and giving Franco a foothold on the shores of the Mediterranean. Movietone showed film of Franco's soldiers dancing in the sea. But Castellon, some sixty miles south of Vinaroz and only fifty miles north of Valencia, was not captured until 14 June, giving Franco his first large Mediterranean port. Paramount and Movietone cameramen were there when Aranda entered the town in triumph, and the story appeared in their issues for 20 June and 23 June respectively. It had been a slow, tortuous victory.

The attitudes of the protagonists in Spain turned, on the face of it at least, to thoughts of peace. Paramount's release for 5 September showed the first exchange of war prisoners at Hendaye, supervised by a British Commission. Almost a year earlier, in October 1937, the Republic had proposed to the British that they negotiate such exchanges, but it was not until September 1938 that a commission arrived under the guidance of Field-Marshal Sir Philip Chetwode. But bigger exchanges were afoot, for on 27 June 1938, the Soviet Ambassador Maisky had agreed to the plan for a withdrawal of volunteers and in October Stalin agreed to the withdrawal of the International Brigades. Furthermore, at Munich.

Mussolini had suggested to Chamberlain that 10,000 Italian volunteers might be withdrawn in order to pave the way for the implementation of the Anglo-Italian Agreement. All the British newsreels covered the withdrawal of the Italian volunteers. Gaumont alone of the newsreels chose not to use any of its footage in a release. Movietone's issue of 13 October perhaps best expressed the ambivalent attitude which had been shown throughout to the presence of these Italians in Spain:

New hopes arise of agreement in the Spanish Civil War, its first fruits being the withdrawal of General Franco's Italian volunteers. Here are official pictures of Italian units in Spain, and members of a contingent being decorated by the Insurgent General.

Very hush-hush has been the attitude over the presence of these foreign volunteers; their numbers have never been published. But if they are to be withdrawn, no reason remains for concealment. So these very pictures may be, in themselves, a sign of hope.

On 20 October, the 10,000 Italians arrived back in Italy at the port of Naples, where they received a personal welcome from King Victor Emmanuel. Paramount's report for 24 October mentioned that 'they had been fighting in the Spanish Insurgent Army' but at the same time made it clear that they were only being withdrawn as a result of successful British diplomacy. In consequence the Anglo-Italian Agreement came fully into force on 16 November, meriting a brief mention in the releases on 21 November by Paramount, Movietone, Universal and Pathé. Pathé, alone of the four, added that 'Italians are still fighting in Spain.'

The last action fought by the International Brigades had taken place on 22 September and they were given an emotional parade of farewell in Barcelona on 15 November, at which laudatory speeches were made about them by La Pasionaria and Negrin, the Republican Premier. Paramount's film of the farewell parade, in issue 808, could not fail to capture the emotion of the occasion, as the flowers showered upon the Brigades from a grateful Republican crowd.

At one point in November, all five newsreels took time off from the apparently peace-ridden proceedings, to report that the Civil War was still raging and had even reached the North Sea. The *Cantabria*, a Republican steamer carrying food supplies, had been sunk seven miles off Cromer by a disguised Nationalist warship,

the *Nadir*. The British merchant ship *Pattersonian* had steered
across the attacking Spanish ship to prevent her picking up one of
the sinking ship's lifeboats, and the men of the Cromer lifeboat had
also helped to rescue the stranded Spanish crew. The newsreels
for 7 November were full of stories about 'The Battle of Cromer'.
And since neither the rescued Spanish captain, Manuel Ardulles,
nor his wife Trinidad, his eight-year-old daughter Gona, nor his
six-year-old son Ramon, spoke much English, the newsreels vied
with each other to interview the remaining people involved in the
incident.

Coxswain Bloggs of the Cromer lifeboat, who turned out to be a
personality in his own right, having won a double vc according to
Gaumont, was undoubtedly in most demand. He was interviewed
by Gaumont, Movietone and Paramount. Universal and Pathé
managed to secure interviews with Captain Blackmore, of the
Pattersonian. And Movietone also included an interview with the
mate of the *Monkwood*, the ship which had first reported the
action. Pathé's concluding comments to their story summarized
the attitude which all the newsreels took about the incident:
'Thanks to the tradition of British seamanship and British courage,
a few more lives have been snatched from the ugly jaws of war.'
The war in Spain still continued but further stories, such as the
one from Paramount on 17 November which announced that
'French volunteers return from Spain', strongly suggested that it
was drawing to a close.

Gaumont for their part continued to propagate generally their
message of peace with strength for Britain. It was perhaps most
clearly expressed during this period by a story that had nothing
to do with Spain at all. Their coverage of the Armistice Day
celebrations for November 1938 ran:

In November 1920 a soldier who had died for his country came home.
He had no name and so he was chosen to represent his million comrades,
known and unknown, who gave their lives for us. Each year we have
remembered those who died. And through all these changing years this
simple service has remained unchanged.

There need never be another Cenotaph if Britain is strong enough to
defy the threat of war. That is why all men and women, however
different their opinions, should work together for the sake of our
Empire. We in Britain have a hatred of war, but to fear war is to

provoke it. It is the duty of our generation to be fit; it is not sufficient today to live in the Empire, we must also serve it. Britain must be strong. If our fighting services are great our youth may live in them today. If they are weak our manhood must die in them tomorrow. Britain must be strong until the world returns to sanity and all men may live together in Peace.

Gaumont now used any occasion to put forward the line that the only way Britain could live in peace was for her to be strong. In the first instance Spain had served to provide such an occasion, then Austria. Now a simple ceremony, which was covered every year by the newsreels, was made use of by Emmett as part of Gaumont's campaign.

Movietone too continued in November with one of their long-standing campaigns. Three times in 1938 Movietone had invited Sir Malcolm Campbell to do editorial stories for them about air-raids and air-raid precautions. As a result a piece on 'Air-Raid Shelters for All' had been included in the issue for 7 March; one on 'ARP Training' had been shown on 24 March; and a further story on 'ARP Progress Reviewed' had been put into the 7 April release. Other stories by Leslie Mitchell had also been included during the course of the year. And the Movietone issue for 21 November now contained aerial scenes from Spain, during the battle for the Ebro, with a commentary from Mitchell which ran:

The problem of the bombing aeroplane remains. That problem extends beyond the boundaries of Spain and affects the whole of mankind.

Franco's bombers raiding Barcelona territory have become a familiar terror to the people of Republican Spain which the rest of us, who have had no experience of air-raids, can only draw in our imagination, stimu-lated by such pictures as these.

As you sit in the theatre, you are visualising the scenes of havoc and heroism below.

Just for once put yourself in the place of the airman. He is an ordinary man doing his job, like the pilots of our own bombing squad-rons. He is no monster of brutality; he regards his work coldly, as duty.

It is just that which makes the bombing aeroplane so terrible a weapon; and the inventor who discovers some way to defeat this Frankenstein will be the benefactor of mankind.

But it was Movietone's next story on aerial bombing, on

8 December, which projected a somewhat different image, at least for one particular release. Their cameramen had secured some unusual film of Franco's aeroplanes dropping bread upon Madrid. In fact Gaumont had also got hold of exactly the same film, through their deal with Movietone, and it was they who made much better use of the material. For Gaumont's report, which was also issued on 8 December, stated openly that their story on 'Madrid bombed by bread' amounted to 'propaganda with a punch, an attempt to indicate to the citizens of Madrid that the Insurgent troops have enough to eat and some to spare.' Several tons of bread, which had been made at the Insurgent forces' bakeries, was shown being loaded on to bombers at a Saragossa airfield; as Emmett characteristically put it, Franco's bombers were loaded up 'not with bombs, but with the staff of life'. The loaves were to be dropped over Government lines and on Madrid. Gaumont had on several occasions commented that the Nationalists were not short of food, as were the besieged Republicans. Here the Nationalists were seen to be flaunting the fact.

Gaumont's next report, released on 12 December, opened with a story on the homecoming of the British contingent of the International Brigades. It noted: 'In the gloom of a winter evening men of the British Battalion of the International Brigade returned to London from Spain.' Then it picked out notable personalities who welcomed them home, including Clement Attlee, Sir Stafford Cripps and Ellen Wilkinson. The film shows the men marching through London before being entertained to dinner. Emmett's final comment is: 'They all seem very carefree, having lived with death round the corner for two years they have probably lost the habit of worrying over trifles.'

The story was followed by one of equal length showing President Roosevelt at a children's hospital in Georgia during Thanksgiving Day celebrations. The President proceeds to read out a speech before the camera and Emmett's first draft noted that it contained 'a message that is particularly appropriate in the world as it is today'. This sentence was excised but the point still remained, particularly since it followed the Brigade story, for Roosevelt went on to say: 'May you and yours have a happy Thanksgiving. I am thankful that I live in a country where our leader sits down on Thanksgiving Day to carve up a turkey instead of a map.' In fact the President was reading from a telegram which had been sent him by Eddie Cantor, the show business personality. The words spoken were not his own, but in the context of the story as it appeared it made little difference for, as Emmett put it, the President chose the opportunity 'to make the Turkey Festival an occasion of international importance.' Indeed the whole of Gaumont's release was given an international emphasis, for the final story was entitled 'The Defence of France, No. 4; Colonial Troops'. The Defence of France was a six-part weekly series which had been compiled by Gaumont presumably to reassure the British people of the strength of our closest ally in the light of post-Munich Europe. The first part had been released on 21 November and had concentrated upon the fortifications along the supposedly impregnable Maginot Line; other stories highlighted the French Air-Raid Precautions, the French Navy, and French Tanks.

Gaumont's final report on Spain came in its Review of the Year on 29 December. It recounted that 'World Affairs in 1938 have been depressing and a frightening problem.' But it was no longer possible to single out the Spanish Civil War from other wars and altercations across the globe. It did still merit a mention as Emmett spotlighted:

China, still wracked with war. The bombing of the American gunboat *Panay* shocked the world. The Japanese aggression marched on, invaders took all the key cities with death and merciless destruction.

Closer to home Emmett commented:

The war situation in Spain reached almost checkmate. Ships were bombed on the high seas. Austria fell to Germany. Czechoslovakia; the story of the Sudeten Germans nearly brought war to the whole of Europe. Britain prepared.

But to conclude, Emmett recalled that 'Agreement was reached when Mr Chamberlain flew to Germany', only to end on an often heard but still prophetic note as he added: 'Then, Re-armament.'

Chapter 7 | The End of the War: Conclusion

At the beginning of January 1939 some newsreels still appeared to have little interest in the actual course of the fighting in Spain. Gaumont and Universal used their releases of 12 January to show film of a memorial service at Earl's Court for men from the British Battalion of the International Brigade who had fallen in Spain. In any case a good deal of newsreel time was being taken up with reporting the events surrounding the visit, early in January, of Chamberlain and Halifax to Rome, where they hoped to persuade Mussolini to act as a moderating influence upon Hitler. In the same release which contained the short report of the memorial service, Gaumont spent most of the time on the story 'Chamberlain leaves for Rome talks'. Paramount also ran a story entitled 'Premier in Rome to appease Duce', and followed this up in the next issue for 16 January with a report which revealed the apparent fruits of Chamberlain's visit by noting: 'Duce tells Premier Italy needs Peace.'

Franco was also enjoying renewed success in Spain and it was this which eventually turned the newsreels' centre of attention back again to the Civil War. On 23 December, Franco had launched a new offensive against Catalonia. The Ebro campaign had severely weakened the Republican forces and within a week of the new year Franco met with a series of immediate victories. Movietone's release for 16 January could now comment that, 'This is one of the biggest battles of the war so far and most critical,' while Gaumont's issue of 19 January reported that 'The fiercest fighting of all Spain's long drawn-out Civil War is taking place in the defence of Barcelona.' But on 19 January at least nobody as yet foresaw an end to the war. Gaumont's commentary went on to add:

There seems to be no end to the manpower of Spain, ready to fill the gaps in the firing line, ready to advance into a new city conquered,

conquered but wrecked beyond recognition. What better evidence could anyone wish of the futility of war?

The might of the Nationalist armour broke the Republican front and on 14 January General Yague drove out from Gandesa along the Ebro and captured Tarragona. Movietone and Gaumont covered the victory on 23 January, with the latter noting that 'Palm-lined streets and grim fighting men make a distressing contrast', but also revealing that normality was at least returning by stating: 'On the day following the entry of the conquering army Mass was said in the public square, attended by the Generals who had directed the offensive.' On the same date Paramount reported that 'Franco's onslaught nears Barcelona' and commented that it appeared to herald 'an offensive which bids fair to end the Civil War'.

The reports began to proliferate again. Cameramen were hurried back to Spain to cover what it was now thought would be an imminent end to the fighting. Once more each release by the newsreels featured coverage of Spain. In one issue for 26 January Gaumont could comment, 'Day by day the march of Franco's army brought conquest nearer to the Government stronghold of Barcelona', and on 30 January they could announce: 'At long last, after two and a half years of Civil War, the Government stronghold in the south of Spain has capitulated.' Barcelona had fallen on 26 January. But with such victories came another endless flow of refugees and the opportunity for Emmett to decry war, as he went on to do in the same story with a concluding invective:

What is the matter with mankind? What foul disease is rotting the brains of our civilisation? What inhumanity impels one half of the living world to make life an intolerable burden for the other?

The contrast between a victorious Nationalist army on the one hand, and a stream of refugees on the other, very much set the pattern for the coverage of the war from this point. Gaumont's next release on 2 February showed the entry of General Yague into Barcelona, with the customary observance of Holy Mass in Catalonia Square at which 'many thousands of men and women were present to watch this religious observance of the victorious troops.' Then the story cut to shots of Franco adding, 'General

Franco seldom permits himself to be filmed, but when he does he seems to prefer to appear as the man of peace in the bosom of his family.' Emmett proceeded to make his point by cutting away to numerous shots of refugees, accompanied by a commentary which ran:

Now take a look at the other side of the story. A constant stream of men, women and children, mostly fellow-countrymen of those same victorious troops, fleeing towards the French border and the hopes of rest and safety.

Most of the men of military age are crippled, crushed in the war machine. The women have the marks of despair seared across their faces, where they should know only the cares of household and motherhood. They seek sanctuary and charity within the frontiers of a neighbour's land.

All the British newsreel companies covered the fall of Barcelona, and in their release Paramount revealed the hardship and plight of many of the refugees en route with a story from the Pyrenees of women and children escaping from Spain through the snow.

For a while the French Government refused to allow Spanish refugees entry into France, because of the heavy cost of maintaining camps to house the swelling numbers of homeless people. They proposed a neutral zone along the Spanish frontier supported by money from foreign relief, but Franco vetoed the plan. As a result the French opened the border on 27 January to civilians and wounded men, and from 5 February they extended the provision to include Republican soldiers provided they surrendered their arms. Again all the newsreel companies in Britain announced the reopening of the frontier in their respective reports for 9 February. In fact by this time the newsreels were almost duplicating each other's coverage. When Solchaga reached the French frontier at Le Perthus with his Nationalist troops, four companies were there to film the event and all four released the film in their issues for 13 February. Gaumont noted: 'The Spanish Royalist flag was hoisted to a telegraph pole and the conquest of Catalonia had become a fact.'

Catalonia was indeed conquered. On 1 February a band of sixty-two members of the Cortes had met at Figueras, the last Catalan town before the French border. Negrin put forward three peace proposals which he hoped would guarantee Spanish independence, the right of the Spanish people to elect their own government, and freedom from persecution. The Cortes duly accepted the proposals, then everybody left for France. The conditions for peace were handed over to French and British ministers in order that they might mediate with the Nationalists. But they need hardly have bothered. Paramount recounted the capture of Figueras, which occurred on 8 February when Navarrese took the town, in a story entitled 'Franco mops up before attacking Madrid', and by 10 February the whole Catalan border with France was in Nationalist hands. Britain was called in to mediate, as well, in Minorca. It too surrendered on 10 February but not before the British Consul in Majorca had been invited, by the Nationalists this time, to arrange the surrender. The Foreign Office agreed, extracting a promise that neither German nor Italian troops would be allowed on the island for a period of two years after the event. On receipt of such a promise HMS *Devonshire* was despatched to ferry the negotiators between Majorca and Port Mahon, as well as to transport Republican sympathisers to Marseilles. Emmett's first draft of his script for release on 16 February intended to say:

Parliament has asked a question about the part played by HMS *Devonshire* in the Minorca peace negotiations but Mr Chamberlain assured the House that all that had been done was to avoid unnecessary bloodshed.

In the event he chose to ignore any notes of disquiet surrounding the incident and instead emphasized its salutary aspects by stating:

Arriving at Marseilles is the British cruiser *Devonshire* landing 450 refugees from Minorca. HMS *Devonshire* has been in the seas of the war zone, taking no part in war, but serving only the interests of humanity.

The other newsreels continued to highlight the plight of the Spanish refugees housed in camps inside the French border at such places as Le Boulou, Argelès and St Cyprien. But these camps needed money to sustain the refugees. The French Government provided thirty million francs, then invited other countries to help either by accepting refugees or by giving donations. Britain helped though on a modest scale. Universal's newsreel for 2 February contained a report on lorries filled with food for the

stricken refugees leaving London under the command of the
Earl of Antrim. It further noted that the convoy 'met with some
lively criticism from British Fascists who didn't quite see eye to
eye with the scheme. The objectors' slogan is "Why feed aliens
while Britain starves", which humanitarian appeal is brought
somewhat under suspicion by its being used to emphasise political
aims.' Paramount's newsreel for 20 February showed the attempts
of one British appeal to raise money in a story entitled 'Artists aid
refugees by painting on hoardings'. It highlighted artists decorat-
ing pleas for money on hoardings near Tower Bridge. As a result of
appeals such as this the British Red Cross collected a sum of
£50,000 with which to provide food and medical supplies for the
refugee camps. And they sorely needed such supplies, as Movietone
showed on 16 February and Paramount on 23 February with film
which revealed the squalor and destitution of one such camp, the
shanty town which had been erected at Argelès.

The war itself was clearly almost at an end. Movietone's release
for 20 February spotlighted Senator Léon Berard consulting with
Georges Bonnet, the French Foreign Secretary, before leaving on a
mission to Burgos. As the commentary put it: 'The question of
French and British recognition of the Nationalist victors in Spain
is the big international question of the moment.' And on 27 February Britain and France officially recognized Franco. In their
releases for that date the newsreels had coverage of Franco's
victory parade through Barcelona. Pathé went through all the contingents on parade, including 'the war-worn uniforms and forage
caps of Aragon, the berets of Navarre and the fezes of Morocco'.
But all reports singled out the Italian Black Shirt Divisions 'who
figure prominently in the victory march'. Some time later, on
18 May, Paramount went on to show 'Franco's farewell to foreign
pilots', at which it was acknowledged that he was reviewing and
awarding medals to both Italian and German airmen who had
fought for him throughout the war.

On Gaumont's part, their next report for 2 March contained a
'Review of the War' which encapsulated their thinking on the
events in Spain, accompanied by a visual run-through of the highlights of the war. The commentary ran:

The latter years of Spanish history have covered pages and chapters of
unrivalled catastrophe. Riots and unrest culminated in July 1936 in the

unofficial commencement of Civil War. General Franco marched on
Madrid. His early successes on the way to the capital resulted in a stream
of refugees seeking sanctuary in Gibraltar. From then till now that
stream of homeless human beings has never ceased to flow. Madrid
prepared defence; men, women and boys armed themselves to defend
the Government under the command of General Miaja, whom both sides
and the whole world had acclaimed a soldier of genius. In Burgos, the
Nationalist headquarters, General Franco was filmed for the first time.
The Insurgent armies advanced, they captured Irun. The story of the
siege of the Alcazar is one of deathless glory. After terrific resistance,
Toledo fell to Franco's troops.

Parliament in London was gravely beset by concern lest this foreign
flame might kindle the fires of war outside the boundaries of Spain and
destroy all Europe. General conflict was avoided. Then more key cities
fell to Franco, Bilbao, Gijon, and the latest and greatest, Barcelona,
bombarded from land, sea and air.

In Barcelona, the Government army cracked and countless thousands
of military and civilian refugees swarmed through the gates of hospi-
tality into neutral France. The President of the Spanish Republic,
Senor Azana, fled also into France, and he resigned. Then, acting in
accord, France and Britain decided to recognise General Franco, hoping
thereby to stem the tide of killing and destruction. In London, the
Ambassador of Republican Spain left the Embassy and the Duke of
Alba took his place.

This is the fate of Spain. We cannot do better than quote the words of
Britain's Prime Minister, who hoped that once the fighting ended,
Spain would unite to repair the destruction, to build up a happy country
worthy of the glorious past of Spain.

It was a long story, comprising some 199 feet of film, and it was
placed at the very end of the release. But for all its length Gaumont
were compelled to concertina the events portrayed to a very great
extent. They still managed to refer, however, to the one major
factor which had guided their attitude to the Spanish Civil War
throughout. For the fear 'lest this foreign flame might kindle the
fires of war outside the boundaries of Spain and destroy all Europe'
had undoubtedly determined the outcome of Gaumont's newsreel
coverage. In the beginning they had gone out of their way to
emphasize that the war was a local conflict, that it was a civil war
affecting Spaniards alone. But when it began to exercise European
statesmen generally, Gaumont chose not to report the extent of

European involvement in Spain. They only reported peace missions when they appeared to achieve success. And when it became clear that Europe was still being drawn more and more into the Spanish conflict, Gaumont brought Spain into the campaign which they began to conduct for Britain's rearmament.

Paramount chose not to assemble a review of the war in the way that Gaumont had done. Spain had been for Paramount throughout the war a land of lost opportunity. They had acquiesced in the newsreel line on Spain. More so than Gaumont they had shown the death and destruction in Spain itself and strongly endorsed the message that 'War is horrible', while at the same time emphasizing the value to Britain of staying out of the conflict. Yet there had always also been a hint in Paramount's coverage that they were capable of greater things. They had been the ones, for instance, to shoot film of the International Brigades in Spain and to secure a dissenting view from Attlee on Eden's resignation. And yet they had never shown the former material and they had withdrawn the latter only a few hours after release, thereby losing the opportunity to demonstrate a more independent newsreel line throughout the period of the Spanish Civil War. Now, at the very end, they also lost the opportunity to compile a review of the war. So indeed did the remaining newsreels. But at least Movietone and Universal had had their moments. They had both broached the matter of Italian volunteers and Non-Intervention sooner than the rest. Pathé's coverage had been straightforward and predictable, though unadventurous, throughout, and remained so until the end.

In fact the Spanish Civil War had not yet come to a close. On 28 February, President Azana, who was in Paris, resigned and Martinez Barrio took on the role. In Madrid itself, Colonel Casado, the commander of the Republican Army of the Centre, successfully led a revolt against Prime Minister Negrin on 4 March. But the negotiations he tried to conduct with Franco proved to be no more acceptable than those of Negrin. Franco still demanded unconditional surrender and on 26 March the final campaign against Madrid began. By 28 March Colonel Prada surrendered the Army of the Centre in Madrid.

Movietone, Universal and Gaumont announced the surrender in their reports for 30 March. 'For General Franco', Gaumont noted, 'this is the hour of triumph and he rides appropriately with an escort of Moors.' Emmett used the story on Madrid as a prelude to a general review of the state of Europe. Like all the other newsreels he made mention of the fact that Marshal Petain, France's Ambassador to the new regime in Spain, and Franco's old comrade-in-arms in Morocco, had arrived in Burgos to present his credentials. But from there Emmett's story cut to Rome where 'Mussolini shouted "woe to the weak", announced the end of brotherhood and stated that Italy's policy was determined by force.' Before leaving Italy, Emmett chose to mention that King Victor Emmanuel had also made a speech in which 'he emphasised the need for armaments, but stated that Italy desired peace.' Next the story cut to Germany and Emmett commented that as a result of Hitler's ultimatum Lithuania had given back her only seaport to Germany, while 'the battleship *Deutschland* carried Hitler to the scene of his latest conquest, Memel.'

In conclusion Emmett pointed out that 'Britain is not asleep' and to back up this claim showed film of Viscount Gort, Chief of the Imperial General Staff, arriving in France at the invitation of the French Chief of Staff, General Gamelin. 'His object was to establish personal contact and to inspect the wonderful Maginot Line that guards the frontiers of our friendly neighbour across the Channel.' Finally the story came back to London where 'ARP Chief, Sir John Anderson, spoke of the need for preparation at home.' Already the newsreels were moving on to new matters for concern, matters that were to involve Britain a great deal more closely than Spain had done.

The newsreels did return to Spain for further stories in the following months. They showed the return of eight million pounds in gold, which had been deposited in Paris by the Republican Government, to Franco and Spain. They showed victory parades, Count Ciano visiting Franco, Franco visiting naval dockyards, and the mass christening of 200 babies in Madrid. Stories on Spain continued until August in the newsreel issues prepared for release to Dublin. But the overall message contained in the concluding reports for consumption in Britain was perhaps best summarized by Ted Emmett, who commented in one of them for 25 May: 'Let us hope that General Franco will celebrate the fruits of victory by a speedy programme of reconstruction, bringing happiness once more to the sunny land of Spain.'

Optimistic to the end, the newsreels finished with Spain, though not before Movietone's issue of 13 July revived the old, pre-war image with a story entitled 'Pamplona bull fight once again'. They had done their job during the Spanish Civil War as far as they saw it and within the bounds which they had set for themselves.

In an article called 'Spilling the Spanish Beans', published in July and September of 1937, George Orwell came to the conclusion that 'There has been a quite deliberate conspiracy (I could give detailed instances) to prevent the Spanish situation from being understood.'[1] And of course Orwell could have proved his point. He would no doubt have cited the *New Statesman* to back up his argument because it had refused to publish an article which he wrote for it on the events in Catalonia between May and June of 1937, when the Communist Party in Spain had set about the suppression of the POUM. He would also probably have cited newspapers like the *News Chronicle* and the *Daily Worker* because he saw them as part of the same left-wing conspiracy to prevent the facts on Spain from becoming widely known, ostensibly in the cause of presenting a united pro-Republican front to the rest of the world. And finally he would no doubt have instanced the pro-Fascist newspapers as part of a wider conspiracy which prevented the British public from grasping the real nature of the struggle. Though he did on numerous occasions deliberate whether it was not the left-wing newspapers, 'with their far subtler methods of distortion,'[2] which did more damage on Spain than, say, the right-wing newspapers which were guilty of little more, in his words, than 'professing to lump all "reds" together and to be equally hostile to all of them.'[3]

But it is interesting to extrapolate from Orwell's particular statement and to speculate whether the newsreels also formed part of a 'conspiracy', of whatever variety, and of a 'deliberate conspiracy' which attempted to prevent the facts on the Spanish Civil War from being made known to the people of Britain. And on the basis of the evidence available it becomes obvious that the newsreels did deliberately withhold certain pieces of information. Whether the newsreel companies conspired together to withhold this information is debatable and seems, in fact, highly unlikely. In the first instance their response to the Civil War was a basically humanitarian one. They chose to emphasize the destruction and devastation in Spain and they used this footage as part of a more general campaign to show the horrors of modern war. They projected Britain as a stable democracy which, for its own sake, should not involve itself with the conflict. To this end they endorsed the British Government's policy of neutrality, though it took them some time before they admitted the presence of a Non-Intervention Committee, simply because the policy of Non-Intervention was so fraught with troubles and controversies. And above all the newsreels scrupulously avoided controversial issues. Furthermore, they endorsed the Government's tacit approval of Franco. Franco was the figure chosen for approbation by the British Establishment and the newsreels were a part of that Establishment. The newsreel companies did not conspire with the Government of the day before giving their approval. They did not need to do so. The matter quite simply was that, as one newsreel chief put it during the course of a discussion on Official and Political Party Films on 19 May 1938, 'The newsreel companies were always ready to give, and in fact frequently gave, assistance to the Government in portraying matters which were deemed to be of public interest.'[4] When it appeared that Britain was becoming inextricably drawn into a worsening European situation, the newsreels wholeheartedly supported the policy of rearmament, first and foremost in order that Britain's own interests might be adequately safeguarded. Of course on each and every issue there were various and conflicting messages emanating from other quarters, in particular from the press. But the newsreels were committed to consensus, not conflict.

It is impossible to ascertain whether the messages on Spain put forward by the newsreels for the consideration of the British cinemagoing public were successful in their purpose of engendering a consensus response. It should not be forgotten, however, that for many people the cinema newsreel was a major source of information on the pressing issues of the day. The newsreel companies knew that. They also knew that film was a medium which could easily be manipulated, and they knew how to manipulate the medium to best advantage. So if the pictures of Spain, and indeed of Britain, which they presented were limited and partial, then they were deliberately so. If they failed to explain fully the role of Russia, Germany or Italy in the Spanish Civil War,

then again it was for a purpose. If, finally, they failed to explain
what the Spanish Civil War was about, then there can be no doubt
that the newsreels helped to prevent the Spanish situation from
being understood.

Notes

Introduction pp. ix–xii

1 David Wingeate Pike, *Conjecture, Propaganda and Deceit and the Spanish Civil War*, Stanford, California, 1968.
2 K. W. Watkins, *Britain Divided*, London 1963.
3 Franklin Reid Gannon, *The British Press and Germany 1936–1939*, London 1971.
4 Asa Briggs, *Mass Entertainment: The Origins of a Modern Industry*, Adelaide 1960, p. 29.
5 Pike, *Conjecture, Propaganda and Deceit*, p. xv.

Chapter 1. Film as a Primary Source pp. 1–16

1 Fritz Terveen, 'Film as a Historical Document' (translated by C. L. Burgauner), in *Film and the Historian*, London 1969, p. 22.
2 Raymond Fielding, *The American Newsreel 1911–1967*, Norman, Oklahoma, 1972, p. 4.
3 W. K. L. Dickson and Antonia Dickson, *History of the Kinetograph, Kinetoscope and Kinetophonograph*, New York 1895, pp. 51–2.
4 Boleslaw Matuszewski, 'Une nouvelle source de l'histoire' as translated in Frances Thorpe (ed.), *A Directory of British Film and Television Libraries*, London 1975, pp. 49–52, and Jay Leyda, *Films beget Films*, London 1964, p. 15.
5 Leyda, *Films beget Films*, p. 13.
6 Fielding, *The American Newsreel*, p. 8.
7 See M. Lhéritier, 'Rapport présenté sur les rapports de l'histoire avec le cinématographe', *Bulletin of the International Committee of the Historical Sciences*, Vol. 2, 1929–30, pp. 361–4; M. Fruin, 'Memoire sur les Films documentaires', *ibid.*, pp. 454–6; Max Fauconnier, 'Les Archives Cinématographiques', *ibid.*, Vol. 3, 1931, pp. 45–9; M. Fruin, 'Enquête de la commission internationale sur les films historiques', *ibid.*, vol. 4, 1932, pp. 467–74.
8 As translated in Terveen, 'Film as a Historical Document', p. 24.
9 H. R. Kedward, 'Politics, Iconography and Film', *The Brighton Film Review*, No. 18, March 1970, p. 23.
10 See W. T. Waugh, 'History in Moving Pictures', *History*, Vol. 11, January 1927. p. 324; H. Forsyth Hardy, 'Fact or Fiction?', *Cinema Quarterly*, No. 2, Spring 1934, pp. 179–81; 'List of Historical-Biographical Films, 1912–1936', *World Film News*, Vol. 1, No. 12, March 1937, pp. 10–11; F. Wilkinson, 'Can History be taught by film?', *Sight and Sound*, Vol. 2, 1936, p. 91.
11 John G. Bradley, 'Motion picture activities of the Library of Congress' as quoted in John B. Kuiper, 'The historical value of motion pictures', *American Archivist*, Vol. 31, No. 4, October 1968, pp. 385–6.
12 Sir Arthur Elton, 'The film as source material for history', *Aslib Proceedings*, Vol. 7, 1955, pp. 207–16.
13 Christopher H. Roads, 'Film as historical evidence', *Journal of the Society of Archivists*, Vol. 3, 1965–9, pp. 183–91.

14 See John B. Kuiper, 'The historical value of motion pictures', p. 389.
15 Penelope Houston, 'The nature of the evidence', *Sight and Sound*, Vol. 36, 1967, pp. 89–92.
16 J. A. S. Grenville, *Film as History*, Birmingham 1971, pp. 7–9.
17 Arthur Marwick, 'Archive Film as Source Material', *Archive Film Compilation Booklet*, Milton Keynes 1973, pp. 1–5, and 'Notes on the Use of Archive Film Material', *War and Social Change in the Twentieth Century*, London 1974, pp. 226–34.
18 British Universities Historical Studies in Film: No. 1, *The Munich Crisis*, written and researched by John Grenville, directed by Nicholas Pronay, 1968; No. 2, *The End of Illusions*, written and researched by John Grenville, directed by Nicholas Pronay, 1970; No. 3, *The Spanish Civil War*, written, researched and narrated by Paul Addison and Owen Dudley Edwards, edited and directed by Tony Aldgate, 1972; No. 4, *The Winter War*, written and researched by Derek Spring, edited by George Brandt, 1974; No. 5, *The Great Depression*, written and directed by Peter Stead, 1976. And also Archive Series: No. 1, *Neville Chamberlain*, 1975; No. 2, *The Origins of the Cold War*, 1977.
19 The Open University: A301, 'War and Society', academic editor for the series, Arthur Marwick, 1973; A401, 'Great Britain, 1750–1950, Sources and Historiography', 1974.
20 'Film and the Historian', April 1968, University College, London; 'Archive Film in the Study and Teaching of Twentieth Century History', June 1972, Imperial War Museum, London; 'The value of news film to the historian', December 1972, Cumberland Lodge, Windsor; 'Film Propaganda and the Historian', July 1973, IWM, London; 'Making Historical Films for Television', March 1974, Windsor; 'Film and the Second World War', September 1974, IWM, London; 'Film and the Arts', December 1974, Windsor; 'Film and Television in the Study of Politics', September 1976, IWM, London; 'Film Study', University of Warwick, December 1976.
21 See, for example, Paul Smith (ed.), *The Historian and Film*, Cambridge 1976.
22 See Kuiper, 'The historical value of motion pictures', p. 389, and E. Bradford Burns, 'Conceptualising the use of film to study history', *Film and History*, Vol. 4, No. 4, December 1974, p. 1.
23 Grenville, *Film as History*, p. 9.
24 I am very much indebted for this summary on the nature of film to Raymond Fielding's article, 'Archives of the Motion Picture: A General View', in *American Archivist*, Vol. 30, No. 3, July 1967, pp. 493–5.
25 Nicholas Pronay, 'British Newsreels in the 1930s, Part I, Audience and Producers', *History*, Vol. 56, October 1971, p. 416.
26 Hans Magnus Enzensberger, 'Constituents of a Theory of the Media', *New Left Review*, No. 64, November–December 1970, p. 20.

Chapter 2. Inside the Newsreels pp. 17–53

THE EVOLUTION OF THE NEWSREEL, pp. 17–27.

1 Peter Baechlin and Maurice Muller-Strauss, *Newsreels Across the World*, Paris 1952, p. 9.
2 Kenneth Gordon, 'The early days of the newsreels', *British Kinematography*, Vol. 17, No. 2, p. 48.
3 Baechlin and Muller-Strauss, *Newsreels Across the World*, p. 10.
4 Gordon, 'The early days of the newsreels', p. 48.
5 Ex-Ray, *Journal of the Association of Cine Technicians*, August–October 1936, p. 58.
6 Gordon, 'The early days of the newsreels', p. 48.
7 *Ibid.*
8 Baechlin and Muller-Strauss, *Newsreels Across the World*, pp. 10–11.

9 Philip Norman, 'The newsreels', *The Sunday Times Magazine*, 10 January 1971, p. 11.
10 A. J. P. Taylor, *English History, 1914–1945*, London 1965, p. 107.
11 Harold D. Lasswell, *Propaganda Technique in World War I*, Cambridge, Massachusetts, 1971 (1st edn, London 1927), p. 40.
12 *Ibid.*, p. 41.
13 John Grierson, 'That unscrupulous rascal Northcliffe', *World Film News*, Vol. 2, No. 11, February 1938, pp. 16–17.
14 Pathé Gazette Issue No. 577, 3 July 1919.
15 Pathé Gazette Issue No. 578, 7 July 1919.
16 Fred Watts, 'Pioneer recalls struggles of early newsreel', *World Film News*, Vol. 1, No. 4, July 1936, p. 42.
17 Paul Wyand, *Useless if Delayed*, London 1959, p. 30.
18 *Ibid.*, p. 41.
19 Norman, 'The newsreels', pp. 11–12.
20 Wyand, *Useless if Delayed*, p. 29.
21 'Aeroplanes and tape machines cover the world', *World Film News*, Vol. 1, No. 3, June 1936, p. 22.
22 Gordon, 'The early days of the newsreels', p. 50.
23 'Soccer league boycott may follow Cup Final squabble', *World Film News*, Vol. 1, No. 3, June 1936, p. 22.
24 Minute of the Fourth Meeting of the Council of the Newsreel Association of Great Britain and Ireland, Ltd, held on 24 January 1938.
25 Donald Fraser, 'Newsreel, Reality or Entertainment?', *Sight and Sound*, Autumn 1933, pp. 89–90.

THE MONEY BEHIND THE NEWSREEL SCREEN, pp. 27–34.

1 F. D. Klingender and Stuart Legg, *The Money Behind the Screen*, London 1937, p. 23.
2 *Ibid.*
3 *Ibid.*, p. 24.
4 *Ibid.*, p. 25.
5 *Ibid.*, p. 24.
6 Political and Economic Planning, *The British Film Industry*, London 1952, p. 67.
7 The Commentator, 'Newsreel Rushes', *World Film News*, Vol. 1, No. 9, December 1936, p. 40.
8 The Commentator, 'Newsreel Rushes', *World Film News*, Vol. 1, No. 8, November 1936, p. 38.
9 Klingender and Legg, *The Money Behind the Screen*, p. 43.
10 *Ibid.*, pp. 30–1.
11 *Ibid.*, p. 41.
12 PEP, *The British Film Industry*, p. 62.
13 *Ibid.*, p. 70; and also The Commentator, 'Newsreel Rushes', *World Film News*, Vol. 2, No. 1, April 1937, p. 28.
14 The Commentator, 'Newsreel Rushes', *World Film News*, Vol. 2, No. 7, October 1937, p. 35.
15 *Ibid.*
16 The Commentator, 'Newsreel Rushes', *World Film News*, Vol. 2, No. 8, November 1937, p. 37.
17 The Commentator, 'Newsreel Rushes', *World Film News*, Vol. 2, No. 10, January 1938, p. 37.
18 The Arts Enquiry, *The Factual Film*, London 1947, p. 139.
19 Pronay, 'Audience and Producers', p. 416.
20 The Arts Enquiry, *The Factual Film*, p. 139.
21 *World Film News*, Vol. 1, No. 3, June 1936, p. 22.

22 'Films produced within 1937', reprinted from the Board of Trade Journal in *Journal of the Association of Cine Technicians*, May–June 1939, p. 13.

23 It was reported that the amount of money paid to the renters and producers of newsreels during 1950 came to £2,203,000 in PEP, *The British Film Industry*, p. 281.

24 *The Times*, 9 November 1936.

THE ORGANIZATIONAL STRUCTURE OF THE NEWSREELS, pp. 34–43.

1 Nicholas Pronay, 'British Newsreels in the 1930s, Part II, Their Policies and Impact', *History*, Vol. 57, February 1972, p. 63.

2 Nicholas Pronay, 'The use of film in History Teaching', in *A Short Guide to the Use of Film in History Teaching*, by Nicholas Pronay, Betty R. Smith and Tom Hastie, London 1972, p. 9.

3 Ex-Ray, 'The Newsreel War', *Journal of the Association of Cine Technicians*, Vol. 1, May 1935, p. 2.

4 *Kinematograph Year Book*, 1936, p. 296.

5 *Ibid.*, p. 308.

6 *Kinematograph Year Book*, 1937, p. 311.

7 *Kinematograph Year Book*, 1936, p. 298.

8 *Ibid.*, p. 322.

9 'Big Men of the Reel', in *Scoop*, the Monthly Bulletin of Gaumont British News, No. 1, undated.

10 *Kinematograph Year Book*, 1937, p. 385.

11 *Journal of the Association of Cine Technicians*, Vol. 2, December 1936–January 1937, p. 112.

12 *Ibid.*, p. 113.

13 *Kinematograph Year Book*, 1937, p. 384.

14 Pronay, 'The Use of Film in History Teaching', p. 9.

15 'Aeroplanes and tape machines cover the world for newsreel', *World Film News*, Vol. 1, No. 3, June 1936, p. 22.

16 The Commentator, 'Newsreel Rushes', *World Film News*, Vol. 2, No. 1, April 1937, p. 28.

17 The Commentator, 'Newsreel Rushes', *World Film News*, Vol. 1, No. 8, November 1936, p. 38.

18 The survey of newsreel production was drawn from correspondence between myself and Roy Drew, formerly an editor with Gaumont British News between 1929 and 1959, as well as the following sources: Thomas Sugrue, 'Bringing the world to the world', *World Film News*, Vol. 2, No. 3, June 1937, pp. 14–19; William P. Montague, 'Eyes of the World', *World Film News*, Vol. 2, No. 11, February 1938, pp. 3–5; Stuart Chesmore, *Behind the Cinema Screen*, London 1934, pp. 53–61 and Low Warren, *The Film Game*, London 1937, pp. 145–51.

19 British Paramount Issue No. 693, 18 October 1937. 'Franco holds monster youth parade.'

20 Gaumont British Issue No. 532, 2 February 1939. 'Both sides of the war in Spain.'

21 British Paramount Issue No. 571, 17 August 1936. 'Madrid holds out.'

22 Murray Sayle, 'When showbiz goes to war', the Spectrum Column, *The Sunday Times*, 30 January 1972; Edward Behr, 'It's war: TV crew opens fire on TV crew', Letters to the Editor, *The Sunday Times*, 6 February 1972; William McLaughlin, 'CBS Principle', Letters to the Editor, *The Sunday Times*, 13 February 1972.

23 The survey on newsreel commentators was drawn from an interview with Leslie Mitchell, a commentator for British Movietone News between 1937 to 1947 and 1958 to 1974, as well as from the following sources: 'Personality, the problem of commentary', *World Film News*, Vol. 1, No. 5, August 1936,

p. 22; The Commentator, 'Newsreel Rushes', *World Film News*, Vol. 2, No. 9, December 1937, p. 39.

24 Gaumont British Issue No. 350, 6 May 1937. 'Ruins of Guernica.'

25 Glen Norris, 'A wide open letter to Mr G. T. Cummins, Editor of British Paramount News', *World Film News*, Vol. 2, No. 5, August 1937, pp. 30–1.

26 Glen Norris, 'A wide open letter to Mr Gerald Sanger, Production Chief of British Movietonews', *World Film News*, Vol. 2, No. 6, September 1937, pp. 32–3.

27 Philip Howard, 'English as news-readers speak it', *The Times*, 17 August 1972; J. F. C. Brown, 'English as she is spoke', Letters to the Editor, *The Sunday Times*, 17 September 1972; J. R. Colville, 'Correct English', Letters to the Editor, *The Times*, 27 June 1973.

28 Universal News Issue No. 443, 8 October 1934. 'Spanish Riots.'

29 British Paramount Issue No. 481, 7 October 1935. 'War. Italians invade Abyssinia.'

30 Gaumont British Issue No. 299, 9 November 1936. 'The Fall of Madrid.'

THE TECHNOLOGY AND THE TECHNICIANS, pp. 43–53.

1 George Hill, 'Motion Picture Camera Development', *British Kinematography*, Vol. 17, No. 4, October 1950, p. 105.

2 The Commentator, 'Rivalry in Giant Lenses', *World Film News*, Vol. 2, No. 4, July 1937, p. 29.

3 Hill, 'Motion Picture Camera Development', p. 105.

4 Gordon, 'The early days of the newsreels', p. 48.

5 90 feet of 35 mm film at 24 frames per second will last for 1 minute; 180 feet will last 2 minutes; 270 feet will last 3 minutes, etc.

6 Gordon, 'The early days of the newsreels', p. 48.

7 *Ibid.*

8 W. S. Bland, 'The Development of the Sound Newsreel', *British Kinematography*, Vol. 17, No. 2, August 1950, p. 51.

9 G. H. Newberry, 'Some Aspects of Newsreel Recording', *Journal of the Association of Cine Technicians*, February 1936, pp. 85–6.

10 BP Issue No. 599, 23 November 1936. 'Premier takes stock, finds Britain best.'

11 BP Issue No. 730, 24 February 1938. 'Mr Attlee expresses the views of the Opposition party.'

12 Gordon, 'The early days of the newsreels', p. 50.

13 Norman, 'The newsreels', p. 10.

14 Sugrue, 'Bringing the world to the world', p. 19.

15 GB Issue No. 339, 29 March 1937. 'British Prisoners of War in Spain.'

16 GB Issue No. 468, 23 June 1938. 'Zoom Camera.'

17 *Journal of the Association of Cine Technicians*, August–October 1936, p. 41.

18 *Ibid.*

19 *Journal of the ACT*, June–July 1937, p. 68.

20 *Journal of the ACT*, May–June 1938, p. 32.

21 *Journal of the ACT*, February 1936, p. 21.

22 *Journal of the ACT*, April–May 1937, p. 26.

23 *Journal of the ACT*, August–October 1936, p. 41.

24 *Journal of the ACT*, May–June 1939, p. 26.

25 *Journal of the ACT*, January–February 1939, p. 145.

26 *Ibid.*

27 *Journal of the ACT*, March–April 1939, p. 198.

28 George Elvin, 'This Freedom, An Enquiry into Film Censorship', *Journal of the ACT*, January–February 1939, pp. 141–6.

29 'Censored', *Journal of the ACT*, March–April 1939, pp. 202–4.

30 *Journal of the ACT*, May–June 1939, p. 27.

31 *Journal of the ACT*, December–January 1937–8, p. 44.

Chapter 3. Outside the Newsreels pp. 54–90

EXHIBITION AND THE AUDIENCE, pp. 54–64.

1 Simon Rowson, 'A Statistical Survey of the Cinema Industry in Great Britain in 1934', *Journal of the Royal Statistical Society*, Vol. 99, 1936, pp. 67–119.
2 *Ibid.*, p. 70.
3 *Ibid.*, p. 84.
4 *Ibid.*, p. 71.
5 Pronay, 'Audience and Producers', p. 412.
6 Rowson, 'A Statistical Survey of the Cinema Industry', p. 74.
7 *Ibid.*, p. 76.
8 *Ibid.*, p. 71.
9 *Ibid.*, p. 71.
10 *Ibid.*, p. 84.
11 Pronay, 'Audience and Producers', pp. 413–14.
12 The Wartime Social Survey, *The Cinema Audience*, London 1943, pp. 1–24.
13 *Ibid.*, p. 1.
14 *Ibid.*, p. 3.
15 *Ibid.*, pp. 6–7.
16 *Ibid.*, pp. 8–9.
17 *Ibid.*, p. 9.
18 *Ibid.*, p. 22.
19 Chesmore, *Behind the Cinema Screen*, p. 61.
20 PEP, *The British Film Industry*, p. 56.
21 *Ibid.*, p. 66.
22 *Ibid.*, p. 67.
23 *Ibid.*, p. 70.
24 *Ibid.*, p. 56.
25 *Ibid.*, p. 66.
26 *Ibid.*, p. 80.
27 See *World Film News*, Vol. 1, No. 3, June 1936, p. 22, and Vol. 2, No. 10, January 1938, p. 37.
28 Howard Thomas, *With an Independent Air*, London 1977, pp. 131–2.
29 *World Film News*, Vol. 1, No. 8, November 1936, p. 38.
30 Baechlin and Muller-Strauss, *Newsreels Across the World*, p. 88.
31 Fraser, 'Newsreel, Reality or Entertainment?', p. 89; Norman J. Hulbert, 'News films and their public', *Sight and Sound*, Winter 1933, p. 133.
32 'The Cinema: A Symposium', with a foreword, by Sidney Bernstein, and including 'The Newsreel Theatre' by A. G. MacDonald, in *The Architects Journal*, No. 7, 1935, pp. 657–718.
33 *Sight and Sound*, Winter 1936–7, p. 119.
34 *Sight and Sound*, Spring 1937, p. 4.
35 J. Neill-Brown, 'The Industry's Front Page', *Journal of the ACT*, March–April, 1939, p. 199.
36 *World Film News*, Vol. 1, No. 4, July 1936, p. 42.
37 Baechlin and Muller-Strauss, *Newsreels Across the World*, p. 89.
38 'Public to gauge film values', *World Film News*, Vol. 1, No. 2, May 1936, p. 20.
39 Tom Harrisson, 'Social Research and the Film', *Documentary News Letter*, Vol. 1, No. 11, November 1940, p. 11.
40 *Ibid.*, p. 11.
41 Ewart Hodgson, 'Mass Observers', *Documentary News Letter*, Vol. 2, No. 1, January 1941, p. 12; Tom Harrisson replied to this criticism in a letter on page 13 of the same edition of *Documentary News Letter*; for further criticism of Mass Observation's techniques see W. Buchanan-Taylor, 'Mass Observation', *DNL*, Vol. 2, No. 2, February 1941, p. 35; and the subsequent rebuttal by Harrisson in *DNL*, Vol. 2, No. 3, March 1941, p. 49.
42 Harrisson, 'Social Research and the Film', p. 11.

43 *Ibid.*
44 *The Bernstein Questionnaire for Children, 1947*, as reprinted in *Winchester's Screen Encyclopedia*, London 1958, pp. 371–2.

NEWSREEL CONTENT, pp. 64–77.
1 As quoted in Fielding, *The American Newsreel*, p. 226.
2 *Ibid.*, p. 227.
3 John Grierson, *Grierson on Documentary*, London 1966, p. 201.
4 'Are newsreels news?', *The Nation*, 2 October 1935, p. 369.
5 Andrew Buchanan, 'Newsreels or real news?', *Film Art*, Vol. 3, No. 7, 1935, p. 22.
6 *Ibid.*, p. 23.
7 Paul Rotha, *Documentary Diary*, London 1973, p. 27.
8 Stuart Hood, Review of *Documentary Diary* by Paul Rotha, *Sight and Sound*, Vol. 43, No. 1, 1973–4, p. 58.
9 Charles Barr, 'Projecting Britain and the British Character: Ealing Studios', Part I, *Screen*, Vol. 15, No. 1, Spring 1974, p. 97.
10 The Arts Enquiry, *The Factual Film*, p. 140.
11 Edgar Dale, *The Content of Motion Pictures*, first printed New York 1935, reprinted New York 1970, p. 189.
12 *Ibid.*, pp. 190–1.
13 *Ibid.*, p. 191.
14 *Ibid.*, p. 199.
15 *Ibid.*, p. 199.
16 *Ibid.*, p. 201.
17 *Ibid.*, p. 202.
18 Leo Handel, *Hollywood Looks at its Audience*, Urbana, Illinois, 1950, p. 170.
19 *World Film News*, Vol. 1, No. 6, September 1936, p. 31.
20 *World Film News*, Vol. 1, No. 8, November 1936, p. 39.
21 Slade Film History Register, 'Survey on Stories Relating to Germany or Germans, 1933–1939', unpublished (mimeographed copy).

CENSORSHIP, pp. 77–90.
1 The Arts Enquiry, *The Factual Film*, p. 210.
2 *Ibid.*, p. 212.
3 Neville March Hunnings, *Film Censors and the Law*, London 1967, p. 110.
4 *Ibid.*
5 *Ibid.*
6 For one response to the CEA's attitude see p. 51.
7 Hunnings, *Film Censors and the Law*, p. 111.
8 'Horror in News Films', *The Times*, 1 December 1933.
9 *The Times*, 2 December 1933.
10 *Kinematograph Weekly*, 5 November 1934, p. 5
11 Hunnings, *Film Censors and the Law*, p. 112.
12 Home Office Circular 676417/6, *Revision of Model Conditions*, 24 October 1934.
13 *Kinematograph Weekly*, 13 April 1933, p. 43.
14 Hunnings, *Film Censors and the Law*, p. 111.
15 *Kinematograph Weekly*, 23 July 1936, p. 13.
16 *Kinematograph Weekly*, 8 March 1934, p. 4.
17 *House of Commons Debates*, Vol. 293, column 339, 1 November 1934.
18 *Kinematograph Weekly*, 5 November 1936, p. 17.
19 Hunnings, *Film Censors and the Law*, p. 113.
20 *H.C.Deb.*, Vol. 342, c. 1275, 7 December 1938.
21 *H.C.Deb.*, Vol. 341, c. 1727–1728, 23 November 1938.
22 *H.C.Deb.*, Vol. 342, c. 1313, 7 December 1938.
23 *H.C.Deb.*, Vol. 342, c. 583–584, 1 December 1938.

24 BP Issue No. 790, 22 September 1938. 'Europe's Fateful Hour.
25 *H.C.Deb.*, Vol. 342, c. 1261, 7 December 1938.
26 *H.C.Deb.*, Vol. 342, c. 1273, 7 December 1938.
27 Hunnings, *Film Censors and the Law*, p. 113.

Chapter 4. The Newsreels and the Spanish Civil War: Before the War
pp. 91–103

1 Stanley G. Payne, *The Spanish Revolution*, London 1970, p. 37.
2 Raymond Carr, *Spain 1808–1939*, London 1970, p. 504.
3 Lisa Pontecorvo, *Notes on Film Items*, Open University Supplementary Material to A301 Television Programme 7, Milton Keynes 1973, p. 28.
4 Watkins, *Britain Divided*, p. 25.
5 Leah Manning, *What I Saw in Spain*, London 1935, p. 95.
6 Watkins, *Britain Divided*, p. 15.
7 Taylor, *English History*, p. 376.
8 Watkins, *Britain Divided*, p. 27.
9 *Ibid.*, p. 26.

Chapter 5. The Advent of the War pp. 104–48

1 Hugh Thomas, *The Spanish Civil War*, London 1964, p. 143.
2 Such amendments are evident from the typewritten script which accompanies this particular story in the newsreel archive.
3 Brian Crosthwaite, 'Newsreels show political bias', *World Film News*, Vol. 1, No. 7, October 1936, p. 41.
4 It is interesting to note that the British press seem to have been guilty of a similar misrepresentation. See C. L. Mowat, *Britain Between the Wars 1918–1940*, London 1966, p. 579, where he comments: 'A letter protesting against the misrepresentation of the war in the press as one fought against a Bolshevist government rather than a Liberal-democratic government was signed by novelists, historians, poets, artists of all parties and of none.'
5 Boake Carter, Philco Radio Corporation. Broadcast on the Columbia Broadcasting System, 7.45 to 8.00 pm, Wednesday, 18 November 1936 (mimeographed copy).
6 'Scenes too gruesome for public showing', *World Film News*, Vol. 1, No. 7, October 1936, p. 41.
7 Thomas, *The Spanish Civil War*, p. 219.
8 *The Times*, 24 October 1936.
9 'Where do we stand?', *Documentary News Letter*, Vol. 2, No. 6, June 1941, p. 103.
10 P. A. M. van der Esch, *Prelude to War*, The Hague 1951, pp. 36–7.
11 *Ibid.*, p. 35.
12 *The News Chronicle*, 25 August 1936.
13 *The Manchester Guardian*, 2 January 1937.
14 Documentary film-makers like Ivor Montagu and Thorold Dickinson consistently presented an alternative viewpoint on Spain to that put forward in the newsreels, though their films were rarely, if ever, shown in the commercial cinemas. For a more detailed account of the Documentary Film Movement's reaction to the Spanish Civil War see Bert Hogenkamp, 'Film and the Workers' Movement in Britain 1929–39', *Sight and Sound*, Vol. 45, No. 2, Spring 1976, pp. 68–77.
15 Thomas, *The Spanish Civil War*, p. 282.
16 *Ibid.*, p. 286.
17 Ivor Montagu, 'The Siege of the Alcazar', *World Film News*, Vol. 1, No. 10, January 1937, pp. 10–11. Hollywood did of course go on to release a Spanish Civil War film in 1938 called *Blockade*. The script was written by John Howard

Lawson and the film was directed by William Dieterle and produced by Walter Wanger. It starred Henry Fonda and Madeleine Carroll.

18 Furhammar and Isaksson, *Politics and Film*, pp. 50–1.

19 The Commentator, 'Newsreel Rushes', *World Film News*, Vol. 1, No. 9, December 1936, p. 40.

20 The Commentator, 'Newsreel Rushes', *World Film News*, Vol. 1, No. 10, January 1937, p. 39. N.B. Though Edward VIII and Mrs Simpson had openly enjoyed each other's company throughout 1936, the British press did not broach the topic of their relationship until the very beginning of December. Edward abdicated on 10 December and the newsreels reported upon this in their issues for 14 December.

21 Neville March Hunnings cites examples of the few instances where censorship was openly imposed in *Film Censors and the Law*, pp. 111–13.

22 The same opinion is put forward for consideration in Hunnings, *Film Censors and the Law*, p. 110, and in The Arts Enquiry, *The Factual Film*, p. 140.

23 The Commentator, 'Newsreel Rushes', *World Film News*, Vol. 2, No. 4, July 1937, p. 29.

24 The Arts Enquiry, *The Factual Film*, p. 140.

25 Political and Economic Planning, *Report on the British Press*, London 1938, p. 51.

26 *Ibid.*, p. 260.

27 The Commentator, 'Newsreel Rushes', *World Film News*, Vol. 1, No. 11, February 1937, p. 42.

Chapter 6. The Course of the War pp. 149–83

1 G. T. Cummins, 'A Reply to Sketch Editor's Criticisms', *World Film News*, Vol. 1, No. 8, November 1936, p. 39.

2 The Commentator, 'Newsreel Rushes', *World Film News*, Vol. 2, No. 3, June 1937, p. 30.

3 Thomas, *The Spanish Civil War*, p. 358.

4 A. J. P. Taylor, *The Origins of the Second World War*, Harmondsworth 1964 (1st edn, London 1961), p. 163.

5 Taylor, *English History*, p. 427.

6 Thomas, *The Spanish Civil War*, p. 336.

7 BP Library No. 5946. 'International Brigades'. (Not Issued.)

8 BP Library No. 5990. 'Volunteers for Spain'. (Not Issued.)

9 Typewritten scripts to GB Issue No. 338 and to GB Issue No. 339, 29 March 1937, 'British Prisoners of War in Spain', together with handwritten amendments to same.

10 In fact, Taylor, *English History*, p. 396, also agrees that, 'Of the 2,000 odd British citizens who fought for the Spanish Republic, the great majority were workers, particularly unemployed miners.' However Watkins in *Britain Divided*, p. 168, maintains 'The best estimate is that only somewhere between an eighth and a quarter were unemployed, the rest relinquished their jobs, often secure ones, in order to go.'

11 Thomas, *The Spanish Civil War*, p. 419.

12 Gannon, *The British Press and Germany 1936–1939*, p. 113.

13 Hugh Thomas, 'Heinkels over Guernica', *Times Literary Supplement*, 11 April 1975, p. 392.

14 *Ibid.*

15 Gannon, *The British Press and Germany*, p. 115.

16 Charles Loch Mowat, *Britain Between The Wars 1918–1940*, London 1966, pp. 577–8.

17 See Taylor, *English History*, p. 437, note A, where he states that 'All the emphasis was laid on Guernica' in miscalculating the potential effects of German bombing on London.

18 Mowat, *Britain Between the Wars*, pp. 578–9.
19. Thomas, *The Spanish Civil War*, p. 468.
20 Taylor, *English History*, p. 412.
21 *Ibid.*, p. 413.
22 *Ibid.*, p. 423.
23 Thomas, *The Spanish Civil War*, p. 530.
24 BP Library No. 7545. 'Bombing of Granollers'. (Unissued material.)

Chapter 7. The End of the War: Conclusion pp. 184–94

1 George Orwell, 'Spilling the Spanish Beans', first published in *New English Weekly*, 29 July and 2 September 1937, and reprinted in *The Collected Essays, Journalism and Letters of George Orwell Vol. 1: An Age Like This, 1920–1940*, edited by Sonia Orwell and Ian Angus, Harmondsworth 1971, p. 308.
2 *Ibid.*, p. 301.
3 Orwell, Letter to the Editor of *Time and Tide*, 5 February 1938, reprinted in *Collected Essays, Journalism and Letters Vol. 1*, p. 332.
4 Minute of the Seventh Meeting of the Council of the Newsreel Association of Great Britain and Ireland Ltd, held on Thursday, 19 May 1938.

Filmography

The locations of the various newsreel libraries are as follows:

Gaumont British News
British Paramount News
Universal News
Gaumont Graphic
Visnews Film Library, Cumberland Avenue, London NW16

British Movietone News
British Movietone News, North Orbital Road, Denham, Uxbridge, Middlesex

Pathé Gazette
EMI-Pathé Film Library, Film House, Wardour Street, London W1

Gaumont British News

The list below cites all the Gaumont British News issues relating to the Spanish Civil War. It gives the issue number, date of release, a brief summary of the story relating to Spain, and any notes relating to that particular issue. The figures appended reveal the following statistics, with all but (c) in feet:

a. The amount of titles footage to the story on Spain.
b. The amount of film used in the actual story on Spain.
c. The number of items or stories in the whole newsreel issue with the position of the story on Spain in brackets. (See note below.)
d. The amount of titles footage to the whole newsreel issue.
e. The amount of film used on all the stories in the issue.
f. The amount of film used on the whole newsreel issue, i.e. a combined total of the titles footage and the stories footage.

N.B. In (c), where a story on Spain occupies part of the Roving Camera Reports section of a newsreel, then there is no individual titles footage, but the story is given a letter to signify its position within that section. Thus, 7(4b) means: that there are 7 stories in the whole of the newsreel issue; that the Roving Camera Reports section occupies the 4th position in the run of 7 stories; and that the story on Spain is the second story in the Roving Camera Reports section.

GB Issue No. 269, 27 July 1936. Spanish Revolution; Pictures of the fighting in Madrid. (Sent in advance to West End Hall.) 15; 116; 5(1); 116; 717; 833.

GB Issue No. 270, 30 July 1936. Spanish Revolution; Refugees depart on British ships, scenes in Madrid, Guadalajara and Guadarrama. 10; 156; 6(6); 106; 670; 776.

GB Issue No. 271, 3 August 1936. Roving Camera Reports: Civil War in Spain; Scenes at Guadarrama. (Civil War in Spain dropped for Dublin.) —; 25; 7(4b); 126; 612; 738.

GB Issue No. 272, 6 August 1936. Spanish Civil War 4th edition; Scenes of Rebels advancing on Madrid, Refugees at Gibraltar and Spanish ship at Southampton. (Spanish Civil War dropped for Dublin.) 15; 123; 8(8); 107; 706; 813.

GB Issue No. 273, 10 August 1936. Spanish Civil War 5th edition; Government troops go into action near Madrid. 9; 70; 5(3); 98; 717; 815.

GB Issue No. 274, 13 August 1936. The 'Blonde Amazon'; Miss Phyllis Gwatkin Williams speaks to GB News about her experiences in the Spanish Civil War. 16; 230; 5(5); 94; 743; 837.

GB Issue No. 276, 20 August 1936. Spanish Civil War; Scenes in San Sebastian, Seville, Madrid. General Mola meets General Franco in Burgos. 15; 125; 4(1); 101; 699; 800.

GB Issue No. 277, 24 August 1936. Spanish Civil War 7th edition; Seville, Algeciras and Madrid. (No. 2 item is President Roosevelt speaks for peace.) 15; 96; 8(1); 120; 658; 778.

GB Issue No. 278, 27 August 1936. Spanish Civil War 8th edition; Captain Juber with Government troops at Azaila. (Preceded by First British Ambulance leaves for Spain and followed by Wonderful Britain.) —; 82; 6(5); 94; 672; 766.

GB Issue No. 280, 3 September 1936. Rebels take outpost of hilltop near Burgos; Scenes at Irun, Saragossa and San Sebastian in Spain. 18; 100; 7(1); 130; 630; 760.

GB Issue No. 282, 10 September 1936. Spain, Irun in ruins after capture by rebels. 10; 53; 8(5); 123; 633; 756.

GB Issue No. 283, 14 September 1936. Roving Camera Reports: Spanish Rebels go into occupation of Huelva. —; 32; 9(5d); 129; 687; 816.

GB Issue No. 284, 17 September 1936. Spanish Civil War; Refugees depart. Rebels converge on Madrid. Toledo in ruins. (Replaced for Dublin.) 10; 69; 6(2); 107; 674; 781.

GB Issue No. 285, 21 September 1936. Irun in ruins. Rebel troops enter San Sebastian. (Scottish Ambulance Unit for Spain not used.) 13; 70; 10(2); 132; 722; 854.

GB Issue No. 286, 24 September 1936. Spanish Civil War. Insurgents capture defending Government troops. (Replaced for Dublin.) 8; 57; 10(2); 127; 678; 805.

GB Issue No. 287, 28 September 1936. Ruins of the Alcazar. Senor Largo Caballero tours ruined area at Santa Cruz Convent. 8; 84; 12(6); 125; 674; 799.

GB Issue No. 289, 5 October 1936. Toledo relieved by Rebels. Generals Franco and Moscardo. 15; 147; 7(1); 108; 660; 768.

GB Issue No. 295, 26 October 1936. Rebel troops relieve Oviedo. —; 67; 8(4); 50; 695; 745.

GB Issue No. 298, 5 November 1936. Roving Camera Reports: Madrid entrenched awaits attack of the Insurgents. —; 32; 9(5e); 118; 644; 762.

GB Issue No. 299, 9 November 1936. The Fall of Madrid showing Rebels advancing a few miles out. (From Rebels' Library.) 6; 54; 7(3); 88; 664; 752.

GB Issue No. 300, 12 November 1936. Insurgents advance on Madrid while defences are strengthened. 7; 64; 5(2); 78; 707; 785.

GB Issue No. 302, 19 November 1936. Roving Camera Reports: Spanish Insurgents encircle and bomb Madrid. —; 78; 8(4d); 81; 736; 817.

GB Issue No. 303, 23 November 1936. Spanish Government ships leave Malaga. Also Government ships in action at Bilbao. 7; 55; 5(2); 77; 720; 797.

GB Issue No. 307, 7 December 1936. Madrid partially destroyed by Insurgent bombing. 6; 78; 9(8); 133; 621; 754.

GB Issue No. 313, 28 December 1936. Review of the Year: Foreign Affairs; Spanish Civil War. 7; 234; 6(5); 85; 873; 958.

GB Issue No. 315, 4 January 1937. Roving Camera Reports: Christmas celebrations in Spanish Trenches. —; 29; 12(9c); 83; 682; 765.

GB Issue No. 316, 7 January 1937. Anglo-Italian Mediterranean Pact signed in Rome. —; 30; 11(6); 90; 663; 753.

GB Issue No. 318, 14 January 1937. Madrid buildings in ruins. Soldiers amuse themselves with fireworks. Evacuation goes on. —; 59; 6(4); 67; 693; 760.

GB Issue No. 328, 18 February 1937. Spanish Civil War drags on. Insurgents enter Malaga. (Followed by Britain Re-arms.) 7; 88; 5(4); 66; 710; 776.

GB Issue No. 332, 4 March 1937. Defence of Madrid still holds. (Followed by *Llandovery Castle* mined off the coast of Spain.) 6; 54; 9(6); 78; 722; 800.

GB Issue No. 339, 29 March 1937. British Prisoners of War in Spain. 6; 48; 10(9); 98; 733; 831. (Followed by Interview in Spanish trenches and capture of village near Madrid. —; 66; 10(10).)

GB Issue No. 350, 6 May 1937. Ruins of Guernica after air-raid in Spanish Civil War. 5; 52; 9(2); 98; 760; 858.

GB Issue No. 354, 20 May 1937. Basque children evacuated from Bilbao while fighting continues. (Replaced for Manchester and Liverpool by Whitweek procession. Replaced for Glasgow by Church of Scotland.) 7; 102; 4(2); 59; 799; 858.

GB Issue No. 356, 27 May 1937. Fighting in Spain while Basque children are evacuated. 6; 34; 10(3); 89; 776; 865. (Followed by Basque children arrive in England from Spain. —; 66; 10(4).)

GB Issue No. 358, 3 June 1937. British Prisoners of War in Spain and subsequent arrival in England after release. 44; 105; 7(7); 114; 753; 867.

GB Issue No. 359, 7 June 1937. Roving Camera Reports: French commercial airliner brought down by Spanish Insurgent planes. —; 18; 9(5b); 89; 729; 818.

GB Issue No. 361, 14 June 1937. Roving Camera Reports: Dancing in Bilbao during Civil War. —; 32; 9(5c); 80; 711; 791.

GB Issue No. 363, 21 June 1937. Basque Iron Belt falls at Bilbao. 6; 67; 11(4); 88; 763; 851.

GB Issue No. 364, 26 June 1937. Insurgents enter Bilbao. 8; 136; 8(7); 96; 751; 847.

GB Issue No. 368, 8 July 1937. Refugee ship from Santander stopped by warship. 5; 180; 8(6); 81; 738; 819.

GB Issue No. 376, 5 August 1937. Roving Camera Reports: Fighting on the Madrid Front. —; 40; 10(5a); 98; 663; 761.

GB Issue No. 380, 19 August 1937. Roving Camera Reports: Interview with the Captain of the bombed tanker *British Corporal*. —; 67; 9(6d); 101; 699; 800.

GB Issue No. 385, 5 September 1937. Roving Camera Reports: Franco's troops enter Santander. —; 31; 10(5d); 103; 698; 801.

GB Issue No. 389, 20 September 1937. Spanish destroyer and British tanker damaged in Insurgent air raid. 7; 49; 10(7); 91; 711; 802.

GB Issue No. 397, 18 October 1937. Spanish Non-Intervention Committee meets in London. 8; 34; 8(1); 99; 707; 806. (Followed by General Franco reviews 35,000 people at Burgos. —; 27; 8(2). Followed by comparisons in speech-making by Franco, Mussolini and Hitler. —; 17; 8(3). Followed by Mr Chamberlain speaks on Health. —; 121; 8(4).)

GB Issue No. 400, 28 October 1937. Spanish Insurgents enter Gijon. 7; 56; 8(2); 90; 719; 809.

GB Issue No. 401, 1 November 1937. Gijon refugees picked up by HMS *Southampton*. 8; 166; 9(8); 126; 624; 750.

GB Issue No. 402, 4 November 1937. Mussolini speaks on the 16th Anniversary of the Fascist March on Rome. 9; 58; 15(14); 109; 650; 759. (Followed by Anthony Eden speaking with 'We Will Not Be Dictated To' superimposed. —; 16; 15(15).)

GB Issue No. 409, 29 November 1937. Roving Camera Reports: Military engineers complete railway bridge at Salamanca. —; 35; 6(4b); 97; 722; 819.

GB Issue No. 417, 26 December 1937. Review of the Year: Foreign Affairs; Spanish Civil War. 5; 279; 5(4); 102; 897; 999.

GB Issue No. 419, 3 January 1938. Spanish Civil War centres upon Teruel. 8; 61; 9(7); 106; 684; 790.

GB Issue No. 423, 17 January 1938. Snow in different parts of the world including Franco's troops on snow-covered ground near Teruel. —; 30; 9(2b); 105; 693; 798.

GB Issue No. 428, 3 February 1938. Battle planes bring death in peace and war including Wellington Bomber and funeral at Tarragona of bomb victims. —; 41; 7(1e); 96; 792; 888.

GB Issue No. 431, 14 February 1938. Barcelona bombed by Franco, including damaged British ship. 10; 136; 10(9); 122; 687; 809.

GB Issue No. 442, 24 March 1938. Roving Camera Reports: Barcelona in ruins after bombing. —; 32; 7(5a); 94; 678; 772.

GB Issue No. 444, 31 March 1938. Insurgents continue to advance on Aragon Front. 9; 72; 10(9); 112; 687; 799.

GB Issue No. 446, 7 April 1938. Roving Camera Reports: Insurgents batter their way through Catalonia. —; 47; 9(5a); 116; 702; 818.

GB Issue No. 449, 18 April 1938. Roving Camera Reports: Recruits parade in Barcelona. —; 44; 8(3c); 94; 716; 810.

GB Issue No. 450, 21 April 1938. Anglo-Italian Pact signed in Rome. 7; 62; 8(5); 109; 716; 825.

GB Issue No. 457, 16 May 1938. The League discusses Abyssinia, Spain and China. 6; 56; 8(2); 104; 699; 803.

GB Issue No. 507, 7 November 1938. Rescued crew of the sunk *Cantabria* at Cromer. 7; 98; 9(3); 105; 718; 823.

GB Issue No. 516, 8 December 1938. Madrid bombed with bread. 8; 56; 10(6); 98; 680; 778.

GB Issue No. 517, 12 December 1938. International Brigade returns from Spain. 9; 68; 5(1); 100; 667; 767. (Followed by Roosevelt at sick children's hospital. 8; 64; 5(2). And at the end of the release The Defence of France No. 4. —; 337; 5(5).)

GB Issue No. 522, 29 December 1938. Review of the Year: Foreign Affairs. 8; 253; 5(1); 101; 859; 960.

GB Issue No. 526, 12 January 1939. Roving Camera Reports: International Brigade Memorial Service at Earl's Court. —; 30; 6(3c); 86; 770; 856. (Followed by Chamberlain leaves for Rome talks.)

GB Issue No. 528, 19 January 1939. Insurgents advance towards Barcelona. 7; 121; 8(1); 83; 684; 767.

GB Issue No. 529, 23 January 1939. Franco's troops take Tarragona. 5; 55; 7(2); 106; 690; 796.

GB Issue No. 530, 26 January 1939. Franco reaches Barcelona. 8; 55; 8(2); 107; 659; 766.

GB Issue No. 531, 30 January 1939. The Fall of Barcelona. 6; 83; 7(7); 89; 672; 761.

GB Issue No. 532, 2 February 1939. Franco's troops enter Barcelona. Spanish refugees at French frontier. 8; 115; 5(2); 79; 694; 773.

GB Issue No. 534, 9 February 1939. Refugees retreat from Barcelona. 8; 91; 8(5); 100; 675; 775.

GB Issue No. 535, 13 February 1939. Roving Camera Reports: Franco's troops reach the French frontier. —; 31; 6(5a); 106; 718; 824.

GB Issue No. 536, 16 February 1939. Spanish troops repatriated to Franco. HMS *Devonshire* rescues refugees. 7; 55; 8(3); 98; 694; 792.

GB Issue No. 539, 27 February 1939. Roving Camera Reports: General Franco reviews troops. Franco aboard warship. —; 40; 6(5a); 96; 714; 810.

GB Issue No. 540, 2 March 1939. Review of the Spanish Civil War. 7; 199; 8(8); 97; 765; 862.

GB Issue No. 548, 30 March 1939. Madrid surrenders. 7; 57; 12(1); 88; 656; 744.

GB Issue No. 549, 3 April 1939. Franco troops enter Madrid. 16; 193; 6(1); 125; 689; 814.

Gaumont Graphic

The list below cites a selection of the Gaumont Graphic issues relating to Spain during the years when the newsreel was in existence, i.e. from 1910 to 1933. It gives the issue number, date of release, library number and the title of the story

GG Issue No. 684, 8 October 1917. (1768) Barcelona authorities prepare for trouble.

GG Issue No. 1054, 21 April 1921. (4663) Spanish troops encamped at Sidi Dais, Morocco.

GG Issue No. 1099, 30 September 1921. (5115) Spanish troops in Morocco.

GG Issue No. 1304, 8 September 1923. (7009) Revolution in Spain.

GG Issue No. 2095, 20 May 1931. (17231) Spain: New Republic.

British Paramount News

The list below cites all the British Paramount News issues relating to the Spanish Civil War. It also cites a selection of the issues relating to Spain in the years before the Civil War. It gives the issue number, date of release, title of the story and a brief summary of the story relating to Spain. The figures which follow give the library number of the story and the number of the stories in the whole release, with the position of the story on Spain in brackets.

BP Issue No. 14, 16 April 1931. Nation votes for Republic on polling day as King Alfonso abdicates: Madrid. First pictures from Spain. 88.

BP Issue No. 16, 23 April 1931. Alfonso in England: London. King Alfonso arrives. First pictures. 99.

BP Issue No. 481, 7 October 1935. War. Italians invade Abyssinia. 4652.

BP Issue No. 496, 28 November 1935. Fall of Makale: First pictures of Italian entry into town. 4782.

BP Issue No. 520, 20 February 1936. Spain holds election: 3 killed, scores injured. After brisk voting scenes, polling gives parties of the left a clear majority. 4948.

BP Issue No. 540, 30 April 1936. Fete Spanish President: Seville welcomes nation's new head. Senor Barrio accompanies Catalonian President to bullfight. 5110.

BP Issue No. 553, 15 June 1936. Bees rout rheumatics: Madrid. Five stings and you're cured. Spanish professor demonstrates treatment which claims amazing results. 5219.

BP Issue No. 568, 6 August 1936. Spain. Latest war pictures: Government and rebel forces prepare for decisive battle. Fighting on all fronts of civil war. 5310; 3(3).

BP Issue No. 569, 10 August 1936. Spanish War still raging: Rebels bombard Toledo. Government rush 5-day recruits into front line to stem advance on Madrid. 5318; 5(4).

BP Issue No. 571, 17 August 1936. Madrid holds out: Spanish Civil War nears climax. 5351; 3(3).

BP Issue No. 572, 20 August 1936. Rebel attacks converge: Spain. Government armies menaced on three sides. Insurgents take Tolosa, only 15 miles from San Sebastian. 5355; 5(3).

BP Issue No. 573, 24 August 1936. Spanish War deadlock: Victory still eludes both armies. San Sebastian shelled. General Franco in Burgos. Government take Pina. 5359; 5(2).

BP Issue No. 575, 31 August 1936. Moors aid rebels: Spain. Coloured troops reinforce northern army. Graphic pictures of attacks near San Sebastian. 5371; 6(5).

BP Issue No. 577, 7 September 1936. Rebels take Irun: Spain. Terror struck inhabitants flee blazing city. M. Rosenberg, Soviet's first Ambassador to Spain, arrives in Madrid. 5385; 6(6).

BP Issue No. 581, 21 September 1936. Alcazar blown up: Toledo's historic citadel mined. Survivors of fortress garrison still hold out after 63 days' siege. 5414; 5(4).

BP Issue No. 582, 24 September 1936. Alcazar mined. First pictures: British Paramount News brings to you the most dramatic war pictures ever taken. The blowing up of Toledo fortress. 5420; 5(5).

BP Issue No. 585, 5 October 1936. Alcazar relieved: First pictures of survivors as Insurgents take city. General Franco now proclaimed 'Head of Government'. 5457; 6(5).

BP Issue No. 592, 29 October 1936. Madrid cut off. Capture imminent: Spain. Government chances dwindle as General Franco's troops steadily advance. 5498; 6(2).

BP Issue No. 593, 2 November 1936. Scots bombed in Spain. Red Cross Unit hit: Madrid. Exclusive first pictures show Scots Ambulance Unit at work on last trip before they were bombed. 5536; 7(4).

BP Issue No. 597, 16 November 1936. Where Stands Peace? Nations arm and ally: Vienna. Count Ciano visits Austria. Warsaw. Marshal Ritz-Smigly honoured on receiving baton. Moscow. Soviet Union celebrates 19th anniversary with huge military parades. 5570; 6(5).

BP Issue No. 598, 19 November 1936. Outer Madrid a battlefield. Hot fighting: Fierce fighting in city's outskirts as Franco's troops attack Spain's capital. 5573; 7(2).

BP Issue No. 599, 23 November 1936. Premier takes stock, finds Britain best: Mr Baldwin contrasts Britain's improved trade and freedom with conditions abroad. 5583.

BP Issue No. 600, 26 November 1936. Fascists–Red Crisis. Soviets fete Spaniards: Moscow. Spanish delegates to Communist United Front welcomed by Soviet leaders. 5592; 6(5). (Also News Flashes From Everywhere: Valencia. Iron foundries at full pressure making shells for Spanish Government. 5590; 6(3).)

BP Issue No. 603, 7 December 1936. The King: Crisis. (This story had to be withdrawn.)

BP Issue No. 605, 14 December 1936. Refugees fill Valencia as Cortes meets: Valencia. Spanish Parliament meets for first session in southern town after leaving Madrid. Cabinet rejects Anglo-French offer to mediate. Refugees pour into city from capital. (Excepting Ireland.) 5651; 4(1).

BP Issue No. 609, 28 December 1936. Review of Year 1936. 5713.

BP Issue No. 610, 31 December 1936. Embassy quits Madrid. Raids terrify city: Sensational exclusive pictures of Madrid's worst air-raid, secured as bombs showered on city. 5721; 5(5).

BP Issue No. 612, 7 January 1937. News Flashes From Everywhere: Rome. Britain and Italy sign Mediterranean Pact. 5731; 6 (3b).

BP Issue No. 613, 11 January 1937. News Flashes From Everywhere: Santiago. Historic Spanish city inaugurates a Holy Year while Civil War continues. 5753; 5(3a).

BP Issue No. 616, 21 January 1937. US Ban too late to catch Spanish cargo: New York. Spanish ship loaded with arms clears customs and races free as US ban on export becomes law. 5786; 7(1).

BP Issue No. 618, 28 January 1937. Madrid raided as powers ban intervention: Madrid, Malaga and Oviedo. Germany, Italy and Russia agree with France and Britain to ban intervention. Whilst in Spain Madrid reels under worst air-raid yet. 5814; 6(6).

BP Issue No. 625, 22 February 1937. French navy stage battle off Riviera: Nice. Mediterranean squadron goes to battle practice as powers put non-intervention in Spain agreement into force. 5881; 5(1).

BP Issue No. 626, 25 February 1937. Six Power ban on Spanish Intervention: Non-Intervention Committee appoint 1,000 inspectors as cordon round Spain to stop arms and volunteers. 5893; 6(5).

BP Issue No. 628, 4 March 1937. British liner mined. Madrid defies Franco: Port Vendres. Mined *Llandovery Castle* reaches harbour. Madrid. Government forces hold out against fierce attacks and aerial bombardment. 5916; 6(6).

BP Issue No. 629, 8 March 1937. Franco greets Hitler's envoy. Pact rumoured: Salamanca. Newly appointed German Ambassador is welcomed by insurgent leader in Spain. 5918; 6(1).

BP Issue No. 630, 11 March 1937. News Flashes From Everywhere: Off New York. Arms for Spain intercepted. 5928; 5(3a).

Library No. 5946. Not issued. International Brigades in Spain.

Library No. 5990. Not issued. Volunteers for Spain arrested by French boat.

BP Issue No. 636, 1 April 1937. Spain keeps Holy Week despite war: Seville. Elaborate procession marks Holy Week. Under Franco, populace revert to splendour of old times. 5992; 6(1).

BP Issue No. 650, 20 May 1937. 6,000 children evacuated from stricken Bilbao: La Rochelle, France. First batch arrive in France. Humane work of Great Powers saves kiddies from horrors of siege and war. 6232; 3(2).

BP Issue No. 652, 27 May 1937. Basque children arrive in England. 6237; 4(1).

BP Issue No. 660, 24 June 1937. British Paramount News Special. Bilbao falls. First Pictures: Bilbao, Spain. Vivid pictures show final stages of attack and fall of beleaguered city as terrified refugees stream out. 6448; 4(4).

BP Issue No. 672, 5 August 1937. News Flashes From Everywhere: Near Marseilles. Spanish ships shelled by two unidentified submarines. 6575; 5(3b).

BP Issue No. 681, 6 September 1937. Ships bombed in Gijon air-raid reach Britain: Falmouth. Bombed Spanish destroyer and British *Hilda Moller* arrive for repairs as Cabinet decides to take action. 6678; 6(4).

BP Issue No. 684, 16 September 1937. Bombs enrage French as Piracy Conference sits: Paris. Bombs wreck headquarters of French industrial organisations. Nyon Anti-Piracy Conference plans Mediterranean patrols. 6703; 6(5).

BP Issue No. 685, 20 September 1937. Piracy patrol starts before Nyon ink dries: Sheerness. Nyon. Powers sign Nyon Mediterranean anti-submarine patrol agreement and Britain sends off more destroyers to do her bit. 6709; 8(4).

BP Issue No. 693, 18 October 1937. World fences for peace as Franco acts: Burgos. General Franco holds monster youth parade at his headquarters and assures world Spain will remain Spanish. 6795; 7(5). (Also The Prime Minister Explains: In his first talk since taking office Mr Chamberlain outlines the ideals behind the National Fitness Campaign. 6794; 7(4).)

BP Issue No. 696, 28 October 1937. News Flashes From Everywhere: Gijon. Last Government stronghold in Northern Spain falls to Franco. 6846; 5(3c).

BP Issue No. 714, 30 December 1937. Review of the Year 1937. 7065.

BP Issue No. 716, 6 January 1938. 500,000 Spaniards locked in death fight for Teruel: Aragon. Is it the turning point? Both sides stake all in bloodiest battle of the Civil War. 7080; 5(2).

BP Issue No. 719, 17 January 1938. Rome bloc signs recognition of General Franco: Budapest. After diplomatic hunting party in the snow, Austria and Hungary get together and sign declaration at Italy's invitation. 7108; 6(1).

BP Issue No. 722, 27 January 1938. 138 Killed by Franco Planes' Lightning Raid: Barcelona. The raid which made Europe gasp. 90 seconds of death and destruction. 7146; 7(6).

BP Issue No. 730, 24 February 1938. Mr Attlee expresses the views of the opposition parties: Mr Attlee gives his opinion on the resignation of Foreign Secretary, Anthony Eden, after disagreement with Mr Chamberlain. 7230.

BP Issue No. 738, 24 March 1938. Franco push. End near?: Belchite. Insurgents drive through towards Barcelona. Government forces fall back before fiercest onslaught of the year. 7312; 5(1).

BP Issue No. 740, 31 March 1938. Barcelona faces defeat; Aragon. Franco thrusts towards key defences of Government stronghold. 7336; 6(6).

BP Issue No. 742, 7 April 1938. News in Flashes: Luchon. Spanish Refugees pour into France. 7354; 4(2c).

BP Issue No. 743, 11 April 1938. Lerida. Now victory?: Catalonia. Graphic pictures of final stages as Franco's forces race onwards with victory beckoning. 7369: 6(5).

BP Issue No. 746, 21 April 1938. Britain and Italy sign pact: Rome. Britain and Italy sign pact which removes all past causes of trouble and promises new era of peace for Europe. 7400; 6(2).

BP Issue No. 760, 9 June 1938. 400 killed in air-raid: Granollers. Franco planes driven off from Barcelona, rain death on open market town. 7545; 6(2).

BP Issue No. 763, 20 June 1938. The Fall of Castellon: Spain. Graphic pictures as Franco's men enter Government key town on Mediterranean after heavy fighting. 7571; 5(2).

BP Issue No. 785, 5 September 1938. Spain 'swaps' prisoners: Hendaye. 100 war prisoners march into France in first exchange of war prisoners arranged by British Commission. 7777; 6(2).

BP Issue No. 799, 24 October 1938. Duce calls troops home: Naples. 10,000 troops return home after fighting in Spanish Insurgent Army. They are the first batch to be withdrawn under non-intervention agreement. 7884; 6(1).

BP Issue No. 803, 7 November 1938. Spanish 'war' in North Sea: Cromer. Captain and survivors of *Cantabria* land after their ship was sunk by Franco Q-ship. 7916; 5(2).

BP Issue No. 806, 17 November 1938. News in Flashes: Pyrenees. French volunteers from Spain. 7940; 5(3a).

BP Issue No. 807, 21 November 1938. News in Flashes: Rome. Lord Perth and Count Ciano sign declaration which puts Anglo-Italian Pact into force. 7948; 5(3b).

BP Issue No. 808, 24 November 1938. News in Flashes: Barcelona. International Brigade inspected by Premier Negrin before disbandment. 7955; 5(3c).

BP Issue No. 818, 29 December 1938. Review of 1938. 8077.

BP Issue No. 823, 16 January 1939. Franco's big thrust menaces Barcelona: Catalonia. Spectacular success attends insurgent offensive towards Spanish Government headquarters. 8121; 6(5). (Followed by Duce tells Premier Italy needs peace: Rome. Mr Chamberlain and Foreign Minister Lord Halifax watch display after talks with Duce. 8122; 6(6).)

BP Issue No. 825, 23 January 1939. Franco's onslaught nears Barcelona: Catalonia. Graphic pictures of Spanish Insurgent offensive which bids fair to end Civil War. 8152; 5(2).

BP Issue No. 828, 2 February 1939. Starving refugees pour into France: French frontier. Dramatic pictures show terrible plight of Catalonian refugees as they escape through snow to safety. 8193; 6(6).

BP Issue No. 830, 9 February 1939. France opens frontier to defeated army: Pyrenees. Catalan troops, fleeing before Franco, find safety by surrendering to French. 8205; 5(2).

BP Issue No. 831, 13 February 1939. Franco troops reach French frontier. Victorious troops reach French frontier as rest of Catalan army escapes into France. 8221; 8(8).

BP Issue No. 832, 16 February 1939. Franco mops up before attacking Madrid:

Figueras. Victorious troops take over burning town on heels of fleeing Government troops. 8232; 6(2).

BP Issue No. 833, 20 February 1939. Artists aid refugees by painting hoardings: London. Well known artists turn London streets into studios for vivid publicity scheme for Spanish refugee fund. 8253; 6(2).

BP Issue No. 834, 23 February 1939. Refugees set France difficult problem: Argelès. Thousands of destitute Spanish war refugees live in squalor shanty town on beach. 8271; 7(4).

BP Issue No. 835, 27 February 1939. Victory crowns Franco. Recognition next?: Barcelona. As admiral, Franco reviews his fleet after triumphant entry into Barcelona. 8279; 6(2).

BP Issue No. 845, 3 April 1939. Madrid welcomes end of long siege: Madrid. First authentic pictures of Franco's troops entering city after surrender. 8391; 6(2).

BP Issue No. 858, 18 May 1939. Franco's farewell to foreign pilots: Madrid. Spanish dictator reviews German and Italian pilots on eve of Madrid victory march. 8542; 7(1). (Also Madrid's famished children get relief: Madrid. 100,000 kiddies between ages of 3 and 10 have first meal under public relief system. 8548; 7(5).)

BP Issue No. 860, 25 May 1939. News in Flashes: Madrid. 150,000 troops march past Franco in Victory Parade. 8567; 4(3a).

BP Issue No. 870, 29 June 1939. News in Flashes: Spain. General Franco arrives to inspect naval dockyard. 8633; 5(3a).

BP Issue No. 876, 20 July 1939. News in Flashes: Spain. Count Ciano visits Franco. 8703; 5(3c).

BP Issue No. 881, 8 August 1939. News in Flashes: Madrid. France returns £8 million in gold to Franco. 8751; 5(3a).

BP Issue No. 884, 17 August 1939. News in Flashes: Madrid. Mass christening of 200 babies. 8773; 6(3c).

BP Issue No. 888, 31 August 1939. The Crisis Hour by Hour: Spain. US Prisoners released. 8816; 3(3c).

Universal News

The list below cites all the Universal Talking News issues relating to the Spanish Civil War. It also cites a selection of the issues relating to Spain for the period immediately preceding the Civil War. It gives the issue number, date of release and the title of the story relating to Spain. The figures appended (in feet) reveal the following statistics:

a. The amount of titles footage to the story on Spain.
b. The amount of film used in the actual story on Spain.
c. The number of stories in the whole newsreel issue with the position of the story on Spain in brackets.
d. The amount of film used on the whole newsreel issue including titles and picture footage on all stories.

UN Issue No. 605, 27 April 1936. Bloodless Bullfighting. 15; 101; 6(1); 888.

UN Issue No. 607, 4 May 1936. Spain celebrates. 15; 69; 6(3); 836.

UN Issue No. 611, 18 May 1936. News in Brief: New Spanish President. —; 48; 5(3a); 858.

UN Issue No. 630, 23 July 1936. Civil War in Spain. 16; 58; 7(6); 817.

UN Issue No. 632, 30 July 1936. News in Brief: Rebellion in Spain. —; 79; 6(4d); 823.

UN Issue No. 634, 6 August 1936. In Spain Today. 18; 56; 5(3); 802.

UN Issue No. 635, 10 August 1936. News in Brief: Refugees in Gibraltar. —; 39 6(2d); 836.

UN Issue No. 636, 13 August 1936. News in Brief: War in Spain. —; 62; 6(5a); 827.

UN Issue No. 639, 24 August 1936. Spanish Civil War. 18; 145; 5(1); 822.

UN Issue No. 640, 27 August 1936. News in Brief: Medical Unit for Spain. —; 47; 6(3a); 811.

UN Issue No. 641, 31 August 1936. Spanish Affairs. 13; 152; 5(1); 826.

UN Issue No. 643, 7 September 1936. Troubled Spain. 16; 140; 7(2); 878.

UN Issue No. 647, 21 September 1936. The Spanish Civil War. 17; 153; 6(1); 834.

UN Issue No. 651, 5 October 1936. News in Brief: Scenes around Madrid. —; 43; 6(3c); 828.

UN Issue No. 655, 19 October 1936. Spanish Prison Ship. 11; 91; 6(3); 818.

UN Issue No. 661, 9 November 1936. News in Brief: Spain. Advance on Madrid. —; 46; 7(5c); 815.

UN Issue No. 666, 26 November 1936. Interview with Mr R. H. Rose, lately returned from the Spanish Civil War. 16; 162; 7(3); 795.

UN Issue No. 667, 30 November 1936. Spain. South of Madrid and Valencia. 11; 78; 7(3); 813.

UN Issue No. 675, 28 December 1936. Review of the Year.

UN Issue No. 676, 31 December 1936. News in Brief: Spain. Gavin, Aragon. —; 34; 6(3e); 822.

UN Issue No. 678, 7 January 1937. Anglo-Italian Agreement. 15; 64; 7(6); 826.

UN Issue No. 682, 21 January 1937. News in Brief: Madrid. Damage after bombardments. —; 39; 6(5d); 802.

UN Issue No. 696, 11 March 1937. News in Brief: At sea. *Mar Cantabrico*. —; 40; 4(3g); 812.

UN Issue No. 718, 27 May 1937. Basque children arrive in England. 18; 175; 5(1); 848.

UN Issue No. 746, 2 September 1937. News in Brief: Spain. The *Gironde* aground. —; 25; 7(2e); 854.

UN Issue No. 751, 20 September 1937. RAF Piracy squadron leaves. 7; 67; 9(5); 838.

UN Issue No. 752, 23 September 1937. Spanish War. Troops enter Santander. 7; 99; 8(1); 868.

UN Issue No. 757, 11 October 1937. Attack on HMS *Basilisk* by submarine. 7; 86; 7(4); 913.

UN Issue No. 765, 8 November 1937. Mussolini pays tribute to fallen heroes. 7; 107; 9(3); 884.

UN Issue No. 780, 30 December 1937. Review of the Year.

UN Issue No. 792, 10 February 1938. Trailer for R. E. Jeffrey's visit to Spain.—; 45; 10(10); 835.

UN Issue No. 793, 14 February 1938. R. E. Jeffrey returns from Spain. 7; 368; 4(4); 883.

UN Issue No. 794, 17 February 1938. R. E. Jeffrey on the Spanish Front. 7; 473; 4(4); 917.

UN Issue No. 796, 24 February 1938. The international situation. Mr Eden resigns. 7; 230; 5(5); 859.

UN Issue No. 808, 7 April 1938. Spanish refugees in France. 7; 94; 8(8); 867.

UN Issue No. 839, 25 July 1938. Attack on Sagunto. 7; 72; 4(2); 866.

UN Issue No. 846, 18 August 1938. The World today. 7; 259; 4(4); 826.

UN Issue No. 866, 27 October 1938. Burgos celebrates. 10; 90; 5(2); 830.

UN Issue No. 869, 7 November 1938. Spanish ship bombed off Norfolk. 12; 245; 5(1); 859.

UN Issue No. 884, 29 December 1938. Review of the Year.

UN Issue No. 887, 9 January 1939. War in Spain. Catalan Front. 8; 85; 7(6); 763.

UN Issue No. 888, 12 January 1939. News in Brief: Memorial to International Brigade. —; 35; 6(3c); 864.

UN Issue No. 893, 30 January 1939. Fall of Barcelona. 8; 51; 7(6); 847.

UN Issue No. 894, 2 February 1939. Spanish refugees in France. 9; 152; 6(4); 889.

UN Issue No. 896, 9 February 1939. Catalan army in France. 10; 126; 6(3); 849.

UN Issue No. 910, 30 March 1939. News in Brief: M Petain in Spain. —; 43; 7(3d); 832.

UN Issue No. 914, 13 April 1939. Madrid in Peace. 8; 75; 4(3); 865.

British Movietone News

The list below cites all the British Movietone News issues relating to the Spanish Civil War. It also cites a selection of the issues relating to general events in the period before the Civil War. It gives the issue number, date of release and the title of the story. The figures which follow reveal the number of sections in the issue, with the position of the story in Spain in brackets.

BM Issue Vol. 2 No. 67A, 18 September 1930. The Foreign Secretary at Geneva.

BM Issue Vol. 2 No. 110, 13 July 1931. If the Nations of the World Could See and Speak to Each Other There Would Be No More War.

BM Issue Vol. 3 No. 139A, 4 February 1932. Arthur Henderson presides in Geneva.

BM Issue Vol. 6 No. 300A, 7 March 1935. Is there to be an armaments race?

BM Issue Vol. 8 No. 372A, 23 July 1936. Spain. Civil War follows riot in Spain. 5(4).

BM Issue Vol. 8 No. 373, 27 July 1936. Reports: First films from menaced Madrid. 4(2a).

BM Issue Vol. 8 No. 373A, 30 July 1936. Reports: New pictures from Spain's inferno. 4(1a).

BM Issue Vol. 8 No 374A, 6 August 1936. Spain. Deadlock in Civil War. 4(3).

BM Issue Vol. 8 No. 376A, 20 August 1936. Spain. Grim tide of battle sweeps country in bitter Civil War. 5(4).

BM Issue Vol. 8 No. 377, 24 August 1936. Reports: Behind the scenes in Spain. 5(1d).

BM Issue Vol. 8 No. 377A, 27 August 1936. Spain. Bloodshed continues as Civil War grows more desperate. 5(3).

BM Issue Vol. 8 No. 379A, 10 September 1936. Spain. Anti-Red advance is pushing refugees over into France. 5(2).

BM Issue Vol. 8 No. 380, 14 September 1936. Spain. Occupation of Huelva and Rio Tinto area and Rebel Leaders' talk. 4(2).

BM Issue Vol. 8 No. 380A, 17 September 1936. Spain. War by dynamite and refugees escape in German destroyers. 5(3).

BM Issue Vol. 8 No. 381, 21 September 1936. Spain. Fall of San Sebastian and grim story of Toledo Alcazar. 5(5).

BM Issue Vol. 8 No. 381A, 24 September 1936. Foreign Affairs, Geneva. France, Spain. 5(3).

BM Issue Vol. 8 No. 383, 5 October 1936. Spain. The relief of Toledo ends heroic episode of Civil War. 6(6).

BM Issue Vol. 8 No. 383A, 8 October 1936. Reports: Franco made Head of 'Rebel' State. 5(1a).

BM Issue Vol. 8 No. 384, 12 October 1936. Reports: On the Bilbao Front. 5(1b).

BM Issue Vol. 8 No. 387A, 5 November 1936. Spain. Madrid Government prepares to resist Franco's assault. 6(6).

BM Issue Vol. 8 No. 388, 9 November 1936. Reports: Spanish Civil War. Madrid entered. 5(1f).

BM Issue Vol. 8 No. 388A, 12 November 1936. Reports: Barricades in Madrid. 3(2a).

BM Issue Vol. 8 No 389, 16 November 1936. Reports: Spanish Ambassador arrives in Moscow. 6(1b).

BM Issue Vol. 8 No. 389A, 19 November 1936. Reports: The fight for Madrid. 5(1e).

BM Issue Vol. 8 No. 390, 23 November 1936. Reports: Spanish War by sea. 5(1b).

BM Issue Vol. 8 No. 391, 30 November 1936. Reports: Spain's Young Soldiers. 5(2c).

BM Issue Vol. 8 No. 392, 7 December 1936. Spain. Madrid is battered by shell and bomb as siege goes on. 6(1).

BM Issue Vol. 8 No. 394, 21 December 1936. Preparedness. Grim fate of Madrid brings home moral of air-raid danger. 5(1).

BM Issue Vol. 8 No. 395A, 31 December 1936. Leslie Mitchell looks around. Madrid.

BM Issue Vol. 8 No. 396, 4 January 1937. Reports: Spanish Christmas. 4(2b).

BM Issue Vol. 8 No. 396A, 7 January 1937. Concord. Britain and Italy sign the Mediterranean Agreement. 5(1).

BM Issue Vol. 8 No. 397A, 14 January 1937. Foreign Affairs. Spanish Civil War and its Complications. 5(2). (Preceded by Gas Respirators for all is timely answer to danger of air-raids.)

BM Issue Vol. 8 No. 399A, 28 January 1937. Reports: Spanish Stalemate. 5(1a).

BM Issue Vol. 8 No. 401A, 11 February 1937. Spain. The fall of Malaga marks new phase in the Spanish Civil War. 5(3).

BM Issue Vol. 8 No. 402A, 18 February 1937. Spain. First pictures after fall of Malaga tell cost of Civil War. 4(3).

BM Issue Vol. 8 No. 404A, 4 March 1937. Reports: The *Llandovery Castle*. 5(1b).

BM Issue Vol. 8 No. 405, 8 March 1937. Reports: Salamanca Ceremony. 4(1g).

BM Issue Vol. 8 No. 416A, 27 May 1937. Foreign News: Basque children reach England. 4(3c).

BM Issue Vol. 8 No. 417A, 3 June 1937. Spain. At Bilbao Front and grave incident of *The Deutschland*. 3(1).

BM Issue Vol. 9 No. 419, 14 June 1937. Reports: Behind the lines in Spain. 4(2e).

BM Issue Vol. 9 No. 419A, 17 June 1937. Reports: Bilbao refugees. 5(2b).

BM Issue Vol. 9 No. 420, 21 June 1937. Spain. General Franco's guns assault iron ring around Bilbao. 5(4).

BM Issue Vol. 9 No. 420A, 24 June 1937. Reports: Fall of Bilbao. 5(2a). (Followed by O'Duffy's men back from Spanish Civil War.)

BM Issue Vol. 9 No. 425, 26 July 1937. Reports: Madrid protects its statues. 5(2f).

BM Issue Vol. 9 No. 425A, 29 July 1937. Reports: Battle flares up around Madrid. 4(1a).

BM Issue Vol. 9 No. 426A, 5 August 1937. Reports: Recapture of Brunete. 5(2a).

BM Issue Vol. 9 No. 431, 6 September 1937. Reports: Santander is taken over. 5(2c).

BM Issue Vol. 9 No. 431A, 9 September 1937. Reports: Madrid today. 5(2b).

BM Issue Vol. 9 No. 437, 18 October 1937. Reports: 'Non-Intervention'. 5(2a).

BM Issue Vol. 9 No. 441A, 18 November 1937. Reports: General Franco reviews crack brigade. 5(2d).

BM Issue Vol. 9 No. 443, 29 November 1937. Reports: Franco's men build a rapid bridge. 5(2e).

BM Issue Vol. 9 No. 447A, 30 December 1937. Review of the Year.

BM Issue Vol. 9 No. 448A, 6 January 1938. Reports: In Madrid today. 4(2e).

BM Issue Vol. 9 No. 449A, 13 January 1938. Spain. Struggle for Teruel. 10(4).

BM Issue Vol. 9 No. 454, 14 February 1938. The Front Page: Horror in Barcelona. 4(1a).

BM Issue Vol. 9 No. 456, 28 February 1938. Personality Column: General Franco. 5(2c).

BM Issue Vol. 9 No. 456A, 3 March 1938. Front Page: Ruined Teruel re-captured. 4(1d).

BM Issue Vol. 9 No. 457A, 10 March 1938. News Pageant: Franco's naval loss. 13(3).

BM Issue Vol. 9 No. 458A, 17 March 1938. News Pageant: Franco's sweep towards coast. 2(1d).

BM Issue Vol. 9 No. 459A, 24 March 1938. At home and abroad: Barcelona air-raid havoc. 4(2a).

BM Issue Vol. 9 No. 460A, 31 March 1938. At home and abroad: Franco's advance on Barcelona. 3(1f).

BM Issue Vol. 9 No. 461A, 7 April 1938. At home and abroad: Franco before Lerida and Spanish refugees flee to France. 4(2d).

BM Issue Vol. 10 No. 471A, 16 June 1938. General Franco reaches Mediterranean. 11(1).

BM Issue Vol. 10 No. 472A, 23 June 1938. Spanish Insurgent troops occupy Castellon. 11(6).

BM Issue Vol. 10 No. 488A, 13 October 1938. General Franco reviews Italians. 14(1).

BM Issue Vol. 10 No. 489A, 20 October 1938. Italian volunteers leave Spain. 13(12).

BM Issue Vol. 10 No. 492, 7 November 1938. Spanish merchantman sunk in the North Sea. 10(2).

BM Issue Vol. 10 No. 494, 21 November 1938. Scenes on the Ebro Front. 10(10).

BM Issue Vol. 10 No. 496A, 8 December 1938. Madrid bombarded with bread. 12(1).

BM Issue Vol. 10 No. 497, 12 December 1938. International Brigade at the Cenotaph. 11(6).

BM Issue Vol. 10 No. 501A, 12 January 1939. Franco's advance in Catalonia. 12(4).

BM Issue Vol. 10 No. 502, 16 January 1939. Franco's push continues unabated. 11(2).

BM Issue Vol. 10 No. 502A, 19 January 1939. Franco's advance on Barcelona. 11(10).

BM Issue Vol. 10 No. 503, 23 January 1939. Fall of Tarragona. 11(1).

BM Issue Vol. 10 No. 504, 30 January 1939. The Fall of Barcelona. 10(1).

BM Issue Vol. 10 No. 505, 6 February 1939. French troops man Spanish border. 12(9).

BM Issue Vol. 10 No. 505A, 9 February 1939. Spanish Government troops pour into France. 10(4).

BM Issue Vol. 10 No. 506, 13 February 1939. Franco's troops at French frontier. 13(6).

BM Issue Vol. 10 No. 506A, 16 February 1939. Spanish national prisoners repatriated. 12(6).

BM Issue Vol. 10 No. 507, 20 February 1939. Leon Berard prepares to leave for Spain. 10(2).

BM Issue Vol. 10 No. 508, 27 February 1939. General Franco's victory parade. 10(3).

BM Issue Vol. 10 No. 508A, 2 March 1939. Leon Berard returns to Paris and ex-President Azana leaves Paris. 13(2).

BM Issue Vol. 10 No. 512A, 30 March 1939. Marshal Petain in Burgos as Madrid falls. 16(4).

BM Issue Vol. 10 No. 513, 3 April 1939. Fifth column celebrates as Madrid falls. 9(7).

BM Issue Vol. 11 No. 527A, 13 July 1939. Pamplona bull fight once again. 10(9).

Pathé Gazette

The list below cites all the Pathé issues relating to the Spanish Civil War. It gives the issue number, date of release and the title of the story relating to Spain. The figures which follow reveal the number of sections in the issue, with the position of the story on Spain in brackets, and the length (in feet) of the story on Spain.

PG Issue No. 36/62, 3 August 1936. Spanish Rebellion. Latest pictures. 6(1); 110.

PG Issue No. 36/69, 27 August 1936. Stricken Spain. Latest war pictures. 4(2); 124.

PG Issue No. 36/71, 3 September 1936. Troubled Spain. Fierce fighting near the Portuguese border. 4(1); 132.

PG Issue No. 36/72, 7 September 1936. News in a Nutshell: Spanish Civil War. Fall of Irun. 3(3a); 42.

PG Issue No. 36/73, 10 September 1936. Irun occupied. Vivid pictures of Spanish Civil War. 6(2); 209.

PG Issue No. 36/75, 17 September 1936. News in a Nutshell: Spanish War scenes. 3(3i); 73.

PG Issue No. 36/77, 24 September 1936. Near Madrid. With the Government forces. 4(3); 70.

PG Issue No. 36/81, 8 October 1936. News in a Nutshell: Scenes in Barcelona. 2(2e); 50.

PG Issue No. 36/82, 12 October 1936. News in a Nutshell: Scenes in Spain. 4(3f); 28.

PG Issue No. 36/88, 2 November 1936. Oviedo relieved. General Franco's troops raise siege. 5(1); 80.

PG Issue No. 36/90, 9 November 1936. News in a Nutshell: Scenes in Madrid. 4(4d); 24.

PG Issue No. 36/92, 16 November 1936. The War in Spain. With the Government forces. 3(2); 102.

PG Issue No. 36/93, 19 November 1936. Destructive war in Spain. 4(2); 51. And Moscow's demonstration in support of the Spanish Government. 4(3); 50.

PG Issue No. 36/94, 23 November 1936. Russian provisions for Spain. 4(4d); 55.

PG Issue No. 36/96, 30 November 1936. News in a Nutshell: News from Spain. Valencia and Barcelona. 4(4g); 72.

PG Issue No. 36/98, 7 December 1936. News in a Nutshell: Scenes near Barcelona. 3(3g); 37.

PG Issue No. 37/1, 4 January 1937. News in a Nutshell: Scenes in Spain. 4(3d); 82.

PG Issue No. 37/2, 7 January 1937. News in a Nutshell: Signing Mediterranean Pact. 3(3a); 63.

PG Issue No. 37/3, 11 January 1937. News in a Nutshell: The War in Spain. 2(2c); 87.

PG Issue No. 37/5, 18 January 1937. News in a Nutshell: Food for Spanish Refugees. 7(7b); 93. And Madrid war damage. 7(7e); 71.

PG Issue No. 37/6, 21 January 1937. News in a Nutshell: British Embassy bombed in Madrid. 4(4a); 61. And U.S. Planes for Spain. 4(4f); 35.

PG Issue No. 37/7, 23 January 1937. Hill of the Angels. With Franco's troops near Madrid. 2(1); 123.

PG Issue No. 37/9, 1 February 1937. The advance on Madrid with General Franco's forces. 4(2); 128.

PG Issue No. 37/11, 8 February 1937. News in a Nutshell: Scenes in Spain. 4(4g); 91.

PG Issue No. 37/12, 11 February 1937. In the firing line in Madrid. 4(3); 92.

PG Issue No. 37/13, 15 February 1937. Madrid in flames. Destruction comes from the air. 5(5); 230.

PG Issue No. 37/20, 11 March 1937. News in a Nutshell: The *Mar Cantabrico* fired in the Bay of Biscay. 2(2g); 35.

PG Issue No. 37/25, 30 March 1937. News in a Nutshell: Spanish Refugees. 3(3h); 40.

PG Issue No. 37/30, 15 April 1937. News in a Nutshell: HMS *Hood* off northern Spain. 3(3c); 21.

PG Issue No. 37/42, 27 May 1937. Tragedy of Civil War. Basque children arrive in England. 4(2); 176.

PG Issue No. 37/44, 3 June 1937. News in a Nutshell: German battleship *Deutschland*. 3(2e); 27.

PG Issue No. 37/65, 16 August 1937. Breaking the blockade off northern Spain. 10(1); 122.

PG Issue No. 37/71, 6 September 1937. British destroyers leave for Spain. 9(1); 66.

PG Issue No. 37/72, 9 September 1937. War. With Franco's troops in northern Spain. 12(1); 86.

PG Issue No. 37/73, 13 September 1937. Franco's drive on Gijon. 9(2); 110.

PG Issue No. 37/75, 20 September 1937. Anti-Piracy Patrol. 11(1); 102.

PG Issue No. 37/91, 15 November 1937. Fighters in a foreign land. Italy honours her war dead. 9(3); 114.

PG Issue No. 37/94, 25 November 1937. On the Aragon Front. 13(6); 40.

PG Issue No. 38/1, 3 January 1938. Rebuilding the bridge across Nervion River at Bilbao. 13(6); 61.

PG Issue No. 38/4, 13 January 1938. Spanish War. With General Franco. 12(10); 85.

PG Issue No. 38/7, 24 January 1938. Scenes of fighting at Teruel. 9(8); 76.

PG Issue No. 38/13, 14 February 1938. British ships bombed in Mediterranean. 10(7); 49.

PG Issue No. 38/16, 24 February 1938. Struggle for Teruel in Spain. 10(8); 60.

PG Issue No. 38/20, 10 March 1938. Barcelona. Death rains from the sky. 11(9); 98.

PG Issue No. 38/21, 14 March 1938. Barcelona again. 9(2); 102.

PG Issue No. 38/24, 24 March 1938. Barcelona. Another terrific air-raid. 11(3); 31. And British ship bombed in Tarragona. 11(6); 54.

PG Issue No. 38/28, 7 April 1938. Franco's advance. Spanish Government's preparations. 10(1); 86. And Spanish refugees in France. 10(6); 109.

PG Issue No. 38/34, 28 April 1938. Three Spanish towns. 12(3); 99.

PG Issue No. 38/52, 30 June 1938. Spanish Civil War. Alicante and Barcelona. 10(3); 134.

PG Issue No. 38/56, 14 July 1938. Castellon rejoices. Spain. 9(5); 73.

PG Issue No. 38/66, 18 August 1938. On the Teruel Front. Spain. 12(4); 48.

PG Issue No. 38/81, 10 October 1938. When will Peace come? Spain and China. 8(2); 147.

PG Issue No. 38/84, 20 October 1938. International Brigade. Paris. 9(6); 30.

PG Issue No. 38/85, 24 October 1938. Italian volunteers return home. 9(6); 72.

PG Issue No. 38/89, 7 November 1938. Spanish ship attacked in North Sea. 9(1); 116.

PG Issue No. 38/104, 29 December 1938. Review of the Year. Spanish Civil War. Barcelona.

PG Issue No. 39/4, 12 January 1939. Franco's big drive. 13(3); 88.

PG Issue No. 39/8, 26 January 1939. Attack on Barcelona. 13(2); 63.

PG Issue No. 39/10, 2 February 1939. Spanish refugees in France. 11(1); 102.

PG Issue No. 39/11, 6 February 1939. Spanish refugees struggle to safety. 10(1); 86.

PG Issue No. 39/12, 9 February 1939. Spanish refugees on the French frontier. 16(11); 40.

PG Issue No. 39/13, 13 February 1939. Catalonian army enters France. 10(3); 107. And Nationalist flag hoisted on French frontier. 10(4); 82.

PG Issue No. 39/14, 16 February 1939. The tragedy of Spain. 10(1); 113.

PG Issue No. 39/17, 27 February 1939. General Franco in Barcelona. 10(4); 174.

PG Issue No. 39/19, 6 March 1939. Spanish refugees hospital ship. Marseilles. 12(6); 50.

PG Issue No. 39/34, 27 April 1939. Palm Sunday in Madrid. 12(10); 80.

PG Issue No. 39/42, 25 May 1939. Victory parade in Madrid. 9(3); 40.

PG Issue No. 39/66, 17 August 1939. Gold in Madrid. 9(6); 63.

Bibliography

1. Contemporary Published Materials

BOOKS

Atholl, Katherine, Duchess of, *Searchlight on Spain*, Harmondsworth 1938.
Bardèche, Maurice, and Brasillach, Robert, *The History of Motion Pictures*, London 1938.
Bennett, Colin Noel, *The Handbook of Kinematography*, London 1913.
Borkenau, Franz, *The Spanish Cockpit*, London 1937.
Boughey, Davidson, *The Film Industry*, London 1921.
British Film Institute, *National Film Library Catalogue*, 2nd edn, London 1938.
Buchanan, Andrew, *The Art of Film Production*, London 1936.
Buchanan, Andrew, *Films: The way of the cinema*, London 1932.
Chesmore, Stuart, *Behind the Cinema Screen*, London 1934.
Churchill, Winston S., *Step by Step*, London 1939.
Consitt, Frances, *The Value of Films in History Teaching*, London 1931.
Dale, Edgar, *The Content of Motion Pictures*, New York 1935, reprinted New York 1970.
Dickson, William Kennedy Laurie, *The Biograph in Battle*, London 1901.
Dickson, William Kennedy Laurie, and Dickson, Antonia, *History of the Kinetograph, Kinetoscope and Kinetophonograph*, New York 1895.
Foss, William and Gerahty, Cecil, *The Spanish Arena*, London 1938.
Humfrey, Robert, *Careers in the Films*, London 1938.
Jellinek, Frank, *The Civil War in Spain*, London 1938.
Klingender, F. D., and Legg, Stuart, *Money Behind the Screen*, London 1937.
Koestler, Arthur, *Spanish Testament*, London 1937.
Lasswell, Harold D., *Propaganda Technique in World War I*, London 1937, reprinted Cambridge, Massachusetts, 1971.
Lejeune, Caroline, *Cinema*, London 1931.
Madge, Charles, and Harrisson, Tom, *Britain by Mass-Observation*, Harmondsworth 1939.
Manning, Leah, *What I saw in Spain*, London 1935.
Montagu, Ivor, *Political Censorship of Films*, London 1929.
Orwell, George, *Homage to Catalonia*, London 1938, reprinted Harmondsworth 1966.
Pitcairn, Frank (Claud Cockburn), *Reporter in Spain*, London 1936.
Political and Economic Planning, *Report on the British Press*, London 1938.
Rotha, Paul, *Movie Parade*, London 1936.
Rotha, Paul, *Documentary Film*, London 1939.
Steer, G. L., *The Tree of Gernika*, London 1938.
Tallents, Stephen, *The Projection of England*, London 1932.
Warren, Low, *The Film Game*, London 1937.
Wintringham, Tom, *English Captain*, London 1939.

NEWSPAPERS, MAGAZINES, AND JOURNALS

Bulletin of the International Committee of the Historical Sciences, 1929–1932.

Change No. 2. The Bulletin of the Advertising Service Guild, 1941.
Cinema Quarterly, 1932–1935.
Daily Telegraph, 1936–1939. (Selected readings)
Documentary News Letter, 1940–1947.
Film Art, 1933–1937.
Journal of the Association of Cinematograph Technicians, 1935–1939.
Kinematograph Weekly, 1933–1939.
Kinematograph Year Book, 1936–1939.
Manchester Guardian, 1936–1939. (Selected readings)
News Chronicle, 1936–1939. (Selected readings)
Picture Post, 1938–1945.
Planning (The broadsheet of Political and Economic Planning), Nos 58, 82, 108, 118, 119 and 120.
Scoop (The monthly bulletin of Gaumont British News), No. 1, undated.
Sight and Sound, 1933–1939.
The Times, 1933–1939. (Selected readings)
World Film News, 1936–1938.

ARTICLES

Anonymous, 'Aeroplanes and tape machines cover the world', *World Film News*, Vol. 1, No. 3, June 1936.
Anon., 'Are newsreels news?', *The Nation*, 2 October 1935.
Anon., 'Censored', *Journal of the Association of Cinematograph Technicians*, March–April 1939.
Anon., 'Personality, the problem of commentary', *World Film News*, Vol. 1, No. 5, August 1936.
Anon., 'Public to gauge film values', *World Film News*, Vol. 1, No. 2, May 1936.
Anon., 'Scenes too gruesome for public showing', *World Film News*, Vol. 1, No. 7, October 1936.
Anon., 'Soccer league boycott may follow Cup Final Squabble', *World Film News*, Vol. 1, No. 3, June 1936.
Anon., 'Where do we stand?', *Documentary News Letter*, Vol. 2, No. 6, June 1941.
Bishop, H. W., 'Newsreels in the making', *Sight and Sound*, Winter 1934.
Buchanan, Andrew, 'Newsreels or real news?', *Film Art*, Vol. 3, No. 7, 1935.
Buchanan-Taylor, W., 'Mass Observation', *Documentary News Letter*, Vol. 2, No. 2, February 1941.
Commentator, The (edited by Raymond East), 'Newsreel Rushes', *World Film News*, Vol. 1, No. 8, November 1936, to Vol. 2, No. 10, January 1938 (inclusive).
Crosthwaite, Brian, 'Newsreels show political bias', *World Film News*, Vol. 1, No. 7, October 1936.
Cummins, G. T., 'A Reply to Sketch Editor's Criticisms', *World Film News*, Vol. 1, No. 8, November 1936.
Elvin, George, 'This Freedom, An Enquiry into Film Censorship', *Journal of the ACT*, January–February 1939.
Ex-Ray, 'Newsreel swindle sheet', *Journal of the ACT*, December–January 1937–1938.
Ex-Ray, 'The Newsreel War', *Journal of the ACT*, May 1935.
Fauconnier, Max, 'Les Archives Cinématographiques', *Bulletin of the International Committee of Historical Sciences*, Vol. 3, 1931.
Fraser, Donald, 'Newsreel, Reality of Entertainment?', *Sight and Sound*, Autumn 1933.
Fruin, M., 'Memoire sur les films documentaires', *Bulletin of the Inter. Comm. of Hist. Sc.*, Vol. 2, 1929–1930.
Fruin, M., 'Enquête de la commission internationale sur les films historiques', *Bulletin of the Inter. Comm. of Hist. Sc.*, Vol. 4, 1932.

Grierson, John, 'That unscrupulous rascal Northcliffe', *World Film News*, Vol. 2, No. 11, February 1938.

Hardy, H. Forsyth, 'Fact or Fiction?', *Cinema Quarterly*, No. 2, Spring 1934.

Hardy, H. Forsyth (editor), 'List of Historical-Biographical Films', *World Film News*, Vol. 1, No. 12, March 1937.

Harrisson, Tom, 'Social Research and the Film', *Documentary News Letter*, Vol. 1, No. 11, November 1940.

Hodgson, Ewart, 'Mass Observers', *Documentary News Letter*, Vol. 2, No. 1, January 1941.

Hulbert, Norman J., 'News films and their public', *Sight and Sound*, Winter 1933.

Lhéritier, M., 'Rapport présenté sur les rapports de l'histoire avec le cinématographe', *Bulletin of the Inter. Comm. of Hist. Sc.*, Vol. 2, 1929–1930.

MacDonald, Alistair G., 'The Newsreel Theatre', in 'The Cinema: A Symposium', with a foreword by Sidney Bernstein, *The Architects Journal*, No. 7, 1935.

Matuszewski, Boleslaw, 'Une nouvelle source de l'histoire', as translated (in part) in Leyda, Jay, *Films beget Films*, London 1964, and as translated (in full) in Thorpe, Frances (editor), *A Directory of British Films and Television Libraries*, London 1975.

Montagu, Ivor, 'The Siege of the Alcazar', *World Film News*, Vol. 1, No. 10, January 1937.

Montague, William P., 'Eyes of the World', *World Film News*, Vol. 2, No. 11, February 1938.

Neill-Brown, J., 'The Industry's Front Page', *Journal of the ACT*, March–April 1939.

Newberry, G. H., 'Some Aspects of Newsreel Recording', *Journal of the ACT*, February 1936.

Norris, Glen, 'A wide open letter to Mr G. T. Cummins, Editor of British Paramount News', *World Film News*, Vol. 2, No. 5, August 1937.

Norris, Glen, 'A wide open letter to Mr Gerald Sanger, Production Chief of British Movietonews', *World Film News*, Vol. 2, No. 6, September 1937.

Orwell, George, 'Letter to the Editor of *Time and Tide*', 5 February 1938, reprinted in *The Collected Essays, Journalism and Letters of George Orwell Vol. 1: An Age Like This, 1920–1940*, edited by Sonia Orwell and Ian Angus, Harmondsworth 1971.

Orwell, George, 'Spilling the Spanish Beans', *New English Weekly*, 29 July and 2 September 1937, reprinted in *The Collected Essays, Journalism and Letters Vol. 1*.

Orwell, George, 'The Prevention of Literature', *Polemic*, No. 2, January 1946, reprinted in *The Collected Essays, Journalism and Letters of George Orwell Vol. 4: In Front of Your Nose, 1945–1950*, edited by Sonia Orwell and Ian Angus, Harmondsworth 1971.

Rio, Armand, 'The Battle of the Films', *World's Work*, August 1916.

Rowson, Simon, 'A Statistical Survey of the Cinema Industry in Great Britain in 1934', *Journal of the Royal Statistical Society*, Vol. 99, 1936.

Sugrue, Thomas, 'Bringing the world to the world', *World Film News*, Vol. 2, No. 3, June 1937.

Tallents, Stephen, 'The Birth of British Documentary (Part I)', ('circulated and probably written in 1945'), reprinted in *Journal of the University Film Association*, Vol. 20, No. 1, 1968.

Tallents, Stephen, 'The Birth of British Documentary (Part II)', reprinted in *Journal of the University Film Association*, Vol. 20, No. 2, 1968.

Watts, Fred, 'Pioneer recalls struggles of early newsreels', *World Film News*, Vol. 1, No. 4, July 1936.

Waugh, W. T., 'History in Moving Pictures', *History*, Vol. 11, January 1927.

Wilkinson, F., 'Can History be taught by film?', *Sight and Sound*, Autumn 1933.

GOVERNMENT PUBLICATIONS
Home Office Circular 676417/6, *Revision of Model Conditions*, 24 October 1934.
House of Commons Debates: Vol. 293, 1934; Vol. 341, 1938; Vol. 342, 1938.
Minutes of Evidence Taken before the Departmental Committee on Cinematograph Films, HMSO, 1936.
Tendencies to Monopoly in the Cinematograph Film Industry. Report of a Committee appointed by the Cinematograph Films Council, HMSO, 1944.
Wartime Social Survey, *The Cinema Audience*, An Inquiry made by the Wartime Social Survey for The Ministry of Information by Louis Moss and Kathleen Box, New Series No. 37.b, June–July 1943.

UNPUBLISHED TRANSCRIPTS
Boake Carter, Philco Radio Corporation, Broadcast on the Columbia Broadcasting System, 7.45 to 8.00 pm, Wednesday, 18 November 1936 (mimeographed copy).

UNPUBLISHED MINUTES
Minute Book No. 1 of The Newsreel Association of Great Britain and Ireland Ltd. Minutes 1 to 659 from 11 November 1937 to 17 April 1941.

2. Secondary Sources

BOOKS AND PAMPHLETS
Arnheim, R., *Film as Art*, London 1958.
Arts Enquiry, The, *The Factual Film*, London 1947.
Baechlin, Peter, and Muller-Strauss, Maurice, *Newsreels Across the World*, Paris 1952.
Briggs, Asa, *Mass Entertainment: The Origins of a Modern Industry*, Adelaide 1960.
Briggs, Asa, *The History of Broadcasting in the United Kingdom, Volume II: The Golden Age of Wireless*, London 1965.
British Universities Film Council. *Film and the Historian*, London 1969.
Broué, Pierre, and Témime, Emile (translated by Tony White), *The Revolution and the Civil War in Spain*, London 1972.
Butler, David, and Freeman, Jennie, *British Political Facts 1900–1968*, London 1969.
Carr, Raymond, *Spain 1808–1939*, London 1966, reprinted with corrections London 1970.
Etzioni, Amitai, *Comparative Analysis of Complex Organisations*, Glencoe, Illinois, 1961.
Fielding, Raymond, *The American Newsreel 1911–1967*, Norman, Oklahoma, 1972.
Gannon, Franklin Reid, *The British Press and Germany 1936–1939*, London 1971.
Grenville, J. A. S., *Film as History*, Birmingham 1971.
Grierson, John (edited by H. Forsyth Hardy), *Grierson on Documentary*, London 1966.
Handel, Leo, *Hollywood Looks at its Audience*, Urbana, Illinois, 1950.
Hunnings, Neville March, *Film Censors and the Law*, London 1967.
Isaksson, Folke, and Furhammer, Leif (translated by Kersti French), *Politics and Film*, London 1971.
Leyda, Jay, *Films beget Films*, London 1964.
Lovell, Alan, and Hillier, Jim, *Studies in Documentary*, London 1972.
Low, Rachel, and Manvell, Roger, *The History of the British Film, Vol. 1, 1896–1906*, London 1948.
Low, Rachel, *The History of the British Film, Vol. 2, 1906–1914*, London 1949.
Low, Rachel, *The History of the British Film, Vol. 3, 1914–1918*, London 1951.
Low, Rachel, *The History of the British Film, Vol. 4, 1918–1929*, London 1971.

MacCann, Richard Dyer, *The People's Film*, New York 1973.
Marwick, Arthur, *War and Social Change in the Twentieth Century*, London 1974.
Mayer, J. P., *British Cinemas and their Audiences*, London 1948.
Mowat, Charles Loch, *Britain Between the Wars 1918–1940*, London 1966.
O'Connor, John E., and Jackson, Martin A., *Teaching History with Film*, Washington, D.C., 1974.
Payne, Stanley G., *The Spanish Revolution*, London 1970.
Pike, David Wingeate, *Conjecture, Propaganda and Deceit and the Spanish Civil War*, Stanford, California, 1968.
Political and Economic Planning, *The British Film Industry*, London 1952.
Pronay, Nicholas, Smith, Betty R., and Hastie, Tom, *The Use of Film in History Teaching*, London 1972.
Robinson, Richard A. H., *Origins of Franco's Spain*, Newton Abbot 1970.
Rotha, Paul, *Documentary Diary*, London 1973.
Slade Film History Register (edited by Frances Thorpe), *A Directory of British Film and Television Libraries*, London 1975.
Smith, Paul (editor), *The Historian and Film*, Cambridge 1976.
Taylor, A. J. P., *English History 1914–1945*, London 1965.
Taylor, A. J. P., *The Origins of the Second World War*, London 1961.
Thomas, Howard, *With an Independent Air*, London 1977.
Thomas, Hugh, *The Spanish Civil War*, London 1961.
Van der Esch, P. A. M., *Prelude to War*, The Hague 1951.
Watkins, K. W., *Britain Divided*, London 1963.
Winchester's Screen Encyclopedia, London 1958.
Wollen, Peter (editor), *Working Papers on the Cinema: Sociology and Semiology*, London 1969.
Wyand, Paul, *Useless if Delayed*, London 1959.

MAGAZINES AND JOURNALS
British Kinematography, 1945–1955.
Film and History, 1971–1975.
History (Film Section), 1971–1975.
Journal of the University Film Association, 1967–1975.
Screen, 1971–1975.
University Vision, 1968–1975.

ARTICLES
Aldgate, Anthony, 'British Newsreels and the Spanish Civil War', *Film and History*, Vol. 3, No. 1, February 1973.
Aldgate, Tony, 'British Newsreels and the Spanish Civil War', *History*, Vol. 58, February 1973.
Aldgate, Tony, 'The Production of "Spanish Civil War"', Part I: The Archives and the Newsreels', *University Vision*, No. 11, April 1974.
Aldgate, Tony, 'The Production of "Spanish Civil War"', Part II: A Film in the Making', *University Vision*, No. 12, December 1974.
Barr, Charles, 'Projecting Britain and the British Character: Ealing Studios', Part I, *Screen*, Vol. 15, No. 1, Spring 1974.
Bland, W. S., 'The Development of the Sound Newsreel', *British Kinematography*, Vol. 17, No. 2, August 1950.
Burns, E. Bradford, 'Conceptualising the use of film to study history: A bibliofilmography', *Film and History*, Vol. 4, No. 4, December 1974.
Cavalcanti, Alberto, 'Interview with', *Screen*, Vol. 13, No. 2, Summer 1972.
Ellis, John, 'Made in Ealing', *Screen*, Vol. 16, No. 1, Spring 1975.
Elton, Sir Arthur, 'The film as source material for history', *Aslib Proceedings*, Vol. 7, No. 4, November 1955.

Enzensberger, Hans Magnus, 'Constituents of a theory of the media', *New Left Review*, No. 64, November–December 1970.

Ferro, Marc, '1917: History and the Cinema', *Journal of Contemporary History*, Vol. 3, No. 4, October 1968.

Fielding, Raymond, 'Archives of the Motion Picture: A General View', *American Archivist*, Vol. 30, No. 3, July 1967.

Fielding, Raymond, 'Time Flickers Out: Notes on the Passing of "March of Time"', *The Quarterly of Film, Radio and Television*, Vol. 11, No. 4, Summer 1957.

Fielding, Raymond, 'Mirror of Discontent: The "March of Time" and its Politically Controversial Film Issues', *The Western Political Quarterly*, Vol. 12, No. 1, March 1959.

Gordon, Ken, 'The early days of the newsreels', *British Kinematography*, Vol. 17, No. 2, August 1950.

Hall, Stuart, 'Media and Message: the Life and Death of *Picture Post*', *Cambridge Review*, Vol. 92, 19 February 1971.

Hall, Stuart, 'The Social Eye of *Picture Post*', *Working Papers in Cultural Studies No. 2*, Spring 1972.

Hayward, Edward, 'Production Problems', *Archive Film Compilation Booklet*, Open University Supplementary Material, Milton Keynes 1973.

Hill, George, 'Motion Picture Camera Development', *British Kinematography*, Vol. 17, No. 4, October 1950.

Hood, Stuart, Review of *Documentary Diary* by Paul Rotha, *Sight and Sound*, Vol. 43, No. 1, 1973–4.

Houston, Penelope, 'The nature of the evidence', *Sight and Sound*, Vol. 36, No. 2, 1967.

Kedward, H. R., 'Politics, Iconography and Film', *The Brighton Film Review*, No. 18, March 1970.

Kedward, H. R., 'Images of Peace 1916–1923', *Oxford Visual History of the Twentieth Century*, 1972.

Kuiper, John B., 'The historical value of motion pictures', *American Archivist*, Vol. 31, No. 4, October 1968.

Marwick, Arthur, 'Archive Film as Source Material', *Archive Film Compilation Booklet*, 1973.

Montagu, Ivor, 'Interview with', *Screen*, Vol. 13, No. 3, Autumn 1972.

Norman, Philip, 'The newsreels', *Sunday Times Magazine*, 10 January 1971.

Pontecorvo, Lisa, 'Aspects of Documentary and Newsreel Research', *Archive Film Compilation Booklet*, 1973.

Pronay, Nicholas, 'British Newsreels in the 1930s, Part I, Audience and Producers', *History*, Vol. 56, October 1971.

Pronay, Nicholas, 'British Newsreels in the 1930s, Part II, Their Policies and Impact', *History*, Vol. 57, February 1972.

Roads, Christopher H., 'Film as historical evidence', *Journal of the Society of Archivists*, Vol. 3, No. 4, 1966.

Terveen, Fritz (translated by C. L. Burgauner), 'Film as a Historical Document', *Film and the Historian*, London 1969.

Thomas, Hugh, 'Heinkels over Guernica', *Times Literary Supplement*, 11 April 1975.

GOVERNMENT PUBLICATIONS

Documents on British Foreign Policy, 1919–1939 (edited by E. L. Woodward and Rohan Butler), Third Series, Vol. 3, 1938–9, HMSO, 1949.

Documents on German Foreign Policy, 1918–1945, Series D, Vol. 3, Germany and the Spanish Civil War, 1936–9, HMSO, 1951.

Records of interest to social scientists 1919 to 1939; Introduction, by Brenda Swann and Maureen Turnbull, HMSO, 1971 (Public Record Office Handbooks No. 14).

The British Press, HMSO, 1971 (Central Office of Information Reference Pamphlet No. 97).
Broadcasting in Britain, HMSO, 1973 (Central Office of Information Reference Pamphlet No. 111).

UNPUBLISHED TRANSCRIPTS AND SURVEYS
Slade Film History Register, *Survey on Stories Relating to Germany or Germans, 1933–1939*.
Donald Watt, 'Historians and the camera', broadcast Wednesday, 18 November 1970, BBC Radio 3, 2050–2110.

INTERVIEWS
Interviews were conducted with the following people:
Ted Candy
Formerly cameraman with Gaumont British News, now General Manager of British Movietonews Ltd.
Roy Drew
Joined the Gaumont Company in 1929; chief editor with Gaumont British News until 1959; editor of 'Look at Life' from 1959 to 1969. Now retired.
George Elvin
General Secretary of the Association of Cinematograph Technicians during the period 1936 to 1939; now President of the Association of Cinematograph and Television Technicians.
Leslie Mitchell
Announcer and news-reader for BBC Radio in 1934; Senior Announcer for BBC Television from 1936 to 1939; Commentator for British Movietone News from 1939 to 1947; Commentator for British Movietone News from 1958 to 1974.
Pat Wyand
Member of renowned 'newsreel family' (brother Paul and uncle Leslie were both newsreel cameramen); joined the sound staff of British Movietone in 1934; eventually became Chief of Sound; then Assistant Manager of British Movietonews Ltd. Now retired.

Index